GOD'S GREATEST GIFT

Theodore M. Burton

Published by
Deseret Book Company
Salt Lake City, Utah
1976

Contents

Preface

Some may think it is presumptuous of me to write a book. However, for the past decade I have been given the responsibility of managing the Genealogical Society of The Church of Jesus Christ of Latter-day Saints and of serving as managing director of the Genealogical Department. I am very conscious of the responsibility I bear of teaching the importance of this aspect of gospel doctrine to Church members. I have been appointed to be a watchman on the tower. I have often felt I should have spoken more forcibly in raising my voice in warning the people, though some people already smile at my personal enthusiasm for this particular field of gospel endeavor. It was not always so. When I was first given this responsibility, I knew very little about it. What I have learned has come through the patient teaching of many wonderful, devoted men and women who have taught me what I know. I have studied to become more knowledgeable and finally feel that I have something to say to the members of the Church and to the world in general on this subject that will be helpful to them.

Although many people have suggested I write such a book, I have hesitated to do so before, because so many able and qualified people before me have spoken on this subject. There is really nothing new that can be written, for it has all been said before. Perhaps it will be convenient to have this information assembled in one place.

That is about the only contribution I can make. Some friends have advised me that we do not need another book of motivation, for they say, "The people of the Church already realize their responsibility to do genealogical and temple work. They are already converted. What they need now is not more motivation, but they need to be told *how* to do this work!" This is a challenging thought, but I am not qualified to show people *how* to do genealogical work. There are many excellent books written on this subject by people much more qualified than I am in genealogical research. I question, however, the validity of the statement that "people are already converted." I do not believe they are. If they *were* converted, they would find out *how* to do research of themselves. In fact, absolutely *nothing* could keep them from doing genealogical research and going to the temple to do ordinance work for the dead if they were converted. I am reminded of what Jesus said to Peter: "But I have prayed for thee, that thy faith fail not: and when *thou* art converted, strengthen thy brethren." (Luke 22:32.) I have taken the liberty of emphasizing that one word, *thou*, for Peter could only strengthen others when he was converted himself.

In these last days the Savior said something very similar to the brethren of the Twelve: "And after their temptations, and much tribulation, behold, I, the Lord, will feel after them, and *if they harden not their hearts, and stiffen not their necks* against me, they shall be converted, and I will heal them." (D&C 112:13. Italics added.) I feel that I, like many other members of the Church, have had a rather stiff neck and a rather hard heart in the past concerning my genealogical responsibility. I have felt my own heart change and my own neck bend as I have caught the vision of this work. Perhaps, therefore, with my own conversion I am now in a better position to help others gain a conviction of the importance of this work.

It should be understood that I am writing this book

without being requested to do so by the Brethren. I bear
the total responsibility for what I say. I am not speaking
for the Church. I am not writing this book as the managing director of the Genealogical Department of the
Church or as a General Authority. I am writing·as an individual who has gained a great deal of insight and
experience by reason of my callings. Therefore, what you
are about to read is not an official book of the Church,
but only my own thoughts and interpretations, based on
my understanding. I hope that what I have written will
be in the best interest of the members of the Church, and
that it is as true as I can make it, conscious as I am of
human faults and shortcomings. If there are errors, I will
be grateful if you call them to my attention so I can learn
myself and correct those errors should a future edition
become desirable.

1

Treasures in Heaven

On my way to an official church assignment in the South Pacific, I had to wait for an international flight in the Los Angeles airport. As I was sitting there waiting for my plane, an elderly woman took the seat next to me. As I looked up she said, "Pardon me, but is this the flight to Melbourne, Australia?" I replied, "I don't know. What is your flight number?" When she told me, I informed her that this was the waiting area for that flight number and that she was in the right place. She then explained to me that she could not understand the announcements being made over the loudspeaking system, and was bewildered as to what to do. I offered to help her, inasmuch as I was taking the same flight to Hawaii, but was leaving the flight there to go on to Samoa. She expressed her thanks, then told me how in the past she had relied completely on her husband and that he had always taken care of all travel responsibilities for her. She said she missed him terribly since his death, and was now on her way to see relatives in Australia.

I asked her how long her husband had been deceased, and she told me he had died suddenly only three months ago. She had been visiting her children in California to escape the loneliness of his passing and now hoped this trip to her birthplace in Australia could take her mind away from her loss. I asked her if she loved her husband and children and she replied, "Oh, with all my heart! I never knew how much I loved them until I lost my husband. I hardly know what to do."

I then said, "Now isn't it remarkable that God in his tender mercy toward you should arrange things so you could sit next to one of the very few men on earth who can explain to you how you can have your husband and your family again?"

Rather startled, she looked at me and said, "Who are you?"

"I am Elder Burton, one of the General Authorities of the Church of Jesus Christ. I know not only the way, but I also have the authority to explain to you about the eternal nature of the family relationship when that family is joined together in the Lord's own way."

She protested, "But I was properly married in the church! My children are legitimate!"

I smiled and told her this was true before the law, but I reminded her that the marriage covenant she made as she and her husband took their vows before their minister had been for this life only. Such covenants and vows have no validity after the death of the individuals who make that covenant. They only promise to take each other for the duration of life, and that is all the authority the minister has when he validates that marriage relationship. Then I asked, "Wouldn't you like to have your husband and your children with you eternally instead of just for this life only?"

"I believe in the resurrection," she said, "and that we will love and have each other *after* the resurrection."

I replied, "I am sure you will continue to love your husband and your children, just as you will love every other person who gets to be with you in heaven, but you will not have that warm, close, personal, family relationship with them that evidently you enjoyed with your family here on this earth."

"But," she objected, "there won't be any family relationship in heaven, for I have read in the scriptures that there won't be any marriage in heaven." She was referring to the temptation of Jesus when some of the Sadducees tried to trap him on the question of the resurrection, using a multiple marriage situation as an example. They had tried to show how unreasonable it was to believe in a continuing marriage relationship in the resurrected state, because of the mixed-up marriage relationships that so often occur in earth life. Jesus had answered them: "Ye do err, not knowing the scriptures, nor the power of God. For in the resurrection they neither marry, nor are given in marriage, but are as the angels of God in heaven." (Matthew 22:29-30.)

I explained to her that the key to that passage of scripture lies in understanding the plan of salvation, which Jesus knew and understood so perfectly. I said to her, "What Jesus said was absolutely true. There will be no marriages made in heaven, for all marriage arrangements and covenants must be made in the Lord's own way on earth. That is why Jesus gave Peter and the other apostles the sealing power to accomplish this very thing." I told her that such sealing power had also been restored upon the earth today, and that I held that priesthood sealing power by the laying on of hands of those who had authority to confer it upon me. "I would like to tell you about it," I said.

"No," she replied, "I am a Congregationalist and prefer to stay with my belief. I have faith in my church and in my minister and do not want to change."

I then said, "I don't want to take away from you your faith in God or your belief in righteous principles. I only want to add to your faith and knowledge and help you so you can be comforted in the loss of your husband. I want you to know how you can continue to have him as your husband forever instead of just for a short earthly period."

"I'll take my chances on that," she said. "I prefer not to talk about it any more." I told her I would respect her wishes, and I did so. I helped her with her packages, assisted her to her seat on the plane, and wished her well on her voyage.

I have since wondered what she will say some day

when she stands before the judgment bar and hears how God sent her to one of his special servants to give her help in her hour of need. What will she say when she realizes that she refused to listen when she had an opportunity to do so? Perhaps that airport occasion or the timing was not right. Perhaps at some other time a missionary or a member of the Church will contact her again and the words I told her may have germinated in her heart to the point where she will listen. It may be that one of her children will hear the gospel message and will respond positively, and will, after her death, perform the temple ordinance work that will make it possible for her to accept the gospel when it is presented to her in the spirit world. I did, however, feel sorrowful that I personally couldn't have been more effective in giving her additional comfort while she was still in this world and so much needed that help.

The world can be a very lonesome place when there is no one present with whom we can share our joys, sorrows, and hopes. It is wonderful to have someone to talk to, someone who understands, someone who will listen, someone to share our life with, someone to be with us when we hear beautiful music, someone to share a meal with, someone to be there when we need a companion, or someone just to touch. A family with all the turbulent scenes that sometimes transpire in that relationship constitutes a treasure that we often fail to appreciate until it is too late.

In trying to present the gospel to others, what can we say to such persons that would cause them to pay more attention to spiritual matters? Most persons are so involved with the many problems and concerns of everyday life that they are just not interested in something that to them is neither pertinent nor necessary. If we could only show them how they could be wealthier, happier, stronger, or healthier, perhaps they might pay attention to what we say. When, however, we talk to them about "blessings in heaven," they fail to understand such a generalized statement and figuratively close the door in our faces. Perhaps the reason is that neither we nor they realize that these blessings are far more than a mere figure of speech. It is not generally understood that these blessings constitute a real and tangible treasure. Probably nothing would be more satisfying to a person's ego or more consoling to a troubled spirit than to possess a confirmed knowledge of a glorious past, a noble parentage, and the promise of an infinitely promising future. But all these things in our past life are true, and there is greatness and nobility within us.

It might be well to ponder the question the Lord asked Job when the latter attempted to justify his thoughts and actions: "Where wast thou when I laid the foundations of the earth? declare, if thou hast understanding. . . . When the morning stars sang together, and all the sons of God shouted for joy?" (Job 38:4, 7.) This was not just a rhetorical question. The Lord was teaching Job a great principle. He was telling Job he was one of his spirit sons who shouted for joy when the earth was prepared for the habitation of man. Job, with other spirit children of God in a premortal state, was a partaker of all the beauties, happiness, and tangible treasures that characterized that premortal state where we all lived together as spirit children with our heavenly parents. Those spirits were children of the most glorious parents anyone could ever hope for. Man *does* have a glorious and a rich past, and nobler and greater parents than the mind of any mortal man can conceive. If that message could somehow be conveyed to an individual, it would change his whole attitude about life on this earth and teach him how important this earth life is for his own growth and development. He would realize there is a purpose to life and that the promise of actual treasures to be gained through living a righteous life on this earth is one of the most motivating powers to be found in mortal existence.

What was life like in the presence of God? We don't

5

know, for a veil has been drawn between that life and mortality. It must have been wonderful to live in the presence of our Heavenly Father and mother and to be surrounded by light, glory, and knowledge. We had there all the comforts and joys of everlasting life, for we were immortal spirit beings, children of immortal and exalted parents. In our present state we cannot even imagine how marvelous and wonderful it must have been to dwell amid such surroundings.

6

Man has had a glimpse from time to time of the glory of God, but such glimpses have been strictly limited. Moses is an example of a man who had such an experience. When he sought for greater light and knowledge, there was no prophet or teacher possessing such knowledge who could teach him, so the only way that information could be given him was for God himself to reveal it to him. The scriptures tell us what happened when Moses prayed for light and knowledge. As a result of that prayer Moses

saw God face to face, and he talked with him, and the glory of God was upon Moses; therefore Moses could endure his presence.

And God spake unto Moses, saying: Behold, I am the Lord God Almighty, and Endless is my name; for I am without beginning of days or end of years; and is not this endless?

And, behold, thou art my son; wherefore look, and I will show thee the workmanship of mine hands; but not all, for my works are without end, and also my words, for they never cease.

Wherefore, no man can behold *all* my works, except he behold *all* my glory; *and no man can behold all my glory, and afterwards remain in the flesh on the earth.* (Moses 1:2-5. Italics added.)

The reason for restricting man to only a limited understanding of God's full glory is perhaps that, unless the veil were kept in place, we could see all those treasures and blessings of our former life and we would then not have the courage to continue life in the flesh. We would seek to return to enjoy again all those treasures and that life of happiness and joy we formerly possessed. If we did return, the plan of God would be frustrated and our own growth would be impeded. So, in our own best interest, a veil has been drawn between us and that former life so we would not be overly tempted to make a forcible return. We can, however, well imagine how wonderful such a premortal life must have been.

One of my former missionary companions in Germany was Hugh W. Nibley, recently retired as a professor of ancient scriptures at Brigham Young University. Dr. Nibley wrote an article entitled "Treasures in the Heavens: Some Early Christian Insights into the Organizing of Worlds." I quote from his article: "To neutralize what would otherwise be the overpowering appeal of the heavenly treasure, the memory of its former glories has been erased from the mind of man, which is thus in a state of equilibrium, enjoying by 'the ancient law of liberty' complete freedom to choose whatever it will." (*Dialogue* 8 [1974]: 79.) I believe this expresses well the reason why God cannot let us know the magnitude of the blessings we enjoyed before we came to earth in this life. God permits us to know just enough to give us faith that we are individually valuable and important, that earth life has great meaning and importance, and that we can become even happier and receive greater joy and blessings if we will only follow the directions laid down in the plan of salvation for achieving a much greater treasure than we formerly enjoyed as spirit children of heavenly parents.

Just as the curtain behind us must close in order to assure us a fair trial in mortal life, so the curtain before us must remain closed also. If we could actually see the tangible treasures ahead of us, it would not be a fair trial. The only fair measure of our ability to make intelligent decisions is to put us on our own. God must give guidance by giving us all we need to know in order to make wise decisions and thus be able to direct our earth life in accordance with eternal principles. However, we as individuals must show our willingness and determination to do that which is right, being guided by faith in the word of God. That is why he has given us the following direction:

For you shall live by every word that proceedeth forth from the mouth of God.

For the word of the Lord is truth, and whatsoever is truth is light, and whatsoever is light is Spirit, even the Spirit of Jesus Christ.

And the Spirit giveth light to every man that cometh into the world; and the Spirit enlighteneth every man through the world that hearkeneth to the voice of the Spirit.

And every one that hearkeneth to the voice of the Spirit cometh unto God, even the Father. (D&C 84:44-47.)

So the future treasure we receive or don't receive depends upon our faith in God's word and our willingness to follow that faith by positive and godly actions throughout our mortal lives. If that former life was so wonderful, what on earth could have motivated us to leave such a life of glory to come to this earth with all life's problems and frustrations? It must have been a real sacrifice for us to have left that life for this one. In commenting on this question, I might ask, What is sacrifice? Sacrifice can be defined as giving up something of great value for something of even greater value. That is why we exchange work for money and money for a house, for clothing, or for a car. We make the sacrifice of the one for that which is better and will bring us greater happiness. If we left a life of glory in the premortal state, it could not have been solely for any treasures that can be found in this life only. This life must therefore be an interim period, a key, or a gate by means of which we can enter into still another life of tremendously greater power and promise. We came here, then, not because we were forced to come, but because we wanted to come. We are also here as a reward for the successes we achieved in our former life. Earth life is a blessing or a reward even though we sometimes fail to appreciate it as such. In spite of all life's trials, earth life enables us to grow and develop.

On earth we are tried and tested in a proving process to see whether we can individually be advanced or promoted to receive much greater advantages for the future. Of course, the converse is also possible: If we fail to prove ourselves here, then we will not get all the blessings we could otherwise attain. There is even a possibility that we can lose entirely the blessings we formerly had. Each person has an opportunity, through a meritorious life on earth, of increasing his future treasure in a post-mortal life above that which he had in the premortal life. On the other hand, he also runs the risk of losing that treasure completely by striving during this mortal life solely for earthly treasures of fame, fortune, and pleasures rather than by concentrating his earthly search on heavenly treasures of lasting value. God explained this to Abraham as he told Abraham how important this earth life is as a testing period:

And we will prove them herewith, to see if they will do all things whatsoever the Lord their God shall command them;

And they who keep their first estate shall be added upon; and they who keep not their first estate shall not have glory in the same kingdom with those who keep their first estate; and they who keep their second estate shall have glory added upon their heads forever and ever. (Abraham 3:25-26.)

It is in this conflict of interest that the temptations of Satan find their place. The Lord promises us treasures in heaven, but they are based on faith in God's word. It is true these treasures are greater than any to be found on earth. It is also true that such treasures can only be obtained by the exercise of faith and good works as we strive on earth for those future blessings, however tangible they may be at some later date. On the other hand, Satan offers us a counterfeit imitation. He shows us a clever, shining, earthly treasure, but a treasure that we can hold in our hands and see. The one is here and now and the other is proffered for the future. True, the earthly treasure is not as valuable as that to be had in heaven, but it is here and we *can* hold it in our hands. That, then, is the real test of a person's intelligence. We have to weigh both treasures and choose that one which has the greater intrinsic value, whatever the cost may be to us in this earth life. The Savior advised us carefully on this point: "Lay not up for yourselves treasures upon earth, where moth and rust doth corrupt, and where thieves break through and steal: But lay up for yourselves treasures in heaven, where neither moth nor rust doth corrupt, and where thieves do not break through nor steal: For where your treasure is, there will your heart be also." (Matthew 6:19-21.) In those words, the Savior summarized the choice before man.

We have, therefore, been placed here on earth by a wise and a noble father and mother to prove ourselves by the choices we make. It appears to me that perhaps we are here to prove ourselves to ourselves, more than to prove ourselves to God. I believe God pretty well knows what choices we will make. We lived with him for a long time in that premortal life, and he knows us thoroughly. I believe we need to convince *ourselves* of who we are even more than we need to convince our immortal parents, for they already know who we are. However, we must also verify God's trust in us. I am sure our heavenly parents have had their hearts broken repeatedly by the failure of some of their choicest children, in whom they had great trust, to live up to their expectations. It is therefore true that anyone can fall from grace. Many warnings have been given us not to rely on our own great strength, but to put our trust and faith in the Lord. The scriptures tell us:

. . . we know that justification through the grace of our Lord and Savior Jesus Christ is just and true;

And we know also, that sanctification through the grace of our Lord and Savior Jesus Christ is just and true, to all those who love and serve God with all their mights, minds, and strength.

But there is a possibility that man may fall from grace and depart from the living God;

Therefore let the church take heed and pray always, lest they fall into temptation;

Yea, and even let those who are sanctified take heed also. (D&C 20:30-34.)

There is need to endure to the end and to hold fast to that faith and hope in greater blessings to come through living a righteous life here on this earth.

Since we do have freedom of choice, we need to be careful how we exercise it. Too often we are tempted by the "bird in the hand" to completely disregard that which is of far greater value. The attaining of these greater blessings, however, must be done in the Lord's appointed way. Many times we attempt to take shortcuts or to speed the attainment of these blessings in other ways, but that is unwise. In this connection, we might well ask, Why did Jesus never make a mistake? He told us, in these words, how he avoided mistakes: "For I have not spoken of myself; but the Father which sent me, he gave me a commandment, what I should say, and what I should speak. And I know that this commandment is life everlasting: whatsoever I speak therefore, even as the Father said unto me, so I speak." (John 12:49-50.)

On another occasion, Jesus explained his actions in these words: "Verily, verily, I say unto you, The Son can do nothing of himself, but what he seeth the Father do: for what things soever he doeth, these also doeth the Son likewise." (John 5:19.)

The wise man and woman would follow the example Jesus set for us. Instead of doing "our own thing," we ought to do the things of God. If we follow our own inclinations, follow the teaching or take the advice of others, we subject ourselves to all the dangers that come with mortality. Men are not all-wise. Men do not possess the knowledge nor the experience that God possesses. Even church leaders are only mortal men. Parents and friends are only mortal. We can never rise above the teaching source; therefore, that source becomes most important. If we are going to follow an example or take advice, then it should be from one who knows the end of things from the very beginning. That person is God, or one who speaks in the name of Jesus Christ by the power of the Holy Ghost.

The Lord warned us in the Doctrine and Covenants that "man should not counsel his fellow man, neither trust in the arm of flesh." (D&C 1:19.) In other words, we should not base our actions or our lives on directions and instructions given us by our fellow mortals, be they friends, parents, or church leaders, *unless* they speak by the Holy Ghost. To know whether they are so speaking, we must know the scriptures, which contain the word of God. The Lord has said he has given us a pattern in all things so we will not be deceived. (See D&C 52:14-19.) We are to teach and we are to listen by the power of the Holy Ghost. (See D&C 52:13-24.) When we listen by the power of the Holy Ghost and when a person speaks by the power of the Holy Ghost, the power of the Holy Ghost carries that message right into our hearts. (2 Nephi 33:1-2.) So in searching for heavenly treasures, we should make sure we do not follow our own mortal desires nor the mortal desires of others; rather, we should follow the admonitions and directions of God as they come to us through scriptures, revelation, and inspiration given us through the power of the Holy Spirit.

Thus the former treasures we had in the spirit world can be added upon and even greater treasures can be obtained than have ever entered into the heart of man. This promise was made to ancient prophets. Isaiah wrote: "For since the beginning of the world men have not heard, nor perceived by the ear, neither hath the eye seen, O God, beside thee, what he hath prepared for him that waiteth for him." (Isaiah 64:4.) This was confirmed by Paul, who was blinded by the vision of the glory of God, which he saw, until by the grace of God and by the healing power of the priesthood his sight was restored. He quoted these words from Isaiah and then wrote:

. . . God hath revealed them unto us by his Spirit: for the Spirit searcheth all things, yea, the deep things of God.

For what man knoweth the things of man, save the spirit

of man which is in him? even so the things of God knoweth no man, but the Spirit of God.

Now we have received, not the spirit of the world, but the spirit which is of God; that we might know the things that are freely given to us of God.

Which things also we speak, not in the words which man's wisdom teacheth, but which the Holy Ghost teacheth; comparing spiritual things with spiritual.

But the natural man receiveth not the things of the Spirit of God: for they are foolishness unto him: neither can he know them, because they are spiritually discerned. (1 Corinthians 2:9-14.)

The knowledge of these glories was revealed by the Lord to Joseph Smith and to Sidney Rigdon as the Lord said to them: "For by my Spirit will I enlighten them, and by my power will I make known unto them the secrets of my will—yea, even those things which eye has not seen, nor ear heard, nor yet entered into the heart of man." (D&C 76:10.) As a result of the vision they received and recorded in part, they concluded with these words:

But great and marvelous are the works of the Lord, and the mysteries [I call them treasures] of his kingdom which he showed unto us, which surpass all understanding in glory, and in might, and in dominion;

Which he commanded us we should not write while we were yet in the Spirit, and are not lawful for man to utter;

Neither is man capable to make them known, for they are only to be seen and understood by the power of the Holy Spirit, which God bestows on those who love him, and purify themselves before him;

To whom he grants this privilege of seeing and knowing for themselves;

That through the power and manifestation of the Spirit, while in the flesh, they may be able to bear his presence in the world of glory. (D&C 76:114-18.)

So, we have a glorious promise of future blessings revealed to us by the prophets of God. They are given us as promises of hope and assurances of what and who we are. If we could only catch a vision of all we worked so hard to achieve before we came here, then that vision could guide us here to do those things which will assure us that mighty treasure which God has reserved for us in the future. If we only have faith to believe and work for these things, that treasure will be ours. What a motivating power this is, to take seriously those things of the Spirit which let us know the purpose and the promise of this earth life! Life on this earth is a continuation of the life that went on before, but it is also the beginning of a greater life to come if we will abide by the rules God has defined to lead us to the mightiest treasure of all—eternal life.

14

If we could but remember the loneliness of that woman at the airport, we could realize that man was not designed to stand alone. That treasure in the heaven for which we seek must be a treasure to be shared. It involves family. It involves those we love and those who love us in return. The treasure in heaven must be a family treasure.

2

Marriage in the Lord's Way

I would like to refer again to my experience with the woman at the Los Angeles airport. Had she been interested enough to listen, what might I have said to her about marriage in the Lord's way? I might have been able to interest her by telling her something about herself. All of us are more interested in ourselves than in any other subject. We want to know what people think of us. We want to know what impressions we make on others. We want to be thought of as important. The truth is, we *are* important, each and every one of us. And she was very important also, as is every woman born into this world.

Since she was a Christian and accepted the Bible as the word of God, we might have opened the scriptures to read about the creation of man. God did not make the earth out of nothing, but organized it and organized man out of material already available. If there is one lesson every person learns in life, whether layman or scientist, it is this law: You can't get something from nothing! It is as true of economics or joy as it is of physics or chemistry. The sum total of substance remains the same. We can convert matter to energy or vice versa, but that simply involves organization or manipulation of the materials already available in one form or another. God is a creator or an organizer. He did not create by bringing into primal existence the ultimate elements of the material from which the earth and man were formed. Element is eternal: "For man is spirit. The elements are eternal, and spirit and element, inseparably connected, receive a fulness of joy; And when separated, man cannot receive a fulness of joy." (D&C 93:33-34.)

When God organized man, the scriptures simply state: "And God said, Let *us* make man in *our* image, after *our* likeness; and let *them* have dominion over the fish of the sea, and over the fowl of the air, and over the cattle, and over all the earth, and over every creeping thing that creepeth upon the earth." (Genesis 1:26. Italics added.)

There it is. The Bible is no scientific treatise. No details are given, but just the bare fact that man was organized. We are not told how, but the plan was defined. Some words in the scripture quoted are italicized, words that I feel are very significant. God is plural and man was to be plural. In those plural words I find great significance.

The scripture then continues: "So God created man in his own image, in the image of God created he him; male and female created he them." (Genesis 1:27.) How could a single male God create a female in his own image? However, if God were plural and consisted of male and female, then the creation of man, both male and female, becomes not only possible but also logical, for it preserves the pattern. This is what Eliza R. Snow expressed so beautifully in her hymn "O My Father," as she wrote:

> In the heavens are parents single?
> No, the thought makes reason stare!
> Truth is reason, truth eternal
> Tells me I've a mother there.

I cannot understand how a man can be a father without an accompanying mother. I cannot understand how a god father can be a father unless there is also a god mother to be a mother. How could we be children without having been fathered and mothered? Accordingly, we speak of God the Father as Elohim. He is the father of the spirits of the human race and is the literal parent of our Lord and Savior Jesus Christ.

Professor William H. Chamberlin, who taught at Brigham Young College in Logan, Utah, wrote a valuable little paper on the use of the word *Elohim,* which was included by B. H. Roberts in his book *The Mormon Doctrine of Deity* (Deseret News, Salt Lake City, Utah, 1903). In this article Brother Chamberlin explained that two words *el* and *eloah* were applied generally to God by the Hebrew people. The plural of the first word is *elim* and the plural of the last word is *elohim.* The Hebrew language would allow the people to use the plural form *Elohim* in speaking of God. A few nouns when used by them in the plural seem to magnify the original idea. Just because the word *Elohim* is followed by the singular form of the verb, however, is no proof that the name itself refers to the singular form of God.

17

Joseph Smith, as recorded in the *History of the Church* (vol. 5, p. 2), understood correctly the nature of the creation when he spoke of the Eloheim, or the Gods, which created the earth and in whose presence the righteous will ultimately live. However, when we speak of the Father, we use the word *Elohim,* and this is a plural name. When I personally think of Elohim, or Father, I think of mother also. To my mind they are one because they are one in perfect knowledge, power, purity, all-wise, all-knowing, and all-loving. At least that is how I personally think of my heavenly parents. They are united in all wisdom and in doing what they do together, in effect, acting as a single unit. Just as our friends speak of us as the Burtons in a plural sense in referring to me and my wife, so when I think of Elohim I think of my heavenly father and mother as a single unit. I find no scripture to prove this, but to me it seems reasonable and logical. I do not pray to nor do I worship a heavenly mother, for as Jesus explained to his disciples, "Therefore ye must always pray unto the Father in my name." (3 Nephi 18:19.) In this and the next chapter of 3 Nephi he repeated this instruction thirteen times, so it must be important. Though I worship my Heavenly Father, I realize that he must have an eternal companion by his side. I love and honor and respect her as all sons should respect and love and honor their mothers.

God was not completely satisfied when Adam was created. Something was lacking: "And the Lord God said, It is not good that the man should be alone; I will make an help meet for him." (Genesis 2:18.) I like the wording in the Pearl of Great Price a little better: "And I, the Lord God, said unto mine Only Begotten, that it was not good for man to be alone; wherefore, I will make an help meet for him." (Moses 3:18.) Note that Elohim did not say he would form a helpmate or a helpmeet for Adam. There are two words used. A "help" is an aide or companion and "meet" defines that companion as one who is worthy. *Meet* is a good and powerful English word that can be defined as meaning worthy or equal.

It is interesting to read the account of the creation of Eve, as given in Moses 3:21-22, to learn that in relation to Adam she was taken from "one of his ribs," which of course was figurative, since no details are given of either creation. One need not speculate about the details, for it is not essential to our salvation to know such things, but I think it is significant that Eve was taken from the side of man. She was not taken from in front of Adam or from his head, to take the forefront or to be superior to him in any way. She was not taken from one of his back parts, to stand behind him, or from his feet, as his inferior in any way. She was taken from the side of man, to stand by his side as an equal partner. Being "meet" for the man meant that Eve was just as important as was Adam. She was of similar intelligence, similar ability, similar faith, similar bodily perfection, worthy in every way to stand together at the side of the first man. She was named Eve, the mother of all living men and women. It is small wonder that when Adam saw her he exclaimed: "This I know now is bone of my bones, and flesh of my flesh; she shall be called Woman, because she was taken out of man." (Moses 3:23. See also Genesis 2:23.) What Adam meant when he said those words was that Eve was as important and as necessary to him as his own flesh and bones. She was as loved and treasured as his own life! He recognized her importance and her nobility as an equal, worthy partner.

So God gave Adam and Eve to each other in marriage. We should remember that at the time they were given to each other, they were immortal beings, not subject to death. They had perfect bodies, for death had not yet entered into the world. When God performed their marriage and gave them to each other, that marriage was designed to last forever. It was an eternal marriage or partnership. It was to continue forever and to be cultivated, nurtured, and nourished just as God the Eternal Father treasures and values his eternal companion, our heavenly mother. From now on Adam and Eve could be spoken of as a single unit as they grew together in love and understanding. God explained to them the nature of this unity as he said: "Therefore shall a man leave his father and his mother, and shall cleave unto his wife; and they shall be one flesh." (Moses 3:24. See also Genesis 2:24.) This was the first promise of the eternal nature of the marriage covenant and the beginning of a family relationship, which is the principal theme of this book. The oneness of the marriage covenant cannot be too highly stressed. A couple should truly seek to become one flesh.

One of the tragic consequences of the apostasy from the church established by the Savior in the meridian of time is that along with many other things, the beauty of the marriage relationship was lost. When a marriage is performed in the Lord's way by the power and authority of the holy priesthood, that marriage is sealed not only for life in mortality, but forever. Marriage is an eternal covenant. That is why Jesus Christ, in rebuking the Sadducees, told them they erred, not understanding the scriptures nor the power of God. (Matthew 22:29-30.) Jesus had previously taught the eternal nature of the marriage covenant:

Have ye not read, that he which made them at the beginning made them male and female,

And said, For this cause shall a man leave father and mother, and shall cleave to his wife: and they twain shall be one flesh?

Wherefore they are no more twain, but one flesh. What therefore God [not man] hath joined together, let not man put asunder [divorce]. (Matthew 19:4-6.)

In other words, when a marriage is performed in God's way and by his power, it is an eternal marriage designed to last forever.

The Sadducees, attempting to ridicule belief in the resurrection, and knowing that Jesus and the Jews in general accepted the eternal nature of the marriage covenant, were in effect saying: "How foolish to believe in a resurrection and marriage in heaven when everyone knows that a woman who has had seven husbands could not have them all in a celestial marriage." The ancient law of Israel was that a woman who married two husbands in this world would be restored to the first husband in the next world. Modern so-called Christian ministers are much like the Sadducees who teach that family, marital love, and marriage all cease with the death of the body.

When Jesus then replied that "in the resurrection they neither marry, nor are given in marriage, but are as the angels of God in heaven" (Matthew 22:30), what was he teaching, and to whom was he referring by the word *they*? He was telling the Sadducees that as far as they were concerned and for those who had married as "children of the world" by secular and not by true priesthood authority, marriage does cease at death. There is marrying and giving of marriage in heaven only for those who are willing to accept and live the fulness of God's law as it applies to eternal family life in the manner planned and prepared by God for his children and which is then performed for them by proxy on earth.

The Lord made this very clear in a modern revelation to the Prophet Joseph Smith:

Therefore, if a man marry him a wife in the world, and he marry her not by me nor by my word, and he covenant with her so long as he is in the world and she with him, their covenant and marriage are not of force when they are dead, and when they are out of the world; therefore, they are not bound by any law when they are out of the world.

Therefore, when they are out of the world they neither marry nor are given in marriage; but are appointed angels in heaven, which angels are ministering servants, to minister for those who are worthy of a far more, and an exceeding, and an eternal weight of glory.

For these angels did not abide my law; therefore, they cannot be enlarged, but remain separately and singly, without exaltation, in their saved condition, to all eternity; and from henceforth are not gods, but are angels of God forever and ever. (D&C 132:15-17.)

This, then, is the condition of those who live according to the manner of the world. This single condition represents those who fall short of gaining those blessings which God has reserved for the faithful. This was to be the fate of the woman and her seven husbands. This was to be the state of the Sadducees, who denied there would be a life of resurrection after death. This will be the state of that woman at the Los Angeles airport, who, rather than listen to a servant of God, preferred to live by the philosophies and practices of men. No marriage "until death do you part" can ever enable a couple who truly do love each other to attain that great treasure in heaven which God has reserved for the faithful. They simply do not comprehend the principle of being sealed together in an eternal marriage, not only for time, but for all eternity. They do not understand that what God has joined together, no man should put asunder. (Matthew 19:6.)

If there is one great problem in family life in our modern world, it is the problem of divorce. Marriages are often entered into very lightly. Little thought is given to the spiritual and the eternal nature of the marriage covenant. It is frequently performed by civil servants entirely without any connection or thought of involving God or his authority. One can be almost cynical and say that in many cases marriage has become only a license for sexual gratification. Little thought is given to children resulting from such marriages. Marriages so entered into were never planned to last, and the attitude of many couples is that "if things don't work out—there is always divorce." Divorces are made easy and family life becomes shallow and meaningless. The hurts left in the hearts of both men and women who are subsequently divorced, though often overlooked, are never healed. The broken hearts of children who grow up out of broken homes remain to canker their lives. Their attitude toward marriage in turn reflects their personal experiences with their quarreling and divorced parents. As they approach marriage themselves, not knowing any better, they adopt the philosophies and practices of their parents. So marriage and family love for them never attain those heights of joy and satisfaction which God designed for the marriage of Adam and Eve.

The glory of womanhood is to be a queen. The glory of man is to become a king. As spirit children of God, we ought to seek for and reach that potential which our heavenly parents know we possess as their children. Divorce and the dissolution of the marriage covenant come because of neglect and/or wickedness. When the Sadducees spoke with Jesus, they said unto him, "Why did Moses then command to give a writing of divorcement, and to put her away? He saith unto them, Moses because of the hardness of your hearts suffered you to put away your wives: but from the beginning it was not so." (Matthew 19:7-8.)

Thus marriages to be planned and executed in the Lord's way did not include divorce. Much of the burden of the success of a marriage must fall on the man. If he cultivates and nourishes his marriage and brings attention, happiness, love, and contentment to his wife, she will generally have no interest in seeking attention from another man. When men let business, sports, or other activities consume their interests above that of wife and family, then marriages are endangered. Women too have a similar obligation toward their husbands and their children. If they keep themselves and their homes attractive; if they keep love, attention, and admiration for their husbands burning brightly, few husbands would ever be tempted to stray from their marriage covenants.

23

Whenever I interview a man for a priesthood office, I ask him a series of questions about his personal life and conduct. For instance, I ask, "Are you married?" Almost always the answer is yes. My next question: "Do you love your wife?" Almost impatiently comes the answer: "Certainly!" Then I inquire, "But do you love her with *all your heart?*" This sobers the man and sometimes, with tears springing from his eyes, comes the declaration, "Yes, I do! She means the world to me and I do love her from the very bottom of my heart." I let that sink in for a moment and then ask, "How long has it been since you took her in your arms and said to her, 'I love you'?" The answer is frequently very revealing. Too many men are careless in this respect.

When I once asked this question of a prospective seventy, he took considerable time before answering. He was trying to remember. To help him I asked, "Has it been within the past year?" He slowly nodded. I continued, "Has it been within the past six months?" This time he took a moment before again nodding slowly. Still trying to help, I asked, "Have you told her within the past three months that you love her?" A really puzzled look came into his eyes and he replied, "Well, Elder Burton, I *think* so!" Here was a man who said he loved his wife with all his heart, yet he couldn't remember if he had told his wife he loved her during the past three months! He had been married in the temple in the Lord's appointed manner by one having authority, yet he had been neglectful.

It isn't the marriage ceremony alone that is important, nor the authority with which the covenant is closed, but the way in which that marriage is cultivated and developed that ensures success or failure in marriage. I instructed the man that he should never leave home in the morning without telling his wife he loved her. That should also be his greeting when he returned home in the evening. No day should pass without his wife and children knowing that he loved them. Some men have said to me, "I don't need to tell her, for my wife knows I love her." I feel that such is a very risky attitude to take. How can she know he loves her unless he not only tells her he loves her, but shows it by the way he acts, both privately and publicly?

I cringe when I hear married people make fun of one another, even in jest. Someday when one refers to his or her companion as "the ball and chain" or "the old man" or "the little woman," that other person is going to get up out of the wrong side of the bed and the fat will be in the fire. A harsh word spoken, thoughtless conduct, indifference, or ridicule can leave scars that are very slow to heal. To be treasured, love needs to be shared and demonstrated both in words and in deeds. It is often those little gestures and a continual striving to understand that make two individuals "one flesh."

How different was another experience I had as I interviewed a man about sixty-eight years old who was to be ordained a high priest and a bishop. When I asked him if he loved his wife, his eyes sparkled as he replied, "Indeed I do. I am one of the most fortunate men ever born. I was blessed with a loving wife." When I asked him how long it had been since he told her he loved her, he looked at his watch and said, "Forty-five minutes ago." I replied, "You pass!" He had caught the vision of how to preserve a successful marriage.

I can't read the statement of Adam, that Eve was now

"bone of his bones and flesh of his flesh," without sensing that wave of affection he felt for his noble companion. What great love is expressed in that simple statement that she was as important to him as life itself! Love is the only basis for an eternal marriage. That love must grow as a couple learn to work, worship, and live together as one. Marriage in the Lord's appointed way is a glorious concept and blessing. It is the key to that great family treasure awaiting the faithful in the kingdom of heaven.

No man can receive the fulness of eternity or a fulness of exaltation alone. No woman can receive that blessing alone. But when they are sealed together and they live for it, they can pass on to exaltation and become like their heavenly parents. This is the destiny of mankind and this is what the Lord desires for his children. But this blessing is reserved for those who are willing to keep the commandments of God, not for those who are rebellious.

There is, however, a problem that we must face up to. Whether we accept it or not, this is a man's world as far as courtship and marriage is concerned. A woman cannot be aggressive in finding a husband. As a result, there are many wonderful, faithful, capable, and lovely sisters who through no fault of their own have never married. Such sisters should never feel under any obligation or necessity of accepting a marriage proposal that is distasteful to them for fear they will come under condemnation. They should not hasten into a marriage that can only be a burden to them in the future instead of a joy. Our Heavenly Father will judge them according to the righteous desires of their hearts. If blessings of a noble marriage are withheld from a good woman in this life through no fault of her own, a just God will provide a way before the final judgment is made to give her an eternal companion who will be worthy of her just as she will be worthy of him. That marriage will have to be based on love and affection. In the long view of the eternities, such a couple will have a joyous family life of their own and will raise up children just as will those who have been sealed in life and have remained true and faithful. This is one of the grandest concepts of the new and everlasting covenant.

But what of those who, like my acquaintance in the Los Angeles airport, reject this message? Is there still hope for them? What of those teeming millions of people who have never even heard of Jesus Christ or of the eternal nature of the marriage covenant? Is the door now slammed in their faces? Could a God exist who planned eternal marriage for his children, yet who could be so cruel as to deny those children such blessings due to circumstances often beyond their control? And what of a church that claims to be the church of God, but which does not have the knowledge, power, or authority to perform such eternal marriages nor the ability to provide for those who have lived and died without ever having received such knowledge? Eternal marriage is a basic principle of family life. Unless such questions can be answered clearly and authoritatively, no church can claim to be the true church of Jesus Christ. This leaves us, then, with a desire to know what God has provided for us in his plan of salvation.

3

The Plan of Salvation

Most people feel there is more to life than our existence here in mortality. Most people in their inner hearts believe they lived some kind of a life before they were born. We meet a person we have never seen before and yet that person is somehow familiar to us. We ask ourselves the question, "Where have I seen him or her before?" That familiarity may be a carryover from faint memories of the spirit world that we bring with us when we come here. Perhaps the "love at first sight" concept of which we so often speak is a result of previous spiritual experiences. The instant friendships that spring up between people may be another carryover from a previous life. Even the doctrine of reincarnation, which some people believe in, may be a confused misunderstanding of the true concept of a premortal and a postmortal life, which is part of the overall plan God prepared for his children.

Enough has been stated previously to sustain a belief in a premortal life where we existed as spirit children of a heavenly father and a heavenly mother. There we were children in a heavenly family of spirits. If we were the children of God, then we had to be organized within that divine family as spirit children, or organized intelligences. There we had names by which we were known to one another, and there we differed in intelligence and ability just as do children who are born within a family in mortality.

The firstborn of all the spirit children of God was Jehovah, who was later to be known on earth as Jesus Christ. He was the most able, the most noble, and the most intelligent of all the spirit children of God. When Jehovah explained to Abraham the ranking of intelligent children of God, he said: "These two facts do exist, that there are two spirits, one being more intelligent than the other; there shall be another more intelligent than they; I am the Lord thy God, I am more intelligent than they all." (Abraham 3:19.) I have wondered in my own mind if Jehovah's intelligence was so superior that, when he said "I am more intelligent than they all," he meant than all the rest of us put together. He must have been a wonderfully noble and intelligent spirit for us to accept him to become our God and Father, as we shall later learn.

Another great and noble spirit was Michael, spoken of as the archangel, who was later to be known on earth as Adam. Gabriel, another great and noble spirit, was later known on earth as Noah. One of these earliest children of God was a spirit referred to as a son of the morning, signifying that he was one of those born early among the spirit children of God. His name was Lucifer, which means "the light bearer." There were other great and noble spirit leaders and also a multitude of spirits sometimes referred to as angels.

God the Father prepared a wonderful plan for the development of his children. By following his plan, which is called the plan of salvation, we as children of God can become like our heavenly parents. This plan was indeed carefully prepared and developed in great detail. I have found sixty-one scriptural references referring to laws, conditions, and principles that were all completed or decided on "before the foundation of the earth." As mortals, we have the ability to plan for the future and to plan for alternative actions to be taken should such changes become necessary to meet changing circumstances. God, with infinitely greater wisdom and experience, would also have planned carefully before undertaking anything as complex as the creation. There was nothing hurried or haphazard in the formulation of those plans. He too provided for all types of emergencies and contingencies. When everything was prepared, all alternatives considered, and actions decided on should emergencies develop, the plan was ready for presentation to God's family.

When the Lord talked to Abraham, he explained to him this planned pattern of life on earth known as the plan of salvation. We learn more about it from the following verses:

29

Now the Lord had shown unto me, Abraham, the intelligences that were organized before the world was; and among all these there were many of the noble and great ones;

And God saw these souls that they were good, and he stood in the midst of them, and he said: These I will make my rulers: for he stood among those that were spirits, and he saw that they were good; and he said unto me: Abraham, thou art one of them; thou wast chosen before thou wast born.

And there stood one among them that was like unto God [in fact, it was indeed Elohim, the Father], and he said unto those who were with him: We will go down, for there is space there, and we will take of these materials, and we will make an earth whereon these may dwell;

And we will prove them herewith, to see if they will do all things whatsoever the Lord their God shall command them;

And they who keep their first estate [that is, in the spirit world or in the premortal life] shall be added upon; and they who keep not their first estate shall not have glory in the same kingdom [here on earth] with those who keep their first estate; and they who keep their second estate [in other words, those who prove themselves valiant and faithful on earth] shall have glory added upon their heads for ever and ever. (Abraham 3:22-26.)

There in that great council in heaven, the plan of salvation was clearly defined for the spirit children of God. In that condition as spirits they did not have the power their parents had. Their growth and their power were limited to the spirit condition in which they lived. They could not create offspring. They could not have a fulness of glory or happiness because they were single spirits and did not have powerful bodies of flesh and bone as their parents had. In the spirit world they received an opportunity to show their faith by their works, but they were largely untested and untried as far as being on their own was concerned. They had been taught by their parents, but their parents were there to correct them when they made mistakes. Their parents were available to answer questions and teach them what to do. They saw, they heard, they felt, and they experienced, but always under the careful guidance and direction of parents and instructors. They did what they did because they were taught to do so. But they could only become truly tested and worthy of greater power if somehow they could be separated from their parents in another creation where they could exercise independent judgment and live by faith and not by sight.

God explained to his children that more powerful bodies of flesh and bone would be provided for them. Since these bodies would have creative power, one of the great tests would be to learn how to control them within the bounds and limitations of that creative power. Failure to be obedient in the exercise of that power on earth would disqualify that child from having such power in the eternities. The eternities are ruled by law and order, and any misuse of creative power there could cause havoc and disaster. Hence this temporary existence away from the presence of God would constitute a proving ground for the intelligence, obedience, and ability of each child of God to qualify for godhood.

For this reason, an earth would be prepared for them and they would be placed thereon with a curtain drawn to separate them from their heavenly parents. Communication would be only by prayer, by faith, and by listening to the whisperings of the Holy Ghost. They would have to learn by personal experience to distinguish between truth and error. They would have to learn to choose the truth and live by it, not because they had to, but because they chose and wanted to do so. They would have to learn to choose the right because it was right. They would have to demonstrate their obedience to the concept of divine law and order by exercising the full use of their own free agency. In a like manner God had become God, not because he was forced to be good and just and kind, but because he wanted to be that way. This was to be the pattern of growth. It was beset by many dangers, but the possibility of reaching perfection was there for those who were willing and able to pay the price necessary to reach that objective.

31

When this plan of salvation was presented to us, we shouted for joy. This was the joyful shout that God referred to when he spoke to Job. What a thrill must have permeated those spirit beings when this plan of growth and development was presented to them. They discovered that a way would be opened to them by means of which they could become perfect even as their parents became perfect before them. This was the plan, but it required a separation between God and his children. Thus, if they were to learn to distinguish between good and evil, between joy and sorrow, between happiness and wickedness, they would have to become mortal and become subject to all the dangers and trials of mortal life.

Undoubtedly our heavenly father and mother pointed out to us the dangers inherent in this mortal life. They told us of cold and heat, of hunger and suffering, of sickness and disease, of accidents, wars, injustices, catastrophes of nature, etc. We didn't even realize what they were talking about, for we had no experience to enable us to understand what these words meant. All we could think of was the glorious goal ahead and the plan by means of which we could reach that perfection. In view of our experience in living with our parents and the reality of that spirit life, we must have thought that we could conquer everything and rise above all temptations.

In our inexperience and in our optimism, we gave that great shout of joy and happiness and agreed to follow the Father's plan. Since we would be separated from God, a method would have to be provided to bring us back into his presence. Thus he said that he would provide a Savior for us, one who through his own free-will offering would take upon him the sins of the world and atone for them so we could again regain the presence of God the Eternal Father with perfected bodies of flesh and bone. Again we shouted for joy. That was the plan and we were willing to accept it. Now for the implementation of that plan.

The scriptures tell us what happened after God had presented the plan of salvation to us.

And the Lord said: Whom shall I send [to be this savior]? And one answered like unto the Son of Man [it was the Son of Man, or Jehovah]: Here am I, send me. And another [Lucifer] answered and said: Here am I, send me. And the Lord said: I will send the first.

And the second was angry, and kept not his first estate; and, at that day, many followed after him. (Abraham 3:27-28.)

We are told that one-third of the hosts of heaven chose to accept the plan of Lucifer and joined him in rebellion against the plan of the Father. (Revelation 12:4.) We are even told why the Father rejected the plan proposed by Lucifer. Lucifer's plan would have assured everyone of returning back into the presence of the Father. Not one would be lost, because Lucifer would not permit it. In other words, his plan was that of a dictatorship in which all choices would be made by him. Mankind would have to do exactly what they were told to do. His plan would have substituted safety and security for growth and development.

And I, the Lord God, spake unto Moses, saying: That Satan, whom thou hast commanded in the name of mine Only Begotten, is the same which was from the beginning, and he came before me, saying—Behold, here am I, send me, I will be thy son, and I will redeem all mankind, that one soul shall not be lost, and surely I will do it; wherefore give me thine honor.

But, behold, my Beloved Son, which was my Beloved and

32

Chosen from the beginning, said unto me—Father, thy will be done, and the glory be thine forever.

Wherefore, because that Satan rebelled against me, and sought to destroy the agency of man, which I, the Lord God, had given him, and also, that I should give unto him mine own power; by the power of mine Only Begotten, I caused that he should be cast down;

And he became Satan, yea, even the devil, the father of all lies, to deceive and to blind men, and to lead them captive at his will, even as many as would not hearken unto my voice. (Moses 4:1-4.)

How presumptuous Lucifer was, to think that he knew more than the Father! One must marvel at the foolishness of so many of the Father's children that they would think that a spirit, no matter how powerful he might be, could be more intelligent, more powerful, or have greater wisdom than the Father who created that spirit. It would seem that anyone who took the time to think would realize that a part could never be greater than the whole. People on earth allow themselves to be deceived by similar totalitarian doctrines that rob the individual of agency, just as did those spirits who were so deceived in the spirit world. People can make such mistakes when they harden their thoughts against the truth and refuse to weigh fully the consequences.

This reminds me of a person who came to me to ask advice and yet who told me after stating his position, "No matter what you say to me, I have made up my mind and nothing can change it!" I could not help but say to him, "Tell me, friend, why did you come to me for advice when nothing I can say to you could make you change your mind?" He became angry, got up, and left my office. He had made up his mind. He had stiffened his neck. He had hardened his heart. Under these circumstances, nothing I nor anyone else could say could change him or help him. He would have to wait until the bitter force of circumstance could teach him the error of his ways. Experience is often a bitter and expensive way of learning the truth. No wonder we refer to such experiences as the "school of hard knocks."

The plan of salvation was much more complete than has been outlined above. It included all those plans for the formation of the earth. It included an organization of the spirits as they existed in heaven into projected families for entry into earth life. It included all the preparations for contingencies that should arise on account of wars, accidents, natural catastrophes, diseases, rebellion, and all the other things that could happen to block the plan of God for the salvation of his children. After all, the whole object of this plan of salvation was summarized by the Lord in the following words as he told of his own work assignment: "For behold this is my work and my glory—to bring to pass the immortality and eternal life of man." (Moses 1:39.)

The immortality of man has already been accomplished through the atonement of Jesus Christ. By this means the prison door was opened and death was overcome by a resurrection that can restore to us again our bodies of flesh and bone. Eternal life is just another way of saying "God's life," or the kind of life that God the Father lives. In other words, eternal life refers to a perfect life with eternal increase. What a glorious promise this includes for all mortals born on earth!

It is the object of this book to point out the greatest treasures contained in the plan of salvation. The highest goal and treasure is that of eternal life, which we can refer to as exaltation. It was realized from the very beginning that not all of God's children would reach that exalted state. This is not because it is unattainable, but because some would not be willing to make that much effort to obtain such a treasure. Thus God in his love and tender mercy provided lesser treasures to meet such eventualities. There are many differing degrees of glory, which will be discussed later. God did provide for universal salvation, so that almost every one of his children would find some degree of glory. Each one of these degrees of glory will be better than what we had in the premortal life. We may rest assured that God's desire is that we reach as high as we possibly can. He has provided, through the marvelous law of repentance, that even if we sometimes lose our way for a period and make mistakes, those errors can be corrected and our feet can again be placed in the path leading to exaltation. It is for this reason that we should strive for the ultimate goal of perfection. Our goal should be the ultimate treasure which is eternal life, rather than to settle for any lesser treasure.

Sometimes we think that God's work is being thwarted by evil, but this can never be. There are some who would criticize the plan of God and suggest that God could have done this or that to improve things. But God, speaking through Isaiah, said: "For my thoughts are not your thoughts, neither are your ways my ways, saith the Lord. For as the heavens are higher than the earth, so are my ways higher than your ways, and my thoughts than your thoughts." (Isaiah 55:8-9.) God was able to say this because he knows all things from the very beginning to the very end of time. When Satan sought to destroy the work of God in the beginning, he failed because he did not know the mind of God. When he attempted to destroy the work of God on earth at the temptation of Adam and Eve, again he failed because he did not know the mind of God. In other words, God used the destructiveness of Satan to turn it to good for the very reason that God the Father already had experience in all such things and knew what to do to meet this apparent blocking of his plan. As he said through Isaiah:

Remember this, and shew yourselves men: bring it again to mind, O ye transgressors.

Remember the former things of old: for I am God, and there is none else; I am God, and there is none like me,

Declaring the end from the beginning, and from ancient times the things that are not yet done, saying, My counsel shall stand, and I will do all my pleasure. (Isaiah 46:8-10.)

When we are sometimes tempted to question the Lord, we ought to think on these things and remember that the plan of salvation was authored by Elohim, the Eternal Father, who knows all things. He is omnipotent, all-wise, all-powerful, all-knowing, perfect. Thus the plan of salvation was developed for the good of man to bring about his immortality and his eternal life.

This plan of salvation was and is the divine plan by means of which each spirit child of our heavenly parents can demonstrate his or her reliability and willingness to do those things which are godlike. Without force or being compelled to do so, we can prove our wisdom by choosing that which is right and true; that which will edify and uplift; that which is correct and everlasting— not because we have to, not even because we are told to do so, but because of its intrinsic basic goodness and truth. We can thus demonstrate our ability to handle and use the tremendous powers and gifts of godhood, which is the treasure promised us as a result of successfully meeting the challenges of earth life.

It is this hope of future glory and promise that gives us courage and the will to persist no matter how discouraging life or circumstances may appear to be at the present moment. This hope gives us faith to persevere to the end and to realize that man is not an accident, but that we are children of God with a divine purpose and destiny.

36

4

The Promised Reward

The plan of salvation contains a promise of a great treasure or reward to be attained by those who are willing to follow that plan and pay the price to obtain that blessing. The greater the reward, the more we will sacrifice to obtain it. The treasure that God offered his children was nothing more nor less than eternal life. This is not immortality, but something far more valuable. It is a treasure of such magnitude that it staggers the imagination of man. Actually, it is the glory of God, as we learn from reading the Pearl of Great Price, Moses 1:39.

We are so accustomed to speaking of eternal life in a rather loose manner that we often fail to understand the precise meaning of this expression. Eternal life is too often confused with immortality or the power to live forever. The way the Lord uses the word *eternal* is in a nobler and more powerful sense. He speaks of eternal things as those pertaining to his manner of life. He personalizes this word, as is plain from the following scripture: "For, behold, the mystery of godliness, how great is it! For, behold, I am endless, and the punishment which is given from my hand is endless punishment, for Endless is my name. Wherefore—Eternal punishment is God's punishment. Endless punishment is God's punishment." (D&C 19:10-12.) The same could have been said of reward, treasures, blessings, and powers. Eternal treasures are God's treasures. This is made abundantly plain in a similar scripture from the Pearl of Great Price:

"Behold, I am God; Man of Holiness is my name; Man of Counsel is my name; and Endless and Eternal is my name, also." (Moses 7:35.) Therefore, eternal life must be the kind of life that God the Eternal Father lives.

Using *eternal* as an adjective that refers to God gives us a different understanding of the immensity of that treasure which God the Father offers his children. He said he would give "all that he had" to his children if they would follow his divine plan. As part of the oath and covenant of the priesthood, Jesus explained that "he that receiveth me receiveth my Father; And he that receiveth my Father receiveth my Father's kingdom; therefore all that my Father hath shall be given unto him. And this is according to the oath and covenant which belongeth to the priesthood." (D&C 84:37-39.) Membership in the kingdom or family of God the Eternal Father as exalted sons and daughters of God is the treasure spoken of as "eternal lives."

The ability to live and work and increase the way God our Father does is eternal life, or the kind of life our eternal father and eternal mother live. The increase that results from such a godlike life is expressed by the words *eternal lives,* or continuing increase. Thus the great treasure promised us is a family treasure, referring to the perfected family of God as it will exist in the highest order of the celestial kingdom. As children of God, by perfecting our lives while on this earth, we can eventually develop into gods and goddesses just as children on earth grow up to become adults like their parents. Thus we in turn, as children of God, can have families that can continue to grow as does the family of God. If we catch this vision, we can begin to understand the importance of family life on earth when it is organized as God intended it to be.

In speaking of rewards or treasures promised us for our future lives, we need to remember that these promises were given us in a premortal life. It has been stated before how many scriptural references are made

38

that refer to the planning done "before the foundation of the world." Where did this knowledge first come to us? When God speaks of a time "before the foundation of the world," he was speaking of a premortal life. Many people find this concept difficult to believe. I can't understand how anyone can see the wonderful organization of the universe, life in all its complexities, yet mutually self-supporting, without realizing that it just did not happen by chance—it had to be planned. This complex organization just did not develop by accident. When I contemplate man and his wonderful body and his marvelous mind, it appears self-evident to me that man is marvelously different from other life forms. The intelligence he possesses, his mind, his agency or power to make decisions, set him apart as special. This earth life is only part of an on-going existence. We lived before, we live now, we will live again, for we are eternal beings, sons and daughters of an eternal father and mother. This thought was expressed by David as he sang:

39

When I consider thy heavens, the work of thy fingers, the moon and the stars, which thou hast ordained;

What is man, that thou art mindful of him? and the son of man, that thou visitest him?

For thou hast made him a little lower than the angels, and hast crowned him with glory and honour.

Thou madest him to have dominion over the works of thy hands; thou hast put all things under his feet:

All sheep and oxen, yea, and the beasts of the field;

The fowl of the air, and the fish of the sea, and whatsoever passeth through the paths of the seas.

O Lord our Lord, how excellent is thy name in all the earth! (Psalm 8:3-9.)

I grew up in a family where I was taught from my earliest infancy about a premortal life as a spirit child of immortal parents. I have always believed that I was a child of God. While engaged in missionary work with people not of our faith, it came as a great shock to me to learn that many people and the churches to which they belong do not believe in a premortal life. I was severely criticized for accepting as true such a concept, which to them was obviously ridiculous. To me it was logical and not ridiculous, but I decided I ought to do more than just accept the teaching of my parents. I turned to the scriptures to see if the teachings of our church were that far away from the truth. As a result of such a study, I received an increased testimony of the truth of the concept of a premortal life. I had an added assurance that my parents had taught me correct principles.

40

When the apostle Paul wrote to the Hebrews, he told them they were children of God. Throughout his letter he speaks of the Father. What being is entitled to use that term *father* without having children, sons and daughters who can follow in his footsteps? Paul wrote:

And ye have forgotten the exhortation which speaketh unto you as unto children, My son, despise not thou the chastening of the Lord, nor faint when thou art rebuked of him:

For whom the Lord loveth he chasteneth, and scourgeth every son whom he receiveth.

If ye endure chastening, God dealeth with you as with sons; for what son is he whom the father chasteneth not?

But if ye be without chastisement, whereof all are partakers, then are ye bastards, and not sons.

Furthermore we have had fathers of our flesh which corrected us, and we gave them reverence: *shall we not much rather be in subjection unto the Father of spirits, and live?* (Hebrews 12:5-9. Italics added.)

What spirits did Paul have reference to if not to the spirits of the Hebrews to whom he addressed his letter? In that same chapter, Paul speaks of Jesus Christ as the Firstborn of these spirit children.

But ye are come unto mount Sion, and unto the city of the living God, the heavenly Jerusalem, and to an innumerable company of angels,

To the general assembly and church of the firstborn, which are written in heaven, and to God the Judge of all, and to the spirits of just men made perfect,

And to Jesus the mediator of the new covenant, and to the blood of sprinkling, that speaketh better things than that of Abel. (Hebrews 12:22-24.)

We know there were many born on the earth before Jesus Christ was born into mortality. If Jesus was the Firstborn, then it must have been in that premortal life. If he was the Firstborn, then it follows there must have been other sons and daughters born to God in that premortal life. These spirit children made up that innumerable concourse of angel spirits to which Paul referred in the above scripture. When Paul spoke to the Greeks in Athens, he said, "We are the offspring of God." (Acts 17:29.)

41

When I mentioned this to those who criticized my belief, they pointed out that the name "Firstborn" was given to Jesus because he was the firstborn of Mary. For example, Luke describes how she brought forth her firstborn son and wrapped him in swaddling clothes. However, in speaking of the Savior who was to come, David wrote: "He shall cry unto me, Thou art my father, my God, and the rock of my salvation. Also I will make him *my firstborn*, higher than the kings of the earth." (Psalm 89:26-27. Italics added.) So the Savior was not only the firstborn of Mary in the flesh, but he was also the Firstborn Son of God the Father in the spirit. Paul makes it very clear that being the Firstborn referred to his sonship in the spirit, for Jesus Christ was the Only Begotten Son of the Father in the flesh.

For whom he did foreknow, he also did predestinate to be conformed to the image of his Son, that he might be the firstborn among many brethren. (Romans 8:29.)

Who is the image of the invisible God, *the firstborn of every creature:*

For by him were all things created, that are in heaven, and that are in earth, visible and invisible, whether they be thrones, or dominions, or principalities, or powers: all things were created by him, and for him:

And he is before all things, and by him all things consist. (Colossians 1:15-17. Italics added.)

I have emphasized a portion of these scriptures to indicate that Jesus was the Firstborn of all the spirit sons and daughters of God. This gives him preeminence by birthright. When one reads Moses' account of the opening of the first dispensation, he refers to the future sacrifice of the Only Begotten of the Father who is full of grace and truth. (Moses 5:7.) Through modern revelation we learn that Jesus himself states that he was the Firstborn of the Father, so there should be no doubt concerning his position in the spirit world before the formation of this earth: "And now, verily I say unto you, I was in the beginning with the Father, and am the Firstborn; And all those who are begotten through me are partakers of the glory of the same, and are the church of the Firstborn." (D&C 93:21-22.)

There are numerous biblical passages that refer to the premortal life of the Savior, but there are also many passages that refer to the premortal life of others. Thus we do have biblical evidences for a premortal life of man, as the following scriptures indicate:

Thus the heavens and the earth were finished, *and all the host of them.*

These are the generations of the heavens and of the earth when they were created, in the day that the Lord God made the earth and the heavens,

And every plant of the field before it was in the earth, and every herb of the field before it grew: for the Lord God had not caused it to rain upon the earth, *and there was not a man to till the ground.* (Genesis 2:1, 4-5. Italics added.)

Then shall the dust return to the earth as it was: *and the spirit shall return unto God who gave it.* (Ecclesiastes 12:7. Italics added.)

Again I have emphasized those passages which teach me plainly that the hosts of heaven were the spirit children of God who were created before the foundation of this earth.

When the Lord called Jeremiah to be a prophet, he told him that he had known him long before he was born upon the earth and that he had been foreordained to be a prophet: "Before I formed thee in the belly I knew thee; and before thou camest forth out of the womb I sanctified thee, and I ordained thee a prophet unto the nations." (Jeremiah 1:5.) Similarly, when Job complained to the Lord about his sufferings in the flesh, God answered him as follows:

Gird up now thy loins like a man: for I will demand of thee, and answer thou me.

Where wast thou when I laid the foundations of the earth? declare, if thou hast understanding.

Who hath laid the measures thereof, if thou knowest? or who hath stretched the line upon it?

Whereupon are the foundations thereof fastened? or who laid the corner stone thereof:

When the morning stars sang together, and all the sons of God shouted for joy? (Job 38:3-7.)

Of course the Lord knew that Job had forgotten all these things when he came to earth as a mortal being. He was reminding him, however, that the sons of God were with him when the foundations of the earth were laid. This is similar to the teaching of Paul to the Ephesians:

Blessed be the God and Father of our Lord Jesus Christ, who hath blessed us with all spiritual blessings in heavenly places in Christ:

According as he hath chosen us in him before the foundation of the world, that we should be holy and without blame before him in love:

Having predestinated [foreordained] us unto the adoption of children by Jesus Christ to himself, according to the good pleasure of his will. (Ephesians 1:3-5.)

and to the Thessalonians:

But we are bound to give thanks alway to God for you, brethren beloved of the Lord, because God hath from the beginning chosen you to salvation through sanctification of the Spirit and belief of the truth:

Whereunto he called you by our gospel, to the obtaining of the glory of our Lord Jesus Christ. (2 Thessalonians 2:13-14.)

The doctrine of a premortal life was well understood

43

by the disciples of Jesus Christ. The following scripture makes this clear:

And as Jesus passed by, he saw a man which was blind from his birth.

And his disciples asked him, saying, Master, who did sin, this man, or his parents, that he was born blind?

Jesus answered, Neither hath this man sinned [in the premortal state that he was born blind] nor his parents: but that the works of God should be made manifest in him. (John 9:1-4.)

44

If the concept of a premortal life for the blind man had been an incorrect principle, Jesus would have rebuked the disciples for making such a statement and would have put them straight. The possibility of being disobedient in the premortal life was so real and so well understood by them and by him that he accepted the fact that their concept of a premortal life was correct and needed no further comment or explanation. He went on to explain that "this man's" blindness was only a temporary condition, and that it had been planned in advance to enable Jesus to show his power to the people so they might recognize him as one possessing great priesthood power.

Not all the spirit children of God were faithful in the premortal state. Some actually rebelled against him, as Jude makes plain in the following verse: "And the angels which kept not their first estate, but left their own habitation, he hath preserved in everlasting chains under darkness unto the judgment of the great day." (Jude 6.) More explanation is given in the revelations of John the Beloved:

And there was war in heaven: Michael and his angels fought against the dragon; and the dragon fought and his angels,

And prevailed not; neither was their place found any more in heaven.

And the great dragon was cast out, that old serpent, called the Devil, and Satan, which deceiveth the whole world: he was cast out into the earth, and his angels were cast out with him. (Revelation 12:7-9.)

Modern revelation makes it abundantly clear that we existed as spirit children of God before we were born into mortality:

And now, verily I say unto you, I was in the beginning with the Father, and am the Firstborn;

And all those who are begotten through me are partakers of the glory of the same, and are the church of the Firstborn.

Ye were also in the beginning with the Father; that which is Spirit, even the Spirit of truth;

Man was also in the beginning with God. Intelligence, or the light of truth, was not created or made, neither indeed can be. (D&C 93:21-23, 29.)

45

From these and other scriptural citations, there is sufficient evidence to convince me that through the centuries men of God have known there is more to life than just this mortal existence. Knowing that I existed before I came into this life gives me confidence that what occurs in this life is not the result of blind chance. Some chance is involved, but that is also taken care of in the careful planning of all that is done. When Paul taught the principle of the resurrection, he wrote: "If in this life only we have hope in Christ, we are of all men most miserable." (1 Corinthians 15:19.) I would like to paraphrase that scripture and apply it to this mortal life by saying that if we try to judge the justice and the mercy of God only by what transpires in this mortal life, then we of all men are most foolish. God is a just God who loves all his children, but there are too many things that transpire in mortality that cannot be explained by thinking that life begins for us with our birth upon this earth. Much can be explained, however, if we realize that we have lived before as spirit children of our Father in heaven. Many of the blessings and many of the problems we face upon this earth are the result of the kind of life we lived in the premortal state before we were born into mortality.

In making this statement, we must be most careful not to prejudge people on the evidence of this life alone.

The fact that a person is born with a crippled body or mind does not prove that he or she was less faithful in the previous life than a well-born person. Much of that which transpires in this world is the result of accident or sickness. Disease and accidents over which a person has absolutely no personal control can result in damage to the body or mind, regardless of how noble that spirit may have been in the premortal life. When we consider whole populations, however, instead of individual beings, it appears to be evident that there are blessings and advantages that come to us as groups of people, resulting from the degree of faithfulness of those people as a group in their premortal life. Some, such as the children of Israel, were given special blessings to serve as leaders to point the way for others to follow. We also believe that many are called as prophets and leaders who were foreordained to that work because of their faithfulness in the premortal life. My personal opinion is that no one was foreordained to failure. I believe that all of us were created to achieve much more than any of us actually accomplish. Our potential is almost limitless. Most of the restrictions in our ability to accomplish great achievements on this earth are self-imposed limitations.

When the apostle Paul talked to the Greeks in Athens on Mars Hill, he explained to them that God

hath made of one blood all nations of men for to dwell on all the face of the earth, and hath determined the times before appointed, and the bounds of their habitation;

That they should seek the Lord, if haply they might feel after him, and find him, though he be not far from every one of us:

For in him we live, and move, and have our being; as certain of your own poets have said, for we are also his offspring.

Forasmuch then as we are the offspring of God, we ought not to think that the Godhead is like unto gold, or silver, or stone, graven by art and man's device. (Acts 17:26-29.)

Too often we read only the first part of those verses and do not read the complete thought. When Paul said there were times appointed for us and bounds set for the areas we were to inhabit, he knew what he was talking about. These limitations became part of the universal laws of truth under which we live. If we violate these universal laws, it will be to our own destruction. We have to pay a penalty for disobedience whether we disobey knowingly or unknowingly. We can see that our world was not created by accident, but was thoroughly planned and carefully executed. There actually were times and places appointed for our individual entry into this world. Races, families, and times were appointed for us according to a divine plan. It is to our personal advantage, then, to learn who we are so we can prepare ourselves to receive the blessings reserved for us and achieve that peace of mind and conscience and that degree of freedom for which we all yearn.

47

The truth that persons were chosen for certain work before this earth was formed is found in many places in the scriptures, as cited above. When Moses taught the children of Israel, he made this remarkable statement: "When the Most High divided to the nations their inheritance, when he separated the sons of Adam, he set the bounds of the people according to the number of the children of Israel." (Deuteronomy 32:8.) This informs us that approximately 2500 years before there were any children of Israel, God divided Adam's sons into families to reflect the coming destiny of those same children of Israel. Jesus Christ himself came through definite lineage lines. These are concepts that should be kept clearly in mind as we contemplate the coming of Elijah and the work for the salvation of the dead. This life is the second phase of a life that began in the premortal state long before we entered into life on this earth.

Thus we learn that this life was planned to test our worthiness and our obedience. At the same time God promised us great rewards and treasures for that obedience. If we are successful in following the plan of salvation, there are no limits set to that reward. The scriptures inform us: "Then shall they be gods, because they have no end; therefore shall they be from everlasting to everlasting, because they continue; then shall they be above all, because all things are subject unto them. Then shall they be gods, because they have all power, and the angels are subject unto them." (D&C 132:20.) This means that we were meant to become as our Heavenly Father and our heavenly mother now are, and that we can share their power, their majesty, their knowledge, their joy, for we are their children. We cannot imagine a greater reward or a greater treasure. These were the promises made to the fathers or patriarchs. These are the promises also made to their progeny. These promises, these rewards, this promised treasure are our heritage blessing. Of all the treasures and gifts of God, eternal life is the greatest of all, as we learn from modern scripture: "And, if you keep my commandments and endure to the end you shall have eternal life, which gift is the greatest of all the gifts of God." (D&C 14:7.)

That treasure, then, is worth working for as the ultimate goal of this earth life.

5

Earth Life Begins

The plan of salvation began to operate with the creation of the earth. There are many theories as to how the earth was formed and how man came to be placed upon it. All such theories are interesting, but for the purpose of this writing, I will purposely limit myself to the scriptures. At one time Moses wanted to know the details of how the earth was formed and inquired of the Lord:

And it came to pass that Moses called upon God, saying: Tell me, I pray thee, why these things are so, and by what thou madest them?

And behold, the glory of the Lord was upon Moses, so that Moses stood in the presence of God, and talked with him face to face. And the Lord God said unto Moses: For mine own purpose have I made these things. Here is wisdom and it remaineth in me. (Moses 1:30-31.)

Paraphrasing these words, the Lord said to Moses: "How I created this world is none of your business, and I'm not going to tell you. You couldn't understand it even if I told you. Besides, it isn't necessary for you to know how it was done. It is sufficient for you to know that it was done. That is all you need to know to work out your own salvation." God did, however, add this important piece of information:

. . . by the word of my power, have I created them, which is mine Only Begotten Son, who is full of grace and truth.

And worlds without number have I created; and I also

created them for mine own purpose; and by the Son I created them, which is mine Only Begotten.

And the first man of all men have I called Adam, which is many.

But only an account of this earth, and the inhabitants thereof, give I unto you. For behold, there are many worlds that have passed away by the word of my power. And there are many that now stand, and innumerable are they unto man, but all things are numbered unto me, for they are mine and I know them. (Moses 1:32-35.)

In other words, God gives to man all he needs to know to work out his salvation. We have a promise that later on we will know all things, even as God does. But that knowledge will come only when we have the capacity and the opportunity to use it profitably.

However it was done, the universe was created and an earth prepared so the plan of salvation could become operative. As we learned in Chapter 2, Adam and Eve were placed on the earth as immortal beings and began their earth life in the Garden of Eden. The story of how Adam and Eve fell from their immortal or perfect state is well-known and need not be repeated here. We need only remark that Eve was deceived when she partook of the forbidden fruit. That fruit, whatever it was, caused a change in her physical being so that blood was formed and the seeds of eventual death were sown in her body. She thus became mortal.

Adam then was faced with two alternatives. He could have refrained from eating the fruit and thus have broken the command God gave them to remain together always, or he could have eaten the forbidden fruit and kept that first commandment to remain together. He chose the lesser of the two evils and partook of the fruit so that they could keep the greater commandment and so that he could remain with his beloved companion. He chose wisely and well.

When Adam and Eve partook of the forbidden fruit, they were disobedient to a command of God. Sin entered the world. Sin is nothing more nor less than disobedience.

God then, being a God of justice, had to drive them out of the Garden of Eden so they could not partake of the fruit of the tree of life and by so eating have counteracted that poison in their systems and thus been able to live forever in a state of disobedience or sin. This would have destroyed the plan of salvation. (See Alma 42:2-5.) So they were driven from the Garden of Eden, and we read: "Unto the woman, I, the Lord God, said: I will greatly multiply thy sorrow and thy conception. In sorrow thou shalt bring forth children, and thy desire shall be to thy husband, and he shall rule over thee [in righteousness]." (Moses 4:22.) Too many people misread this scripture and think that God condemned Eve to bear her children in pain, but the scripture does not say so. The companion scripture in Genesis 3:16 uses the same word, *sorrow*. In other words, Eve was to sorrow at the thought of bringing children into the world amid the sin, corruption, temptations, and buffetings of Satan that they would have to face. Her love for her children would be so great that she would suffer in their behalf and spare them if she possibly could. But, as we read later on, God also gave her consolation to temper that sorrow.

The scripture goes on to tell us that Father Adam would sorrow also: "And unto Adam, I, the Lord God, said: Because thou hast hearkened unto the voice of thy wife, and hast eaten of the fruit of the tree of which I commanded thee, saying—Thou shalt not eat of it, cursed shall be the ground for thy sake; in sorrow shalt thou eat of it all the days of thy life." (Moses 4:23.) Here again the word *sorrow* is used, for Adam also was to suffer at the thought that his children would have to be brought up in a world of sin and wickedness. He too would want to spare them that suffering if he could. The sorrow would come when he realized that he could not save them all even though he, like Eve, would love every one of them. The thought of losing even one of these children would be like a knife thrust into their hearts. Indeed, they would suffer sorrow whenever their children became disobedient and cast away their promised heritage blessings. Note that the curse was not placed on Adam, but on the earth. It was the ground that was cursed, not the man. In other words, the cursing of the ground was to be "for thy sake," or to be a blessing to Adam. A good explanation is found in the statement made by the Lord to Joseph Smith when Joseph was a prisoner in the jail at Liberty, Missouri: "My son, peace be unto thy soul; thine adversity and thine afflictions shall be but a small moment; and then, if thou endure it well, God shall exalt thee on high; thou shalt triumph over all thy foes." (D&C 121:7-8.) So Adam likewise, if he endured it well, would find the cursing of the ground to be a blessing to him in the end. It is quite unlikely that Adam understood this when the Lord first uttered that promise, but he must have given this promise greater consideration as the Lord gave him further instruction.

As Adam and Eve received children in mortality, they asked the Lord for further light and knowledge and it was given them:

And Adam and Eve, his wife, called upon the name of the Lord, and they heard the voice of the Lord from the way toward the Garden of Eden, speaking unto them, and they saw him not; for they were shut out from his presence.

And he gave unto them commandments, that they should worship the Lord their God, and should offer the firstlings of their flocks, for an offering unto the Lord. And Adam was obedient unto the commandments of the Lord. (Moses 5:4-5.)

There is a great message to be learned in this scripture as one reflects on it. Adam and Eve were told to offer the "firstlings of the flock" unto the Lord. Today we are also told to offer an offering unto the Lord in righteousness; however, many do not offer the "firstlings," but the last fruits of their labor to the Lord. Probably that is why so many people are not as prosperous as they otherwise could be. They take care of all their personal obligations first and then from what they have left over they attempt to pay their offering unto the Lord. The problem is that often nothing is left, and the offering to the Lord then becomes shortchanged. If a person would do as Adam and Eve did and offer the firstlings instead of the last fruits of their labor, the Lord could bless them as he did our first parents.

I was talking one day with some bishops who were friends of mine, and our conversation turned toward helping the poor and needy. One bishop said, "Almost invariably the persons in my ward who are in need are those very persons who do not pay tithing nor fast offerings and who are not diligent in attendance at meetings or in priesthood assignments." The other bishops in turn said that this was also true in their wards. The Lord in justice cannot give blessings to those who do not earn them, but he does bless those who keep their covenants. This also applies to those who, having their hearts turned to their fathers and mothers, take care of their genealogical priesthood assignments and obligations. They put things in proper perspective and realize that family obligations, both for the living and for the dead, should take precedence over selfish personal desires.

53

We are not told how long Adam and Eve were obedient to the commandments of the Lord. Adam lived for almost a thousand years and certainly had plenty of opportunity to show his devotion over a long period of time. The scriptures state that Adam and Eve had sons and daughters born to them and began to multiply and replenish the earth, so many years must have been spent in gaining experience and demonstrating their obedience. We can be sure that this testing period was long enough to satisfy the Lord that they would do whatever they were told to do. They proved their faith by their works. The scripture then goes on to inform us:

And after many days an angel of the Lord appeared unto Adam, saying: Why dost thou offer sacrifices unto the Lord? And Adam said unto him: I know not, save the Lord commanded me.

And then the angel spake, saying: This thing is a similitude of the sacrifice of the Only Begotten of the Father, which is full of grace and truth.

Wherefore, thou shalt do all that thou doest in the name of the Son, and thou shalt repent and call upon God in the name of the Son forevermore.

And in that day the Holy Ghost fell upon Adam, which beareth record of the Father and the Son, saying: I am the Only Begotten of the Father from the beginning, henceforth and forever, that as thou hast fallen thou mayest be redeemed, and all mankind, even as many as will. (Moses 5:6-9.)

Thus for the first time in mortality the promise was given to Adam and Eve that a Savior would be provided for them and that the consequences of their original disobedience could thus be compensated. This redemption was to be theirs on the basis of repentance, and then the mercy of God could be made manifest in their behalf.

One of the most beautiful explanations of the mercy of God and how it functions to aid mankind is given in the Book of Mormon. The prophet Amulek explains how the mercy of God operates to overpower justice, but only on the condition of repentance:

> For it is expedient that an atonement should be made; for according to the great plan of the Eternal God there must be an atonement made, or else all mankind must unavoidably perish; yea, all are hardened; yea, all are fallen and are lost, and must perish except it be through the atonement which it is expedient should be made.
>
> For it is expedient that there should be a great and last sacrifice; yea, not a sacrifice of man, neither of beast, neither of any manner of fowl; for it shall not be a human sacrifice; but it must be an infinite and eternal sacrifice.
>
> Now there is not any man that can sacrifice his own blood which will atone for the sins of another. Now, if a man murdereth, behold will our law, which is just, take the life of his brother? I say unto you, Nay.
>
> But the law requireth the life of him who hath murdered; therefore there can be nothing which is short of an infinite atonement which will suffice for the sins of the world.
>
> Therefore, it is expedient that there should be a great and last sacrifice; and then shall there be, or it is expedient there

should be, a stop to the shedding of blood; then shall the law of Moses be fulfilled; yea, it shall be all fulfilled, every jot and tittle, and none shall have passed away.

And behold, this is the whole meaning of the law, every whit pointing to that great and last sacrifice; and that great and last sacrifice will be the Son of God, yea, infinite and eternal.

And thus he shall bring salvation to all those who shall believe on his name; this being the intent of this last sacrifice, to bring about the bowels of mercy, which overpowereth justice, and bringeth about means unto men that they may have faith unto repentance.

And thus mercy can satisfy the demands of justice, and encircles them in the arms of safety, while he that exercises no faith unto repentance is exposed to the whole law of the demands of justice; therefore only unto him that has faith unto repentance is brought about the great and eternal plan of redemption. (Alma 34:9-16.)

This, then, was the promise given to Father Adam and Mother Eve by means of which they now knew that forgiveness and restoration into the presence of God the Father was possible. This is summarized by Alma in these words as he spoke to his son Corianton:

I say unto thee, my son, that the plan of restoration is requisite with the justice of God; for it is requisite that all things should be restored to their proper order. Behold, it is requisite and just, according to the power and resurrection of Christ, that the soul of man should be restored to its body, and that every part of the body should be restored to itself.

And it is requisite with the justice of God that men should be judged according to their works; and if their works were good in this life, and the desires of their hearts were good, that they should also, at the last day, be restored unto that which is good.

And if their works are evil they shall be restored unto them for evil. Therefore, all things shall be restored to their proper order, every thing to its natural frame—mortality raised to immortality, corruption to incorruption—raised to endless happiness to inherit the kingdom of God, or to endless misery to inherit the kingdom of the devil, the one on one hand, the other on the other—

55

The one raised to happiness according to his desires of happiness, or good according to his desires of good; and the other to evil according to his desires of evil; for as he has desired to do evil all the day long even so shall he have his reward of evil when the night cometh.

And so it is on the other hand. If he hath repented of his sins, and desired righteousness until the end of his days, even so he shall be rewarded unto righteousness. (Alma 41:2-6.)

When these glorious principles were explained to Adam and Eve, there was no end to the joy and happiness they felt. A way had been opened to them as the promise was given that they, by following these principles, could find exaltation into the very presence of God the Eternal Father again. They had lived in his presence before the fall. They knew him intimately as they had also known his son Jehovah. They had walked with them in the garden and had known the joy of their companionship. They had profited from their counsel as these eternal beings had instructed them. The very clothes they wore were garments of skins made for them by their hands. Their joy knew no bounds. "And in that day Adam blessed God and was filled, and began to prophesy concerning all the families of the earth, saying: Blessed be the name of God, for because of my transgression my eyes are opened, and in this life I shall have joy, and again in the flesh I shall see God." (Moses 5:10.) Eve, his wife, was also filled with this same joy, and they blessed the name of God, and made all things known to their sons and daughters. They wanted their children to know about these promises and to feel the same joy they felt. They wanted to pass on to them these promises as their eternal blessings.

This, then, is the first recorded promise made to the fathers. It applies to all the families of the earth. It was to be a promise for all mankind, a promise to be shared and enjoyed by all. There were no limits set for any of God's children who were to inherit mortal bodies. They could all be restored again in their proper families, as they had been organized to come to the earth. However, this was to be accomplished only if those children obeyed the restrictions given to our first parents. Salvation is dependent upon the laws on which it is based.

6

The Story of Cain and Abel

From the standpoint of family relationships and priesthood heritage, there are few stories in the scripture more important than the story of Cain and his brother Abel. Many read this account only as an interesting story and sum up its moral in the phrase that we ought to be our brother's keeper. To treat this story so casually is to miss its true value. The scriptural story has great spiritual significance. It carries a warning to us that no matter how strong we were as spirits and no matter how strong and faithful our parents or progenitors are, as individuals we must follow God's plan if we are to succeed.

We agreed to follow the plan of salvation as it was presented to us in the premortal world. There are no shortcuts and there can be no substitutions. This was a God-given plan which, if followed, would bring us back into the presence of God, ready to receive the treasure he promised us. This was something that Cain overlooked. God tried to explain it to him and remind Cain that he had lived before, and therefore God knew his weaknesses as well as his strengths.

Our Heavenly Father has given us a similar warning for our day to remind us of our weaknesses:

Behold, there are many called, but few are chosen. And why are they not chosen?

Because their hearts are set so much upon the things of

this world, and aspire to the honors of men, that they do not learn this one lesson—

That the rights of the priesthood are inseparably connected with the powers of heaven, and that the powers of heaven cannot be controlled nor handled only upon the principles of righteousness.

That they may be conferred upon us, it is true; but when we undertake to cover our sins, or to gratify our pride, our vain ambition, or to exercise control or dominion or compulsion upon the souls of the children of men, in any degree of unrighteousness, behold, the heavens withdraw themselves; the Spirit of the Lord is grieved; and when it is withdrawn, Amen to the priesthood or the authority of that man. (D&C 121:34-37.)

That withdrawal of the priesthood happened to Cain and it can happen to us if we forget the eternal or godlike covenants we have made. On the other hand, if we keep those covenants, that marvelous eternal treasure is freely given us at the conclusion of our testing period.

Now let us pick up the story of Cain and Abel. As Adam and Eve realized the promises God had given them by means of which they and their children could be restored again into the presence of God the Eternal Father, they made these things known unto their sons and daughters:

And Adam and Eve blessed the name of God, and they made all things known unto their sons and their daughters.

And Satan came among them, saying: *Believe it not;* and they believed it not, and they loved Satan more than God. And men began from that time forth to be carnal, sensual, and devilish. (Moses 5:12-13. Italics added.)

In those three words, "Believe it not," the whole mission of Satan is defined. It is a negative doctrine. It is destructive and is the very opposite of the doctrine of Jesus Christ. The doctrine of Jesus Christ is positive, uplifting, and constructive. It can be summarized in one word: "Believe!" It is relatively easy to distinguish between

59

these two doctrines because of their opposite nature. As Nephi explained it:

Wherefore, men are free according to the flesh; and all things are given them which are expedient unto man. And they are free to choose liberty and eternal life, through the great mediation of all men, or to choose captivity and death, according to the captivity and power of the devil; for he seeketh that all men might be miserable like unto himself. (2 Nephi 2:27.)

When Satan lies to us and tries to make us as miserable as he is, how can we tell what is truth and what is error? Nephi tells us (2 Nephi 9:9) that Satan can transform himself almost into an angel of light, and in this guise Satan has deceived many. There have been many men and women who, after receiving the truth, have allowed themselves to be deceived by this powerful being or his angels. In an attempt to teach the brethren holding the priesthood of this danger, the Lord revealed the following:

. . . I the Lord ask you this question—unto what were ye ordained?

To preach my gospel by the Spirit, even the Comforter which was sent forth to teach the truth.

And then received ye spirits which ye could not understand, and received them to be of God; and in this are ye justified?

Behold ye shall answer this question yourselves; nevertheless, I will be merciful unto you; he that is weak among you hereafter shall be made strong.

Verily I say unto you, he that is ordained of me and sent forth to preach the word of truth by the Comforter, in the Spirit of truth, doth he preach it by the Spirit of truth or some other way?

And if it be by some other way it is not of God.

And again, he that receiveth the word of truth, doth he receive it by the Spirit of truth or some other way?

If it be some other way it is not of God.

Therefore, why is it that ye cannot understand and know that he that receiveth the word by the Spirit of truth receiveth it as it is preached by the Spirit of truth?

Wherefore, he that preacheth and he that receiveth, understand one another, and both are edified and rejoice together. (D&C 50:13-22.)

That which does not edify, strengthen, build, or uplift is not of God, but is of the devil.

There are many people today who attempt to gain a testimony of truth in their own way, or, perhaps better said, by the methods and power of man. In other words, they attempt to gain a testimony by the power of reason. They forget that anything a person can be reasoned into, he can be reasoned out of. An intellectual testimony is no stronger than the intellect that possesses it. Another person with a greater intellect can come along and by his superior reasoning power he can rob that person of his testimony. When, however, a testimony is obtained by the power of the Spirit and testified to by the Holy Ghost, that testimony burns into the person's heart and is not easily destroyed. As Nephi explained it:

. . . for when a man speaketh by the power of the Holy Ghost the power of the Holy Ghost carrieth it into the hearts of the children of men.

But behold, there are many that harden their hearts against the Holy Spirit, that it hath no place in them; wherefore, they cast many things away which are written and esteem them as things of naught. (2 Nephi 33:1-2.)

Not only do they cast away valuable things that are written, but they also reject precious truths that are taught them in verbal communications. The best testimony, then, is one based on intellect and on personal feeling as it is sealed in a person's heart by the power of the Holy Ghost.

There is a method given us by means of which we may determine the truth of all things:

Wherefore, take heed, my beloved brethren, that ye do not judge that which is evil to be of God, or that which is good and of God to be of the devil.

For behold, my brethren, it is given unto you to judge that

61

ye may know good from evil; and the way to judge is as plain, that ye may know with a perfect knowledge, as the daylight is from the dark night.

For behold, the Spirit of Christ is given to every man, that he may know good from evil; wherefore, I show unto you the way to judge; for everything which inviteth to do good, and to persuade to believe in Christ, is sent forth by the power and gift of Christ; *wherefore ye may know with a perfect knowledge it is of God.*

But whatsoever thing persuadeth men to do evil, and believe not in Christ, and deny him, and serve not God, *then ye may know with a perfect knowledge it is of the devil;* for after this manner doth the devil work, for he persuadeth no man to do good, no, no one; neither do his angels; neither do they who subject themselves unto him. (Moroni 7:14-17. Italics added.)

Using this key, any person can know whether a teaching or doctrine is of God or of the devil. All one needs to do is to ask: Is it positive, uplifting, beautiful, ennobling, constructive, and edifying, or is it negative, demeaning, ignoble, ugly, destructive, and hurtful?

No one will ever know the heartbreak it must have cost Adam and Eve to see and hear their own children reject those truths which they knew with such personal assurance. Undoubtedly they told their children how they had lived in the Garden of Eden, that they had spoken with the Father and the Son, and that they knew them personally, just as their children knew one another through close personal association. The majesty and power of the Father and Son had been made manifest in their eyes. By personal experience they knew of the truth of these teachings and the actuality of the promises given them. There were no doubts either in the minds or the hearts of Adam and Eve as to these truths. But their children hardened their hearts and would not believe their parents. One may speak today of a generation gap between parents and youth, but probably no greater lack of communication between generations ever existed than occurred at that time. Despite the pleadings of their

62

parents, the children would not listen. Adam and Eve had to look on and observe as their children, whom they loved, walked down the road leading to their own destruction.

Adam and Eve then pleaded with God to give them children who would have the faith to believe their teachings so that the promises of eternal life they had been given might be passed on to future generations. As a result of this prayer and the intense yearning of their hearts, they received another son, and they rejoiced in the Lord that in answer to prayer he had given them a son who would surely believe. Thus Cain, who was born to them in answer to this prayer, must have been one of the choicest spirits God had to send them. But the scriptures (Moses 5:16) inform us that he too rejected the instructions of his parents and said in a most insolent manner, "Who is the Lord that I should know him?" This must have broken their hearts.

Then they received of the Lord another son, whom they named Abel. He was the first of their many children who had the good judgment to love the Lord, to respect him and follow his teachings as these truths were explained to him by his parents. How they must have rejoiced in that obedient son!

They still had a problem with Cain: "And Cain loved Satan more than God. And Satan commanded him, saying: Make an offering unto the Lord. And in process of time it came to pass that Cain brought of the fruit of the ground an offering unto the Lord." (Moses 5:18-19.) Note here two things: First, Cain made his offering, not because the Lord had commanded him to do so, but because Satan had asked him to do so. In other words, he made his offering for the wrong reason. Second, he made his offering from the fruit of the ground instead of doing as God had commanded, to offer the firstlings of the flock. Not only was the purpose wrong, but even the method was wrong. How different was the offering made by Abel: "And Abel he also brought of the firstlings of his

63

flock, and of the fat thereof. And the Lord had respect unto Abel, and to his offering; But unto Cain, and to his offering, he had not respect. Now Satan knew this, and it pleased him. And Cain was very wroth, and his countenance fell." (Moses 5:20-21.) Abel's offering was not only made for the right reason, but it was made in the right manner. In fact, Abel went the extra mile, for not only did he offer the firstlings of his flock but he also chose the very best animals he had, to make sure his offering would be pleasing to the Lord.

One can readily understand how the Lord would be pleased with Abel's attitude and why he would be displeased with Cain's offering. Satan knew that the Lord would have to reject Cain's offering, and he must have chuckled within himself as he contemplated what effect this would have on Cain. Cain also made the terrible error of becoming angry about it. When a man becomes angry, he loses all sense of perspective. No longer can he think and reason. He is led wholly by his emotions and thus is subject to greater error. Naturally this rejection made Cain unhappy, and his face showed it. When we are unhappy it shows in our countenance. I can tell, when a person walks in my door, whether he is in trouble or not, for his face shows it. When a person sins, he becomes unhappy. He does not smile. His eyes are not glistening, but dull. In fact, there is a negative or dark atmosphere about him that he brings into the room when he enters. I know even before he speaks that he is troubled in his heart. When we feel unhappy and troubled in our hearts, it is a clear signal to us that we ought to take stock of our lives and look within ourselves to see what that trouble is. Cain couldn't look within himself, for he was too angry to do so.

Then Jehovah gave Cain a clear warning. He explained to Cain that the problem was within himself. He explained that, because Cain had a body while Satan had none, he would rule over Satan. He explained to Cain that, because Satan has no body, he is powerless to act unless a person allows his body to be used by Satan to fill Satan's desires. He said, therefore, that if lies should come it would be because Cain was the mouth for those lies and would be Satan's spokesman. Cain must have held the high priesthood, which he undoubtedly received from his father, or he could not have spoken with Jehovah the way he did. Therefore, Cain knew personally that Jehovah was real, just as he knew that Satan was real. He was making a deliberate choice of Satan over God. He was acting in the full light of his knowledge by denying God when he knew, just as well as he knew the sun was shining overhead, that God lived. It was a deliberate choice of evil in spite of his priesthood knowledge. In other words, he was sinning against the Holy Ghost. Thus he would be committing an unforgivable sin. The Lord reminded Cain that he knew him from his previous experiences with him in the premortal life. He knew his weaknesses just as he knew and recognized his strengths. There was still time to repent if Cain would only listen, but if he would not listen, then Jehovah would have to turn him over to the buffetings of Satan. Read now how plainly the Lord spoke with him:

And the Lord said unto Cain: Why art thou wroth? Why is thy countenance fallen?

If thou doest well, thou shalt be accepted. And if thou doest not well, sin lieth at the door, and Satan desireth to have thee; and except thou shalt hearken unto my commandments, I will deliver thee up, and it shall be unto thee according to his desire. And thou shalt rule over him;

For from this time forth thou shalt be the father of his lies; thou shalt be called Perdition [a title of damnation applied also to Satan and those who follow him, as stated in D&C 76:26]; for thou wast also before the world.

And it shall be said in time to come—That these abominations were had from Cain; for he rejected the greater counsel which was had from God; and this is a cursing which I will put upon thee, except thou repent. (Moses 5:22-25.)

We might well ask why Satan desired to win Cain over to him even more than he desired other sons and

65

daughters of Adam and Eve. It must have been because Satan recognized his potential greatness. Satan's work is destructive in nature. Cain stood at the threshold of man's mortal existence, and from him would come many generations of men and women yet unborn. The course of life on the earth had been carefully preplanned in the council in heaven so that the various families of men would follow lineage lines. Cain could have been one of the patriarchal sons of Adam; he could have stood at the head of generations of men and women who would come from his lineage line, who would serve the Lord. If Satan could bring Cain to fall, Satan thought he could destroy God's adopted plan of action and thus bring his work to naught.

It is for this reason that Satan makes a special attack on everyone who has great potential. He would rather capture a bishop than a member of the ward, because if he can bring the bishop to destruction, he will tear away many with him. Satan would rather destroy a stake president than any other priesthood leader in the stake, because if he can bring the president, his wife, or his children to fall, they will tear away many with them. He places greater temptation in the path of a General Authority than in the path of a member of a stake presidency, for his area of influence is greater. The more promising the future of the person, or the more responsible the position, the greater the temptation will be. On the other hand, the greater the responsibility that person has, the greater the faith and the determination he possesses, along with the power of the priesthood office given him, to resist evil and accomplish good.

The problem with Cain was that he was angry, and in this angry mood he was not inclined to listen to the Lord, much less to others;

And Cain was wroth, and listened not any more to the voice of the Lord, neither to Abel, his brother, who walked in holiness before the Lord.

And Adam and his wife mourned before the Lord, because of Cain and his brethren.

And it came to pass that Cain took one of his brother's daughters to wife, and they loved Satan more than God. (Moses 5:26-28.)

One cannot read this without sensing the heartbreak of Adam and Eve as they mourned the loss of this chosen son, who had so hardened his heart that even in spite of greater light and knowledge, he would no longer listen to truth. The warnings of his parents fell on deaf ears. He had hardened his heart and could no longer be touched.

Under these conditions the time was now ripe for Satan to tempt Cain with one of those temptations which man finds hardest to resist. He tempted him with greed and power. He was now ready to show Cain a method whereby he could not only become wealthy, but also how he could take away the power of his brother, which Abel would normally pass on to his posterity, and transfer that heritage and power to his own posterity. So Satan whispered into Cain's ear a partial truth. If he would murder his brother, he could remove Abel's posterity from their inheritance and it would automatically be transferred to Cain's posterity. Also, all the wealth that Abel possessed would fall into the hands of Cain, and Cain would have not only his own lands and crops, but the flocks and herds of his brother Abel as well. However, Satan warned Cain that he was not to tell this to Adam. If Cain would swear to him with an oath not to reveal it to anyone else, Satan would show him how this could be accomplished. The reason Satan did not want Cain to talk to his father was that Adam would have seen the hole in Satan's argument and would have warned Cain of that trap. By keeping this matter a secret from Adam, who had both wisdom and knowledge, Cain would be left to his own limited knowledge. Because of Cain's lack of experience and lack of inspiration now that he had cut himself off from the Lord, he became the dupe or tool of Satan.

And Satan said unto Cain: Swear unto me by thy throat, and if thou tell it thou shalt die; and swear thy brethren by their heads, and by the living God, that they tell it not; for if they tell it, they shall surely die; and this that thy father may not know it; and this day I will deliver thy brother Abel into thine hands.

And Satan sware unto Cain that he would do according to his commands. And all these things were done in secret.

And Cain said: Truly I am Mahan, the master of this great secret, that I may murder and get gain. Wherefore, Cain was called Master Mahan, and he gloried in his wickedness. (Moses 5:29-31.)

The real problem was that Satan had told Cain a partial truth. It is true that anyone can murder and get gain. When a person is murdered and robbed, the murderer not only has what he already possesses, but he also now has the money or goods he stole from his victim. However, Satan had not told the whole truth, and Adam would have pointed this out to Cain had he received an opportunity to speak with him about his contemplated action. You can murder and get gain, but as you become wealthier and have told others this same secret, they in turn will seek your life and take from you your increased wealth to build their own wealth and strength and power. So a chain of murder begins that has no end. Adam would have told Cain that he would have to pay dearly for the slight advantage murder would have brought him. As for Cain's claim to the heritage of Abel's posterity, that would be removed from him by his excommunication from the priesthood. The power and the blessings connected therewith would be passed on to another who would value them in the proper way.

The story of how Cain went into the field with Abel his brother and slew him there is well known. Abel's flocks did fall into Cain's hands just as Satan had promised him. It appeared to Cain that Satan indeed had told him the truth. "And Cain gloried in that which he had done, saying: I am free; surely the flocks of my brother falleth into my hands." (Moses 5:33.) But Cain was not free, for he now was called upon to pay the price for his actions. The Lord explained to him the consequences of his sin and how he would now have to pay for what he had done and how he would now become the object of his brothers' greed. Cain had foolishly revealed to his brothers the secret of how one can murder and get gain. Now they in turn would seek his life so they could become richer and more powerful than he. The chain of destruction was already beginning to lengthen.

And the Lord said unto Cain: Where is Abel, thy brother? And he said: I know not. Am I my brother's keeper? [The Lord did not even bother to answer this smart-aleck question. Cain's impudence was simply ignored.]

And the Lord said: What hast thou done? The voice of thy brother's blood cries unto me from the ground [one can't hide anything from the Lord].

And now thou shalt be cursed from the earth which hath opened her mouth to receive thy brother's blood from thy hand.

When thou tillest the ground it shall not henceforth yield unto thee her strength. A fugitive and a vagabond shalt thou be in the earth. (Moses 5:34-37.)

Cain finally realized the enormity of what he had done and how he had endangered his own life and that of his posterity by this cruel murder. Typically, he now tried to justify himself. The hardest part of repenting from sin is to confess that what one has done is wrong. We all rationalize our actions and try to find excuses or mitigating circumstances to justify the action we have taken. Instead of freely admitting that what we did was wrong, we try to put the blame on someone else to free ourselves from the burden of sin. This Cain now attempted to do. First he tried to justify himself, saying that Satan had tempted him; thus he tried to put the blame on Satan. Then he tried to excuse his actions because he had lost his temper and had performed the deed in anger. Finally he tried to put the blame on the Lord himself, because the Lord had accepted Abel's offering and not his own. To all these excuses, the Lord just shook his head. Cain had only himself to blame. When Cain realized he was now on his own and subject to grave dangers, he asked for protection, and this the Lord granted him by putting a sign on him that would warn

69

others against making this same mistake.

And Cain said unto the Lord: Satan tempted me because of my brother's flocks. And I was wroth also, for his offering thou didst accept and not mine; my punishment is greater than I can bear.

Behold thou hast driven me out this day from the face of the Lord, and from thy face shall I be hid; and I shall be a fugitive and a vagabond in the earth; and it shall come to pass, that he that findeth me will slay me, because of mine iniquities, for these things are not hid from the Lord.

And I the Lord said unto him: Whosoever slayeth thee, vengeance shall be taken on him sevenfold. And I the Lord set a mark upon Cain, lest any finding him should kill him. (Moses 5:38-40.)

The realization of what he had done would be an eternal burden upon Cain's mind and upon his posterity. The riches he had gained in life could not be taken with him into the spirit world. The treasures of family and priesthood to which he had been heir and which he could have taken with him into the spirit world were now stripped from him. He had lost the heritage blessings not only for himself, but also for his whole lineage line. What a terrible price to pay for a moment of weakness! Yet he had been carefully warned. Had he only not hardened his heart, all this unhappiness would never have come to him or to his family.

Undoubtedly one of those constituent or substitute plans that God had prepared for just such emergencies was now called into play. The righteous spirits who would normally have come through Cain's priesthood line would have to be transferred to another lineage line where their priesthood rights would be preserved. The Lord would also transfer to Cain's line the spirits of those who were not entitled to receive priesthood blessings as a lineage right. This was not to condemn such spirits to the same damnation pronounced on Cain. They could still attain exaltation, but they would have to work harder for it, make greater sacrifices, and show greater patience and faith on earth in order to attain exaltation than they had shown in the premortal life. The goal and the blessings would still be theirs to obtain, but they would have to work harder for those treasures to make up for their lack of faith and works in the premortal life where they had been careless rather than valiant. The way would still be open, but the path would be difficult.

The more I ponder this story, the more important it becomes to me. I can see why it was placed in the scriptures. Every man and woman who lives on this earth has to face temptations such as those faced by Cain. How we respond can affect not only our own lives, but the lives of our family. There is never such a thing as a victimless crime. Even those sins that some of us feel involve only our own lives also affect the lives of others, just as Cain's actions did. It is a thought that everyone should ponder carefully.

7

The Sins of the Parents

I never read the opening verses of the Book of Mormon without pausing to thank God for my own parents. Nephi simply begins: "I, Nephi, having been born of goodly parents, therefore I was taught somewhat in all the learning of my father; and having seen many afflictions in the course of my days, nevertheless, having been highly favored of the Lord in all my days; yea, having had a great knowledge of the goodness and the mysteries of God, therefore I make a record of my proceedings in my days." (1 Nephi 1:1.) It is indeed a rich blessing to have parents who love you and teach you of the great treasures God has reserved for you.

This instruction becomes an even greater blessing when those parents teach by example as well as by precept. It is one thing to be a progenitor (a creator), but another, more difficult thing to be a father or mother. The latter designation is a far greater honor. We refer to God the Father and address him by that title rather than as God the Creator. Fatherhood and motherhood carry with them a connotation of teachers of righteousness, both by precept and by example. The Lord so teaches us, and so ought we to teach our children. In fact, this responsibility to teach our children is a command God has given us as parents.

And again, inasmuch as parents have children in Zion, or in any of her stakes which are organized, that teach them not to understand the doctrine of repentance, faith in Christ the Son of the living God, and of baptism and the gift of the Holy Ghost by the laying on of the hands, when eight years old, the sins be upon the heads of the parents.

For this shall be a law unto the inhabitants of Zion, or in any of her stakes which are organized. (D&C 68:25-26.)

Thus the Lord appoints the age of accountability for children at eight years of age. By that time a child has reached such maturity that he can begin to exercise his own agency to know good from evil.

It is imperative that parents understand how important the first eight years are in the life of a child. During these early years he learns much of what he will retain throughout the balance of his life. This is more particularly true of attitudes and attributes than it is of skills or knowledge. Honesty, love, obedience, happiness, ability to cooperate, to live with and understand others are concepts we learn or fail to learn in those earliest years. A child taught to keep himself physically clean and to live in neat and clean surroundings will tend to keep himself clean and have a neat and clean home when he grows up. The reverse, of course, is also true.

A child who is taught to learn and develop his mind at an early age will tend to continue in that direction when he is older. Parents who teach their children that they are noble sons and daughters of God build into those children a sense of nobility that will guide them through their later years. Parents who teach their children of the promised treasures of heaven, which are reserved for them as a heritage right, set goals in their minds that will aid them one day to attain those treasures. How fortunate a child is who has goodly parents to teach him truths and to set him a good example!

A most interesting conclusion can be drawn after reading the following scripture: ". . . behold, I say unto you, that little children are redeemed from the foundation of the world through mine Only Begotten; Wherefore, they cannot sin, for power is not given unto

73

Satan to tempt little children, until they begin to become accountable before me." (D&C 29:46-47.) From this scripture we learn that parents have an eight-year head start in teaching their children righteousness. During this period Satan is powerless to affect the lives of those children. Yet the parents can and often do teach their children to do evil, or they fail to teach them to be righteous. During this early period, though Satan has no influence on children, parents can teach their children wicked habits and practices. They can feed them harmful foods, and expose them to accidents, disease, or injury both of body and of mind. They can also harm their children by failure to teach them righteousness. When parents do such things, those children are conditioned to failure and unhappiness. In such cases the parents must bear the blame and the responsibility for the child's subsequent failure. The tragic thing is that in the process the child is destroyed. My personal belief is that where a child is so harmed through no fault of his own, a righteous God will provide some way in the future for that child to recover from that damage. It is regrettable, however, that the child has to suffer such a handicap. It is a blessing to be born of goodly parents, for children reproduce in their own characters the teachings received from their parents.

There is another scripture that teaches us how, as the poet wrote, we come into this life trailing clouds of glory from that premortal state where we lived with our heavenly parents:

Every spirit of man was innocent in the beginning; and God having redeemed man from the fall, men became again, in their infant state, innocent before God.

And that wicked one cometh and taketh away light and truth, through disobedience, from the children of men, and because of the tradition of their fathers.

But I have commanded you to bring up your children in light and truth. (D&C 93:38-40.)

For this very reason, I deeply resent those who speak disparagingly of "illegitimate" children. What blame should ever be attached to an innocent child who had nothing to do with his own birth? I feel we could well speak of illegitimate parents, but never of an illegitimate child. Children are born innocent, regardless of race or color or creed. But parents are commanded to care for them and teach and train them.

And ye will not suffer your children that they go hungry, or naked, neither will ye suffer that they transgress the laws of God, and fight and quarrel one with another, and serve the devil, who is the master of sin, or who is the evil spirit which hath been spoken of by our fathers, he being an enemy to all righteousness.

But ye will teach them to walk in the ways of truth and soberness; ye will teach them to love one another, and to serve one another. (Mosiah 4:14-15.)

Fortunate indeed is the child who is raised in an atmosphere of love in a righteous family and who is taught correct principles in the home.

When Abinadi, the prophet, taught the people of the wicked King Noah, he warned them about their wicked practices. Specifically he warned them about idol worship and the dangers involved therein. Not only were they leading each other astray, but they were also teaching their children to be disobedient. Abinadi taught them:

Thou shalt not make unto thee any graven image, or any likeness of things which are in heaven above, or which are in the earth beneath, or which are in the water under the earth.

And again: Thou shalt not bow thyself down unto them, nor serve them; for I the Lord thy God am a jealous God, visiting the iniquities of the fathers upon the children, unto the third and fourth generation of them that hate me;

And showing mercy unto thousands of them that love me and keep my commandments. (Mosiah 13:12-14.)

He was quoting the words God had given Moses when the Ten Commandments were written for the guidance of the people of Israel. It would be wise to review what the Lord told Moses on that occasion:

And the Lord passed by before him, and proclaimed, The

Lord, The Lord God, merciful and gracious, longsuffering, and abundant in goodness and truth,

Keeping mercy for thousands, forgiving iniquity and transgression and sin, and that will by no means clear the guilty; visiting the iniquity of the fathers upon the children, and upon the children's children, unto the third and to the fourth generation. (Exodus 34:6-7.)

The reason the problem continues to the third and fourth generation is that behavioral patterns that are set up in families continue for a long time. When parents teach their children righteousness, that righteousness tends to persist in the family generation after generation. When parents teach their children evil, either by word or by action, those evil patterns also tend to persist generation after generation. Children of such parents teach their children in turn those same patterns of conduct, and hence that manner of living continues to reproduce itself.

From the beginning the Lord taught our first parents righteous principles. Adam and Eve in turn taught their children that they were of noble lineage. Through them and through their seed should come those spirit children of God who were to be tested during their earth life to see if they would remain valiant. We learned in the previous chapter that some of the children believed their parents and some did not. Those who rejected these teachings lost their birthright. Those who believed and practiced the teachings of God as those principles were taught them by their parents preserved their heritage rights. Great promises were given them that their descendants would be leaders among the nations of the earth. Their children by reason of their priesthood heritage rights would form the line of patriarchs and prophets who would point the way for others to follow to attain the promised treasure of eternal life.

At various times during the history of the world, the opportunity for mankind to receive the blessings of the gospel has been denied them. For instance, during the apostasy, which followed the ministry of the Savior and his apostles down to the time of the restoration of the gospel, there was no opportunity for men to receive a remission of their sins by baptism or to participate in other ordinances essential to salvation. The divine church with its true doctrine, and possessing duly appointed ministers having priesthood authority, was not on the earth. Similar conditions have existed on the earth during other periods of time and in other places. Even when the priesthood has been on the earth, as it is at the present time, and when every effort has been made to bring a knowledge of the truth to all men, many have died without ever hearing the name of Jesus Christ. Many such people would have accepted the gospel had they only had an opportunity and privilege to hear it explained to them in words they could understand.

This leads us to an answer to the question: What is meant by the "promises made to the fathers" as this statement is used in the scriptures? From before the foundation of the world it was known that limiting conditions would exist from time to time, as stated in the previous paragraph. Hence, from the very beginning plans were made to solve this problem. The plan of salvation was explained to all those in the spirit world. A promise was given to the early fathers on earth that those who died without a knowledge of the gospel and without an opportunity to receive the sealing ordinances of the priesthood would be provided with such an opportunity in the future. The promise was given them that their righteous descendants in the latter days would perform vicariously such ordinances for them as could make possible their exaltation. They would be given an opportunity either on earth or in the spirit world to hear the gospel and to accept gospel truths, as well as to accept the saving ordinance work done in their behalf that would make that exaltation possible.

It has been stated before that God's work and his glory is to bring about the immortality and the eternal life of man. This being true, the promise was given the fathers that *all* men and women must have an opportunity to hear the gospel either on earth or in the spirit world. As Joseph Smith explained the matter in a revelation:

All who have died without a knowledge of this gospel who would have received it if they had been permitted to tarry, shall be heirs of the celestial kingdom of God; also all who die henceforth without a knowledge of it, who would have received it with all their hearts, shall be heirs of that kingdom, for I, the Lord, will judge all men according to their works, according to the desire of their hearts. And I also beheld that all children who die before they arrive at the years of accountability, are saved in the celestial kingdom of heaven. (Pearl of Great Price, Joseph Smith—Vision of the Celestial Kingdom 7-10.)

This promise was given because God is merciful and just and will not deny these blessings to any of his children for reasons over which they personally have no control.

A record of some of the promises made to the fathers is found in the scriptures. Thus Isaiah, referring to the Savior, said: "I the Lord have called thee in righteousness, and will hold thine hand, and will keep thee, and give thee for a covenant of the people, for a light of the Gentiles; To open the blind eyes, to bring out the prisoners from the prison, and them that sit in the darkness out of the prison house." (Isaiah 42:6-7.) Later on Isaiah prophesied again of the Savior's mission to the dead: "The Spirit of the Lord God is upon me; because the Lord hath anointed me to preach good tidings unto the meek; he hath sent me to bind up the brokenhearted, to proclaim liberty to the captives, and the opening of the prison to them that are bound; To proclaim the acceptable year of the Lord, and the day of vengeance of our God; to comfort all that mourn." (Isaiah 61:1-2.)

These references to the prisoners who are bound refer to those who are dead, who were held back until they could hear and accept the gospel in the spirit world. Thus, through the preaching of the gospel they could be freed from their spiritual prison and be redeemed. Further light is given in regard to this principle of having an opportunity to hear the gospel preached in the spirit world. Isaiah explains how they can be released from this spirit prison: "And it shall come to pass in that day, that the Lord shall punish the host of the high ones that are on high, and the kings of the earth upon the earth. And they shall be gathered together, as prisoners are gathered in the pit, and shall be shut up in the prison, and after many days shall they be visited." (Isaiah 24:21-22.)

A similar passage containing a promise made to the fathers is found in the Pearl of Great Price. In speaking of those who lived in the days of Noah, the Lord said: "But behold, these which thine eyes are upon shall perish in the floods; and behold, I will shut them up; a prison have I prepared for them. And that which I have chosen hath plead before my face. Wherefore, he suffereth for their sins; inasmuch as they will repent in the day that my Chosen shall return unto me, and until that day they shall be in torment." (Moses 7:38-39.)

Thus, though the sins of the parents shall be visited on their children, a just God has prepared a way that justice can be done to all his children. Through his mercy, a way has been opened so that all his children who desire to do so can recognize light and truth. Through belief, repentance, and good works, they can eventually obtain that great heavenly treasure. This also calls to mind the great obligation we have of doing vicarious work for those of our ancestors who have gone before us and who have prepared the way for us to hear these truths. We are obligated to them in a very personal way. The very bodies we enjoy, the blood that flows in our veins, and the heritage blessings we enjoy are made possible to us only through our ancestors who lived before us. It is our great privilege and blessing, then, to be the means whereby those promises made to our fathers can be fulfilled.

8

The Blessings of the Fathers

The death of Abel ended his family line. All those just spirits who had been promised a heritage through Abel were now left without a parent to lead them to the earth. To have directed them to come through the lineage of Cain was now impossible, for Cain had been excommunicated and his priesthood had been taken from him. Those spirits who were to come through Abel had lineage rights to the treasures of heaven and had been given a promise of being born to goodly parents who would train them to receive those priesthood blessings. On the other hand, to have given the priesthood to those spirits who were destined to become Cain's descendants would have given those spirits precedence and an unfair advantage over those scheduled to come through Abel and who now would have to come to earth through another line of parentage. This had been one of the very things Cain had desired in cutting off Abel's line of posterity. In order to preserve justice and to keep the promises of lineage rights to priesthood blessings, certain changes had to be made in the order in which those spirits were sent to the earth.

In all fairness, the priesthood blessings would have to be withheld from Cain's descendants until the spirits who were righteous and had been originally scheduled to come through Cain and Abel had an opportunity to come to earth through another line where they would have an opportunity to receive or reject those priesthood heritage blessings under favorable circumstances. This would take time. The birth of Seth, a righteous son of Adam and Eve, made a continuation of the line of the patriarchs possible.

And Adam knew his wife again, and she bare a son, and he called his name Seth. And Adam glorified the name of God; for he said: God hath appointed me another seed, instead of Abel, whom Cain slew.

And God revealed himself unto Seth, and he rebelled not, but offered an acceptable sacrifice, like unto his brother Abel. And to him also was born a son, and he called his name Enos.

And then began these men to call upon the name of the Lord, and the Lord blessed them;

And a book of remembrance was kept, in the which was recorded, in the language of Adam, for it was given unto as many as called upon God to write by the spirit of inspiration;

And by them their children were taught to read and write, having a language which was pure and undefiled.

Now this same Priesthood which was in the beginning, shall be in the end of the world also.

Now this prophecy Adam spake, as he was moved upon by the Holy Ghost, and a genealogy was kept of the children of God. And this was the book of the generations of Adam, saying: In the day that God created man, in the likeness of God made he him;

In the image of his own body, male and female, created he them, and called their name Adam, in the day when they were created and became living souls in the land upon the footstool of God. (Moses 6:2-9.)

The patriarchal priesthood of the generations of Adam is an especially important division of the Melchizedek Priesthood. A partial genealogy of this higher priesthood is given from Moses to Adam in Doctrine and Covenants, section 84, verses 6-15. We learn that Abel is in this line, as indicated in the following scripture: "And from Enoch to Abel, who was slain by the conspiracy of his brother, who received the priesthood by the commandments of God, by the hand of his father Adam, who was the first man—Which priesthood continueth in the church of God in all generations, and is without beginning of days or end of years." (D&C 84:16-17.) There is no question that Abel was one of these patriarchs, though he was murdered by his brother. He was ordained by his father, Adam, who also ordained Seth in whom now the patriarchal family lineage continued.

We have been instructed that the patriarchal order of the priesthood was confirmed to be handed down from father to son (D&C 107:39-40) and rightly belongs to the literal descendants of Adam through Seth, thus constituting the promises made to the fathers that were to be brought to the attention of the children of the covenant in the last days. The scripture goes on to tell us more about Seth, that great son of Adam:

This order was instituted in the days of Adam, and came down by lineage in the following manner:

From Adam to Seth, who was ordained by Adam at the age of sixty-nine years, and was blessed by him three years previous to his (Adam's) death, and received the promise of God by his father, that his posterity should be the chosen of the Lord and that they should be preserved unto the end of the earth;

Because he (Seth) was a perfect man, and his likeness was the express likeness of his father, insomuch that he seemed to be like unto his father in all things, and could be distinguished from him only by his age. (D&C 107:41-43.)

Seth must have been a most remarkable man and a worthy patriarch.

One of the most interesting ideas to come from the verses previously quoted is the reference to a book of remembrance. This book contained a genealogy of the people and showed how much they valued the importance of their heritage rights to the priesthood. However, this book of remembrance was much more than just a genealogy of this priesthood line. It included a history of the people, and it included revelations and an account of their spiritual experiences as these leaders were inspired of God to write them.

Adam and Eve were not ignorant or primitive

savages, but intelligent, highly qualified, and gifted human beings. God gave them a perfect language and taught them how to speak, read, and write it. They were taught moral and ethical principles and had a philosophy of life taught them by the greatest teacher of all, Jehovah. They were taught that perfect language so they could pass vital information on to their children: "And a book of remembrance was kept, in the which was recorded, in the language of Adam, for it was given unto as many as called upon God to write by the spirit of inspiration; And by them their children were taught to read and write, having a language which was pure and undefiled." (Moses 6:5-6.)

83

The language was a powerful language (Moses 7:13) and was used by mankind until the time of the confusion of tongues, which took place at the tower of Babel. Thus, using this perfect language, a pattern was given for a book of remembrance written by the finger of God himself: "For a book of remembrance we have written among us, according to the pattern given by the finger of God; and it is given in our own language." (Moses 6:46.)

This is how Abraham later on was able to write about the creation of the world, for he possessed a written record: "But the records of the fathers, even the patriarchs, concerning the right of Priesthood, the Lord my God preserved in mine own hands; therefore a knowledge of the beginning of the creation, and also of the planets, and of the stars, as they were made known unto the fathers, have I kept even unto this day, and I shall endeavor to write some of these things upon this record, for the benefit of my posterity that shall come after me." (Abraham 1:31.) It was through such accounts written in the book of remembrance that the promises made to the fathers were preserved for posterity. The same procedure was followed in Book of Mormon days, for they also wrote a book of remembrance: "Then they that feared the Lord spake often one to another, and the Lord hearkened and heard; and a book of remembrance was written before him for them that feared the Lord, and that thought upon his name." (3 Nephi 24:16.)

In our day also we have been commanded to write a book of remembrance (D&C 85:9). This book of remembrance written for the Church is sometimes referred to as the book of the law from which the people are to be judged at the last day. Each patriarchal family head should write and/or maintain a family book of remembrance to guide, bless, and inspire his posterity to know of the promises made to their fathers that constitute the inheritance of all members born into that family. There is little doubt that Moses had a book of remembrance at hand when he wrote his account of the creation of the world as found in our Bible today.

From the Bible we can obtain some interesting information about the lineage of the patriarchs. It is easy to understand how knowledge was passed from one to another. Wherever possible, God uses natural everyday means to increase our knowledge. It is not necessary that each one of us should receive a personal revelation of information that is readily available to us from other sources. It would be a waste of God's time to give the same revelation to a host of individuals when all those persons need to do is to consult a living prophet or to read what the Lord has already revealed to such prophets. These revelations which the prophets have received are made available to us in the form of scriptures, and in their writings and speeches as recorded, and are made available to all who will take the time to read them. This scripture constitutes the word of the Lord and the will of the Lord to us as individuals.

During those early days in the world, the ruling line, in a political sense, the patriarchal line, and the prophetic or church administrative lines were all combined in one central lineage. How this patriarchal lineage was passed on from one to another is made apparent by examining Chart 1. This chart was constructed from the account in Genesis, chapters five and ten. These "begats," as some people call them, are often regarded as

Life and times
of the early patriarchs

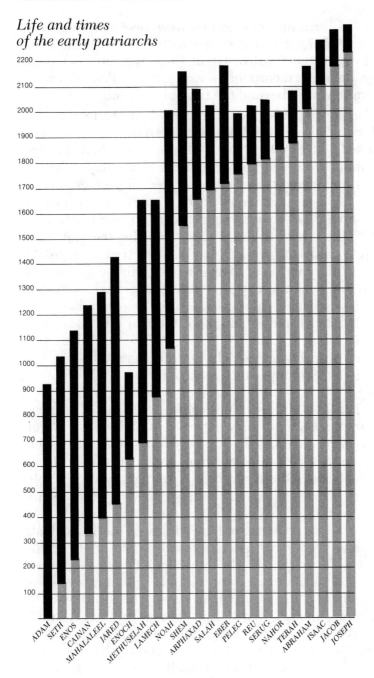

things of little importance and have been skipped over.
Yet it is impressive that in the sixth chapter of the book
of Moses in the Pearl of Great Price is found that same
fairly detailed record of lineage from Adam down to
generations well beyond the time of the flood.

The genealogies given in the Book of Mormon in the
book of Ether again show the importance of preserving
lineage lines. Surely God would not have had this information preserved and revealed for our day unless it
was of importance. The tables of genealogies preserved
in the Bible are testimony of the importance of lineage
relationship. Of course, people can go overboard and
confuse the tool with the purpose for using the tool. This
the Jews did in the days of Paul, by trying to justify
themselves by virtue of their genealogical lineage instead
of justifying themselves through righteous achievements
of their own. This caused Paul, in righteous indignation
at their lack of understanding of the real purpose of lineage accounts, to say: "Neither give heed to fables and
endless genealogies, which minister questions, rather
than godly edifying which is in faith. . . ." (1 Timothy
1:4.)

When one considers that Moses received his genealogical information by revelation about 2,500 years after
the days of Adam, and the Lord saw fit to give such
details in his scriptural account, there must have been
real significance to such a record. An important principle
must have been involved for this genealogy to become
part of scripture. Giving the matter a little thought, we
recognize that it preserved the rights of the individuals
concerned to receive special blessings. The rights in this
case are the rights to the blessings of the priesthood,
which are as important for us today as they were for
Abraham and Moses in their days. The Lord said to
Abraham: "Behold, I will lead thee by my hand, and I
will take thee, to put upon thee my name, even the
Priesthood of thy father, and my power shall be over
thee. As it was with Noah so shall it be with thee; but

through thy ministry my name shall be known in the earth forever, for I am thy God." (Abraham 1:18-19.)

From a study of the accompanying chart, showing the life and times of the early patriarchs, we can realize how many of these men were contemporaries. In other words, since they were living at the same time and could be in contact with each other, they could pass on to their descendants a firsthand account of their personal witness of God as a divine being. Thus Adam could have borne his testimony to his seventh-great-grandson, Lamech. The knowledge of God as a divine being was passed on by these righteous men not only to the patriarchs themselves, but also to the then-known world. There was no need of new revelation to explain the relationship of God to man, because this knowledge was already available in the world by the mouths of living witnesses. The promises made to the fathers could be passed on to his descendants by Adam as a personal witness, who had lived in the presence of God and who knew God personally as we know members of our own family through frequent personal association.

Noah had personal witness borne him of the divinity of God from six patriarchal fathers who had known Adam personally for many years. In fact, Adam had been dead only 130 years when Noah was born. Noah was acquainted with all the fathers except Adam, Adam's son Seth, and Enoch, who was translated. Noah, in turn, was able to bear his own personal witness of what had been taught him to his sons and children down to his eighth-great-grandson, Terah, the father of Abraham. Abraham knew the patriarchal fathers back to his seventh-great-grandfather, and Noah had been dead only about two years when Abraham was born. Abraham was able to know and talk with many of his forefathers and to have firsthand knowledge of his own rights to priesthood blessings.

The blessings of the fathers for which Abraham sought were obtained from Melchizedek. When

Abraham returned after his war with the kings at Chedorlaomer, he met that great high priest and received a blessing from him: ". . . Abraham received the priesthood from Melchizedek, who received it through the lineage of his fathers, even till Noah." (D&C 84:14.)

The following account from Joseph Smith gives us a better understanding of what transpired:

And Melchizedek, king of Salem, brought forth bread and wine; and he break bread and blest it; and he blest the wine, he being the priest of the most high God,

And he gave to Abram, and he blessed him, and said, Blessed Abram, thou are a man of the most high God, possessor of heaven and of earth;

And blessed is the name of the most high God, which hath delivered thine enemies into thine hand.

And Abram gave him tithes of all he had taken. (Inspired Version, Genesis 14:17-20.)

The story now continues:

And Melchizedek lifted up his voice and blessed Abram.

Now Melchizedek was a man of faith, who wrought righteousness; and when a child he feared God, and stopped the mouth of lions, and quenched the violence of fire.

And thus, having been approved of God, he was ordained an high priest after the order of the covenant which God made with Enoch,

It being after the order of the Son of God; which order came, not by man, nor the will of man; neither by father nor mother; neither by beginning of days nor end of years; but of God;

And it was delivered unto men by the calling of his own voice, according to his own will, unto as many as believed on his name. For God having sworn unto Enoch and unto his seed with an oath by himself; that every one being ordained to this order and calling should have power, by faith, to break mountains, to divide the seas, to dry up waters, to turn them out of their course;

To put at defiance the armies of nations, to divide the earth, to break every bond, to stand in the presence of God; to do all things according to his will, according to his command, subdue principalities and powers; and this by the will of the

Son of God which was from before the foundation of the world.

And men having this faith, coming up unto this order of God, were translated and taken up into heaven. (Inspired Version, Genesis 14:25-32.)

One cannot read this recital of powers, strengths, and blessings without having an understanding of the magnitude of the treasures God has reserved for us if we would only have faith to understand that these are offered us as a personal inheritance. What hope should burn in each one of us as we contemplate the magnitude of the blessings that Abraham sought and obtained. While others were translated to be with Enoch in the city of Zion, Abraham was left on earth possessing this great power:

89

And now, Melchizedek was a priest of this order; therefore he obtained peace in Salem, and was called the Prince of peace.

And his people wrought righteousness and obtained heaven, and sought for the city of Enoch which God had before taken, separating it from the earth, having reserved it unto the latter days, or the end of the world;

And hath said, and sworn with an oath, that the heavens and the earth should come together; and the sons of God should come together; and the sons of God should be tried so as by fire.

And this Melchizedek, having thus established righteousness, was called the king of heaven by his people, or, in other words, the King of peace.

And he lifted up his voice, and he blessed Abram, being the high priest, and the keeper of the storehouse of God;

Him whom God had appointed to receive tithes for the poor.

Wherefore Abram paid unto him tithes of all that he had, of all the riches which he possessed, which God had given him more than that which he had need.

And it came to pass, that God blessed Abram, and gave him riches and honor, and lands for an everlasting possession; according to the covenant which he had made, and according to the blessing wherewith Melchizedek had blessed him. (Inspired Version, Genesis 14:33-40.)

The identity of Melchizedek is more or less obscure. It may be that he is Shem, the son of Noah. There is an unsupported tradition in Jewish literature to this effect. It could be possible, for Shem was still living 500 years after the flood. For 350 years of that time, he lived with his father, Noah. Shem therefore lived in the days of Abraham, and Abraham was 150 years old when Shem died.

Since Melchizedek, spoken of as the high priest, and Shem, the righteous son of Noah, were living at the same time, it might well be that they were one and the same person. It is rather unlikely that there would have been two high priests holding that presiding office at the same time. Thus, one could draw the conclusion that Melchizedek (Prince of peace) is a title that could have been given to Shem because of his greatness and the position he held in the patriarchal order. Shem did reign under his father, Noah, as was also written of Melchizedek (Alma 13:18). Whether Melchizedek and Shem were one and the same person or were different persons is not pertinent to an understanding of priesthood lineage. Had this knowledge been necessary, God would have made this information known. It is only significant for us to remember that the patriarchal order within the Melchizedek Priesthood is extremely important and that it comes to us as a lineage right.

These fathers, or patriarchal leaders, were men who loved God with all their hearts. The scriptures speak of them as "fearing" God. From the Hebrew tongue, that word which meant "to reverence with humility" has been translated as "fear." The use of this word has continued to the present time, but the thought could better be expressed as love and reverence combined. Those faithful patriarchs were promised a knowledge of the mysteries and the treasures of God, as we read from the following scripture:

For thus saith the Lord—I, the Lord, am merciful and

gracious unto those who fear me, and delight to honor those who serve me in righteousness and in truth to the end.

Great shall be their reward and eternal shall be their glory.

And to them will I reveal all mysteries, yea, all the hidden mysteries of my kingdom from days of old, and for ages to come, will I make known unto them the good pleasure of my will concerning all things pertaining to my kingdom.

Yea, even the wonders of eternity shall they know, and things to come will I show them, even the things of many generations.

And their wisdom shall be great, and their understanding reach to heaven; and before them the wisdom of the wise shall perish, and the understanding of the prudent shall come to naught.

For by my Spirit will I enlighten them, and by my power will I make known unto them the secrets of my will—yea, even those things which eye has not seen, nor ear heard, nor yet entered into the heart of man. (D&C 76:5-10.)

These are the promises of the fathers that are to be called to the remembrance of their children in the last days. As their heirs, these promises made to the fathers become our promises. What a grand and glorious message this is! These blessings are ours if we will work for them and accept them as they are offered to us.

9

Abraham's Search for Treasures

I have commented on the great treasures promised to the children of the covenant. The search for these treasures is well exemplified in the life of Abraham. While he lived in Ur of the Chaldees, Abraham learned of his inherited right to those treasures. We are not told how he learned of his heritage rights, but he does tell us that he possessed the records of his fathers, the patriarchs: "But the records of the fathers, even the patriarchs, concerning the right of Priesthood, the Lord my God preserved in mine own hands. . . ." (Abraham 1:31.) His own parents evidently possessed valuable scriptural records, perhaps even had a family book of remembrance, but had abandoned the truths of the gospel and turned to idol worship. In a like manner many people today turn to worship modern idols, such as fame, fortune, and influence. They neglect and abandon the scriptures and the tradition of faith and good works found in the true gospel. They have the scriptures, but neither use them nor follow them. When those scriptural records came into the hands of Abraham, his heart was touched. He recognized their value to him personally and sought for the promises and blessings contained therein.

Referring to those promises not only of heavenly, but also of earthly treasure, he wrote:

And, finding there was greater happiness and peace and rest for me, I sought for the blessings of the fathers, and the right whereunto I should be ordained to administer the same;

having been myself a follower of righteousness, desiring also to be one who possessed great knowledge, and to be a greater follower of righteousness, and to possess greater knowledge, and to be a father of many nations, a prince of peace, and desiring to receive instructions, and to keep the commandments of God, I became a rightful heir, a High Priest, holding the right belonging to the fathers. (Abraham 1:2.)

One cannot read this life goal of Abraham without recognizing his wisdom in searching for those treasures which of all the treasures of the earth have the greatest worth to man.

Even though his own immediate family regarded God's priesthood power as a thing of little worth, the royal blood of leadership flowed in Abraham's veins. He had leadership vision and exercised, of his own will and choice, his right to receive these blessings for himself and for his posterity. He explained how these blessings were to be received:

It was conferred upon me from the fathers; it came down from the fathers, from the beginning of time, yea, even from the beginning, or before the foundations of the earth to the present time, even the right of the firstborn, on the first man, who is Adam, our first father, through the fathers unto me.

I sought for mine appointment unto the Priesthood according to the appointment of God unto the fathers concerning the seed. (Abraham 1:3-4.)

In this scripture we learn another truth: that, in order to obtain them, we must actively seek for these blessings regardless of any rights we have to receive them by virtue of our birth. Blessings do not come automatically. First we have to know what things are available to us; then we must catch a vision of their worth and value; and finally, knowing we have a right to receive them, we must actively search for them in order to obtain them. So it was with Abraham. He had to leave his home in Ur of Chaldea to go and seek out those righteous men who had the power to confer those priesthood powers and blessings on him.

Full priesthood power includes authority to seal on earth and in heaven and thus to be a spokesman for God.

93

This authority was held by the ancient patriarchs. A promise was given to Abraham and to his seed after him that they should become a specially chosen people to do the work of the Lord. We speak of them as being children of the covenant. God so designated them as he changed Abram's name to Abraham and said: ". . . I will establish my covenant between me and thee and thy seed after thee in their generations for an everlasting covenant, to be a God unto thee, and to thy seed after thee. . . . And God said unto Abraham, Thou shalt keep my covenant therefore, thou, and thy seed after thee in their generations." (Genesis 17:7, 9.)

94

Abraham was a faithful man, and so loyal that the Lord said he could not hide from Abraham the things he would do to preserve Abraham's family as a righteous people. God knew they would serve him faithfully. The Lord said: ". . . Abraham shall surely become a great and mighty nation, and all the nations of the earth shall be blessed in him. For I know him, that he will command his children and his household after him, and they shall keep the way of the Lord, to do justice and judgment; that the Lord may bring upon Abraham that which he hath spoken of him." (Genesis 18:18-19.)

This promise of greatness to come for the children of the covenant was made by the Lord, who knew, right from the beginning, the things that would transpire even to the end of the world. The Lord said to Abraham:

My name is Jehovah, and I know the end from the beginning; therefore my hand shall be over thee.

And I will make of thee a great nation, and I will bless thee above measure, and make thy name great among all nations, and thou shalt be a blessing unto thy seed after thee, that in their hands they shall bear this ministry and Priesthood unto all nations;

And I will bless them through thy name; for as many as receive this Gospel shall be called after thy name, and shall be accounted thy seed, and shall rise up and bless thee, as their father. (Abraham 2:8-10.)

We should realize that in accepting the gospel of Jesus

Christ, we have become the children of Abraham, or children of the covenant, with all the obligations, responsibilities, and blessings this great promise brings us.

A question, however, is raised as to just how we should act in this office as children of the covenant. What are we to do? The Lord explained to Abraham how members of his family were to serve as children of the covenant:

And I will bless them that bless thee, and curse them that curse thee; and in thee (that is, in thy Priesthood) and in thy seed (that is, thy Priesthood), for I give unto thee a promise that this right shall continue in thee, and in thy seed after thee (that is to say, the literal seed, or the seed of the body) shall all the families of the earth be blessed, even with the blessings of the Gospel, which are the blessings of salvation, even of life eternal. (Abraham 2:11.)

So again we hear the promise of a great treasure of eternal life that is to come through the exercise of priesthood power. We often fail to realize that our priesthood comes to us through the lineage of our fathers and mothers. Whenever I see the word *patriarch,* a vision of Abraham comes to my mind. Yet he was only one of the many patriarchs. All leaders who held the keys of the priesthood from Adam down to Abraham were truly patriarchs.

It is interesting to review the life of Abraham and see how this priesthood power was passed on to his progeny. Abraham was troubled because he had no heir, and he realized that all he possessed, upon his death, would go to his steward Eliezer. When he prayed to the Lord for a son to carry on his name, he was promised an heir and was told that his progeny would be as plentiful as the stars in the heaven. From Abraham we can also learn the value of patience in obtaining the fulfillment of future promises. The Lord told him, for example, that he was to have the land from the Nile to the Euphrates as an inheritance for himself and for his posterity. Yet more than 400 years were to pass before that promise would be fulfilled. The promised land in the days of Abraham was already populated and belonged to the people of Ammon who lived there. God would never take the land from them to give to Abraham or to anyone else so long as the people remained righteous. Yet there comes a time when God, even with all his patience, can no longer strive with man. Abraham's descendants were to be in bondage in Egypt for 400 years before that prophecy came into fulfillment, yet it did come to pass. By that time the Amalekites held the land of Canaan. They were a wicked people also, but the Lord gave them full opportunity to repent. It was only when they failed to repent that King Saul was sent by the prophet Samuel to take over the land by force for an inheritance for the Israelites. When the wickedness of the people had reached a point at which they no longer had a right to claim the land, it was taken from them and given to the descendants of Abraham.

Knowing of Abraham's desire to have a son, Abraham's wife Sarah gave him one of her maids, Hagar, to be his wife. A son was born from that union, and he was named Ishmael. Abraham loved Ishmael and asked God to establish him as his heir. The Lord answered that Abraham's heir was to come from the royal line through Sarah and not from Hagar. The Lord explained: "And as for Ishmael, I have heard thee: Behold, I have blessed him, and will make him fruitful, and will multiply him exceedingly; twelve princes shall he beget, and I will make of him a great nation. But my covenant will I establish with Isaac, which Sarah shall bear unto thee at this set time in the next year." (Genesis 17:20-21.) So important was this son to be that God revealed to Abraham, before the boy was born, that he was to be named Isaac. The covenant promises were to come through this son. Ishmael was fourteen years old when his brother Isaac was born.

At that time Abraham lived near Sodom and Gomorrah, but these cities were so wicked that God sent three men to investigate. They were received by Abraham and given hospitality. At the time of their visit, these men confirmed the promise God had made to Abraham that Sarah would give him a son. Sarah, being ninety years old, knew this impossible and laughed at the thought. She was rebuked and chastened as the Lord reminded her and Abraham, "Is anything too hard for the Lord?" (Genesis 18:14.) This question is a promise all of us should remember in our search for our covenant blessings. No matter how handicapped or how incapable we might sometimes feel when life with all its demands and vicissitudes presses on us, the promises of God will be fulfilled if we will only have the faith to live for them.

97

The importance of the influence of even a few righteous people on the lives and destinies of others can be learned from the story of Sodom and Gomorrah. While the men went to make their investigation, Abraham stood before the Lord and conversed with him:

And Abraham drew near, and said, Wilt thou also destroy the righteous with the wicked?

Peradventure there be fifty righteous within the city: wilt thou also destroy and not spare the place for the fifty righteous that are therein?

That be far from thee to do after this manner, to slay the righteous with the wicked: and that the righteous should be as the wicked, that be far from thee: Shall not the Judge of all the earth do right?

And the Lord said, If I find in Sodom fifty righteous within the city, then I will spare all the place for their sakes. (Genesis 18:23-26.)

As I read this, I smile at the presumptuousness of Abraham in telling the Lord what he ought to do. Yet there was no rebuke, and the Lord must have been pleased with Abraham's tender heart in wanting to save the people from destruction and for pleading mercy in their behalf.

Abraham then went on to bargain with the Lord, asking him if he would spare the city if only forty-five righteous people could be found. The Lord agreed. Then Abraham continued his pleas for forty, then thirty, then twenty, and each time the Lord agreed to spare them if that many righteous persons could be found. Finally Abraham said: "Oh let not the Lord be angry, and I will speak yet but this once: Peradventure ten shall be found there. And he said, I will not destroy it for ten's sake." (Genesis 18:32.)

Thus the mercy of God is made evident, and this should encourage us as we strive to convert the people of the world to a knowledge of the eternal treasures awaiting them. Nothing is impossible to the Lord, and though there be but few of us to carry the message, we can be that leaven which will cause the whole of mankind to rise and be edified.

When not even ten righteous people could be found within the cities, Sodom and Gomorrah were destroyed because of their extreme wickedness. Lot and his family were warned to flee and did so before the cities were consumed by fire. Lot's wife, however, after leaving the city, looked back and regretted the decision she had made. She thought how foolish it was to leave their city life and now to have to begin all over again without the friends and comforts she had known in her city home. She was destroyed as a result of her lack of true repentance. So, too, some of us think the price we have to pay to attain our inheritance is too great. Some of us become dissatisfied and full of regret. When we waver in our faith and look back, we stop our forward progress and lose all we might have had. Someday in the future, when we remember what we might have attained, we will regret our lack of faith and fortitude, but it will be too late. In the words of Samuel, the great Lamanite prophet, the Lord will say: "But behold, your days of probation are past; ye have procrastinated the day of your salvation until it is everlastingly too late, and your destruction is made sure; yea, for ye have sought all the days of your life for that which ye could not obtain; and ye have sought for happiness in doing iniquity, which thing is contrary to the nature of that righteousness which is in our great and Eternal Head." (Helaman 13:38.)

98

10

Faith Demonstrated

A whole book could be written on the life of the patriarch Abraham. Regardless of Abraham's greatness of character, he yet needed to be tested and proved to see if he would remain faithful under even the most trying circumstances. This principle of trial is expressed in the following scripture: "For of him unto whom much is given much is required; and he who sins against the greater light shall receive the greater condemnation." (D&C 82:3.) We should note that this greater faith is not just expected of us—it is required. It has already been demonstrated how disobedience can rob us of inherited blessings. Abraham had been taught the principles of righteousness. If he were to stand at the head of the promised lineage, his faith and constancy needed to be tested.

One of the principles of righteousness is the concept of sacrifice or a willingness to demonstrate our obedience by giving a part of our means, time, energies, or even of ourself to prove our constancy. When Adam and Eve were driven from the Garden of Eden, they were told to sacrifice the firstlings of the field for an offering unto the Lord. When they were obedient to this command, an explanation was given them as to why sacrifice is necessary. It was explained to them by an angel of the Lord that such a sacrifice was a similitude of the sacrifice of the Only Begotten of the Father, who is full of grace and truth. (Moses 5:7.) Thus, sacrifice is a principle of the

plan of salvation and was provided from the very beginning. However, this concept of sacrifice became cor-
rupted over the centuries as the doctrines of men replaced the doctrines of God.

Abraham had been taught the principles of
obedience. He had lived amid idol worshipers, had seen
their wickedness, and had been taught most emphatically
that the sacrifice of human beings was an abomination to
the Lord. Abraham's own life had been threatened, for he
was prepared as one of these sacrifices. Only by the intervention of an angel of God was his life preserved. Thus
100 Abraham knew from personal experience how horrible
human sacrifice could be. If there was one doctrine he
had learned thoroughly, it was the horror of idol worship
with its accompanying human sacrifice. He understood
thoroughly that mankind constituted the children of
God. The whole purpose of earth life was to provide a
mortal experience for these children of God. To rob them
of this experience by murder in the name of religion was
to destroy the very purpose of the plan of salvation. No
wonder idol worship, with its accompanying human
sacrifice, is a doctrine of Satan and an abomination to
God.

One day when Abraham's son Isaac was a young man,
the Lord spoke to Abraham and told him to take Isaac
into the land of Moriah and there offer him to the Lord
as a burnt offering. This was human sacrifice, the very
thing God had taught him was the greatest of all evils. It
was murder of the worst type. Abraham might well have
protested this extraordinary command from God as being
totally inconsistent with everything he had been taught.
He might well have delayed action in the hope that the
Lord would change his mind. He dared not tell Sarah or
anyone else of this commandment. Neither did he dare
delay action lest his heart fail and cause him to falter in
his determination to obey the Lord. Instead, Abraham
arose early the next morning and, taking two young men-
servants and Isaac with him, set out to do as he had been
commanded. His willingness to do whatever God asked

of him, regardless of consequences, was a sign of his faith and absolute trust in God. He made his decision to be obedient to the Lord. Of course, that resolve could weaken, as happens so often with us. We resolve to comply, but our determination weakens along the way. This test applied also to Abraham, for surely every step and every minute of that journey to Mount Moriah must have tortured his mind as he anticipated what he would have to do.

When they came to the designated place, Abraham told the servants to remain. "And Abraham took the wood of the burnt offering, and laid it upon Isaac his son; and took the fire in his hand, and a knife; and they went both of them together." (Genesis 22:6.) We should remember that Abraham was an old man by this time. Isaac, a young man, carried the heavy burden of wood up the mountain. The scriptures say that Abraham lived in the land of the Philistines "many days." In fact, Josephus, in his book *Antiquities of the Jews*, reports that Isaac was twenty-five years old at the time this journey was made. When they reached the top of the mountain, they built a stone altar and put the wood in order, and Abraham then bound Isaac and placed him on the altar. I am impressed by this statement, for Abraham, according to Josephus, would have been 125 years old. Had Isaac not agreed to be bound, Abraham could never have bound him. We speak of the faith of Abraham, but I also think of the faith and obedience of Isaac. Isaac had such faith and confidence in his father and in the Lord that even if it meant giving up his life, he would do as he was asked, and so he permitted his father to bind him and place him upon the stone altar.

We can well imagine the anguish of heart and the suffering of mind as Abraham raised the knife to plunge it into the heart of his beloved son. God had promised him this son in his old age. Isaac was his heir and had received the promise to stand at the head of Abraham's progeny. All the promises of the future rested on this young boy. This offering represented the destruction of

Abraham's hopes for the future and the end of life for this son whom he loved as he loved his own life. How could he ever explain this sacrifice to Sarah? It is probably impossible for us to understand fully how his heart must have broken as he raised that knife to take the life of his beloved son Isaac.

As he thus demonstrated his obedience and his trust in God, the voice of the angel of God called to him out of heaven and said, "Lay not thine hand upon the lad, neither do thou any thing unto him: for now I know that thou fearest God, seeing thou hast not withheld thy son, thine only son from me." (Genesis 22:12.) Abraham lifted his eyes and saw that God had provided a ram for the sacrifice. As Isaac was released from his bonds, those two great men were further strengthened in their knowledge of the power of God to save. As a result now of their demonstrated complete willingness to do whatever the Lord commanded, they received the promise of a great posterity:

By myself have I sworn, saith the Lord, for because thou hast done this thing, and hast not withheld thy son, thine only son:

That in blessing I will bless thee, and in multiplying I will multiply thy seed as the stars of the heaven, and as the sand which is upon the sea shore; and thy seed shall possess the gate of his enemies;

And in thy seed shall all the nations of the earth be blessed; because thou hast obeyed my voice. (Genesis 22:16-18.)

This testing of Abraham and Isaac was a harbinger of the situation that would occur at the atonement of Jesus Christ. God the Father at that time would have to permit the death of his Beloved Son, and Jesus Christ would have to give his life willingly. Not even Abraham and Isaac could understand the anguish this would cause them. Abraham and Isaac had been freed of the ultimate sacrifice that had originally been requested of them. There was, however, no way for the Father and the Son to escape their anguish and suffering in fulfilling their

portion of the plan of salvation. For the Father and the
Son there could be no ram provided with his horns
caught in the thicket. The ultimate sacrifice was required
of them. Later on Jesus was to teach: "This is my commandment, that ye love one another, as I have loved you.
Greater love hath no man than this, that a man lay down
his life for his friends." (John 15:12-13.) He demonstrated
his great love for us by giving not just a part of himself,
but his life, that we might be returned to the Father.
How wholeheartedly grateful we ought to be for this
greatest expression of love that could ever be made for
us! If we are that precious to them, should we not remember who we are and act accordingly?

103

So Abraham and Isaac returned home to take up their
lives again. As Isaac matured, it became necessary for
him to take a wife and begin raising a family of his own.
But Abraham, realizing how important blood lines are,
would not permit Isaac to take a wife locally as his
brother Ishmael had done. Abraham sent his steward
back to the Chaldees as God had instructed him to do, so
that the lineage of Isaac's posterity could remain pure according to the promise. The Lord directed the steward to
the house of Rebekah, who was Isaac's first cousin, once
removed. Rebekah became Isaac's wife, and the scriptures record that he loved her. (Genesis 24:67.) Isaac was
forty years old when he took her to wife.

From this union came twin sons, but the Lord told
Rebekah that the older son, Esau, should serve the
younger son, Jacob. Esau married local girls, but his
parents did not want Jacob to do as his brother had done.
Isaac sent Jacob back to take a wife of noble lineage from
among the family of the ancient patriarchs, where the
promise of inherited rights to the priesthood blessings
was part of their lineage rights. This had been the pattern of his father and his grandfather before him. There
in that land Jacob served Laban, his great-great-uncle,
for fourteen years before he was able to marry Rachel, his
first cousin twice removed. His first marriage to Leah
came as a result of Laban's deceit, but Jacob's love for

Rachel was so great that the years of servitude "seemed unto him but a few days, for the love he had to her." (Genesis 29:20.)

Faith and obedience were characteristic of Jacob's family, and when Jacob demonstrated his faith and obedience, the Lord changed his name to Israel. From Jacob came twelve sons, and all of them were sons of the covenant with rights to priesthood blessings. Some were more faithful than others, and the blessings given them came according to what they were willing to do. Normally, the patriarchal right should have been given to Reuben, the oldest son. When he became disqualified because of disobedience, the mantle of the patriarch was given to Joseph, the eldest son of Rachel. Since all the children of Israel were children of the covenant, we speak of these children of the promise as the children of Israel, a people chosen to serve others and to point the way for others to follow. Their stewardship is that of leadership. God does expect more from them because of who they are. I cited before the scripture found in Doctrine and Covenants, section 82, verse 3, which expresses their stewardship responsibility in strong terms. The children of Israel have been given many promises and much power and authority. They are not only expected, but are required, to demonstrate leadership. The same instruction was given by the Savior in his time as he told his disciples of their stewardship responsibility as leaders: ". . . For unto whomsoever much is given, of him shall be much required: and to whom men have committed much, of him they will ask the more." (Luke 12:48.) Note again that the Lord did not say much is *expected*, but that much would be *required*. Where we have been given so much information about our lineage responsibilities, we in turn will be required to give an account of that stewardship and make a report of what we have done to protect and foster our family relationship.

The line of priesthood authority passed from Joseph to Ephraim. Manasseh also had priesthood authority, for he too was a blood descendant of the patriarchal line. He also will be great, but the leadership responsibility fell on Ephraim and his descendants, who are to lead out, supported by Manasseh and all his descendants. In fact, *all* of the descendants of Israel have a family responsibility to bring a knowledge of the divinity of God and of the promises inherent in the plan of salvation to every one of God's children who have dwelt on this earth.

Chart 2 shows an interesting phenomenon. When Adam and Eve were made mortal, they had almost perfect bodies and lived almost one thousand years, as God had promised them. As men became less obedient and sin entered into the world, those almost perfect bodies became contaminated. Because men failed to follow God's laws, disease and illnesses entered into the world and the length of their lifespan continually decreased. If this decrease in length of life took place in the patriarchal line, we can well conceive that it became accentuated among those less faithful and less obedient. We have no record of the length of life of those not of the patriarchal lineage. It is interesting to read in the scriptures how God gave dietary regulations from time to time to protect the health and preserve the life of his children. Long life is a blessing, as are health and happiness. If we could remain well and strong and our lives could be preserved and lengthened, think how much more we could learn and do during our lifetime on this earth. Not only would we have the necessary experiences and the time to improve our own characters, but we would be able to help others to increase their knowledge and their joy and happiness on the earth. When righteousness prevails and knowledge increases as they will do in the Millennium, we are told: "In that day an infant shall not die until he is old; and his life shall be as the age of a tree." (D&C 101:30.) People then living on the earth will be able to accomplish much more, for they will have time, experience, and opportunity to make the most of life.

Length of life
of early patriarchs

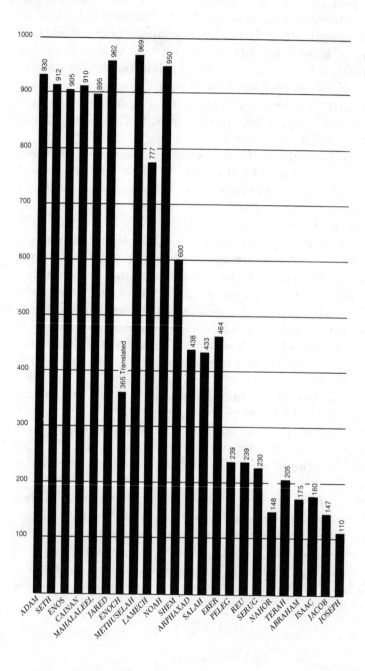

Abraham, Isaac, and Jacob were great men. When we think of their blessings, we must realize that these patriarchal blessings are also ours to enjoy if we are willing to pay the price to obtain them. For this reason all of us should strive to qualify ourselves so that we can have these promises sealed on our heads as our inherited family right, just as these promises were given our patriarchal fathers. This is our inheritance as children of the promise.

11

A Mess of Pottage

One of the saddest experiences in life is to see a person one loves, a person who has tremendous potential and ability, waste away that potential and never achieve the greatness within him. That happened to Cain, and that is why his story becomes one of importance to every one of us. Somehow or in some way we must understand that each of us, no matter what our status in life may be, can accomplish much more than we think we can. If we could only catch this vision, each of us could accomplish more and be happier in the process. Perhaps additional stories of lost opportunities of other men can help us realize that we individually can obtain great blessings if we avoid making the same mistakes they did.

Isaac, the son of Abraham, was named before he was born, and through the wisdom of his parents, obtained a special wife of noble birth. She was a descendant of the same patriarchal lineage Isaac held. Thus a pure blood lineage for their children was preserved. The scriptures record that Isaac loved her; such love is the prime foundation for an eternal marriage. Isaac's marriage to Rebekah was sealed for eternity through the special power of the priesthood, as was Abraham's marriage to Sarah. Abraham's other wives are referred to as concubines, and though his marriages to them were valid throughout mortality, those for time only did not carry with them that same eternal promise which made Isaac, as a covenant son, different from Abraham's other sons.

Rebekah, the wife of Isaac, bore twin sons. The firstborn, Esau, would normally have inherited the patriarchal right; however, before they were born the Lord told Rebekah that Jacob, the second son, would predominate over Esau. That knowledge she kept hidden in her heart during the following years. Isaac was sixty years old when these boys were born, and it was little wonder that he had a special love for Esau, his firstborn. One day when Esau returned from a long and strenuous hunt, he was faint with hunger and asked his brother Jacob for a portion of the food Jacob was cooking in a pot. Jacob said he would trade some of the food for Esau's birthright. The scriptures do not say whether Jacob made that statement in jest or in earnest, but Esau, thinking only of his present hunger and willing to trade that intangible promise of the future for the tangible present treasure of food for his famished body, agreed to the exchange, and with an oath he rejected his right of inheritance. He sold his birthright to eternal blessings for nothing more important than a meal.

What we should realize in this story is that Esau, by reason of his birth, had a right to that birthright blessing. When God told Rebekah that Jacob would prevail over Esau, it was because from the very beginning he knew of a flaw in Esau's character. Had Esau overcome that flaw in mortality, he would have reserved for himself that promise and prevailed over Jacob. Esau's flaw was his indifference to priesthood authority and his lack of appreciation of his family heritage. He regarded his priesthood blessings as of no more value than a pot of lentil soup. A further testimony of Esau's disregard for his priesthood blessings was his marriages to Hittite wives. The scriptures record that these "were a grief of mind unto Isaac and to Rebecca." (Genesis 26:35.) This grief came because the children from these marriages could not hold the priesthood. Thus Esau threw away his own birthright and also the right of his children to hold the priesthood. He was not only indifferent, but also disobedient. He never overcame that flaw in his character, which God knew and recognized in the spirit world before Esau was born.

The thought comes to my mind: How many of us have similar flaws in our characters? God gives us many opportunities to overcome these flaws. Like Esau of old, some of us are born into the finest of families. We have good and faithful parents, and every opportunity is given us to overcome our weaknesses. We are born in a time, at a place, and under conditions in which everything is conducive to our growth and development. Yet when everything is said and done, whatever happens depends upon our obedience and willingness to conform. Being born in a good family will not alone assure us of exaltation. Even being born in the Church or born in the new and everlasting covenant as an heir to the priesthood does not assure us of exaltation. The treasures we achieve depend on the use we make of those opportunities which God gives us.

Following the rebellion of Esau, Jacob obtained Esau's birthright. Jacob did as his mother instructed him to do; he went to his father clothed in garments like those that Esau wore and asked for his father's blessing. Though he obtained the birthright blessing by subtlety, it would not have had any validity whatsoever had not the Lord approved it. The Lord did approve it and the blessing was valid. As Isaac told Jacob:

Therefore God give thee of the dew of heaven, and the fatness of the earth, and plenty of corn and wine [these were temporal blessings to him and his posterity]:

Let people serve thee, and nations bow down to thee: be lord over thy brethren, and let thy mother's sons bow down to thee: cursed be every one that curseth thee, and blessed be he that blesseth thee [these were the spiritual blessings that were to come]. (Genesis 27:28-29.)

So Jacob obtained the birthright blessing and the priesthood heirship that pertains thereto.

What about Jacob's marriage and the rights of his posterity? Rebekah's statement to Isaac gives us information as to what should follow in Jacob's life: "I am weary of my life [in other words, discouraged and heartsick that her grandchildren were denied the priesthood, which is one of the great purposes of life] because of the daughters of Heth [the wives of Esau who were Hittites]: if Jacob take a wife of the daughters of Heth, such as these which are of the daughters of the land, what good shall my life do me?" (Genesis 27:46.) In others words, the whole purpose of her life in mortality would be more or less wasted if her descendants were to be denied the priesthood of God. So Isaac instructed Jacob "and blessed him, and charged him, and said unto him, Thou shalt not take a wife of the daughters of Canaan." (Genesis 28:1.) That statement reminds us again of Moses 7:8, the statement made to Enoch about the people of the land of Canaan, and we are reminded in verse 12 that the gospel was carried to all people in that day except those living in the land of Canaan.

111

It is common knowledge how Jacob was sent back to Abraham's ancient home to obtain a wife from the patriarchal lineage. On his way the Lord confirmed the blessing given him by his father Isaac, saying, ". . . in thee and in thy seed shall all the families of the earth be blessed." (Genesis 28:14.) Jacob then went on to Padanaram, and at a well in that land he met and fell in love with Rachel, the daughter of Laban, who was Rebecca's uncle. There Jacob agreed to serve Laban seven years for his daughter Rachel. Laban agreed, but on the wedding night he substituted his oldest daughter, Leah, for Rachel. Jacob served yet another seven years for Rachel, so great was his love for her. Each of these girls gave him their maids as wives, but we are not told whether or not these maids were wives of the eternal priesthood covenant as were Leah and Rachel. They may have been, or they may have been wives for mortality only. When I first thought about this problem, I considered Jacob's marriages to these maids to be marriages only for time. Presently I am inclined to think that they might well have been eternal marriages, for all the children of Israel are spoken of as children of the covenant. As God made his covenant with Jacob, Jacob's name was changed to Israel (Genesis 35:9-10) because of his faithfulness and obedience. The twelve sons are listed as follows:

LEAH	RACHEL	BILHAH (Rachel's Maid)	ZILPAH (Leah's Maid)
1. Reuben	11. Joseph	5. Dan	7. Gad
2. Simeon	12. Benjamin	6. Naphtali	8. Asher
3. Levi			
4. Judah			
9. Isachar			
10. Zebulun			

Although Leah became the first wife by subterfuge, she was a daughter of the covenant. Her firstborn son, Reuben, by right of birth inherited the patriarchal right as heir to succeed his father as head of the family. Things happened later on to show that he was unfit for that office, but he did have that birthright; and had he proved faithful, that blessing would have been his by right of covenant. So all of us are born with almost unlimited possibilities. What we make of them depends on our willingness to prove ourselves worthy of these blessings by what we think and then do. In other words, though God can and does give us opportunities for growth, unless we magnify these offices and opportunities, they do us little good.

What happened under Reuben's leadership? His sister Dinah was ravished by Shechem, a son of Prince Hamor the Hivite. Shechem, who was more honorable than all the rest of his father's house, desired to marry Dinah, so he and his father went to Jacob seeking her hand in marriage. However, the sons of Israel were very angry that he had defiled their sister. Hamor and Shechem offered to produce any dowry requested for Dinah no matter what it might cost them. The sons of Jacob agreed that if Hamor and all his house would be circumcised as were the male descendants of Abraham, they would accept them as equals. This they were willing to do, and so all the males of the house of Hamor were circumcised. But on the third day afterwards, Simeon and Levi took their swords and murdered all the men, spoiled their city, stole all their property, and made slaves of their wives and children. "And Jacob said to Simeon and Levi, Ye have troubled me to make me to stink among the inhabitants of the land, among the Canaanites and the Perizzites. . . ." (Genesis 34:30.)

Thus they lost their right to rule because they were not only dishonest, but murderers as well. We have been taught in the Church that murder is an unforgivable sin and that our word should be as good as our bond. These are words we should remember if we want to protect and preserve our priesthood heritage. Reuben lost his birthright when Jacob took his family to Bethel. There, after the death of Rachel when Benjamin was born, Reuben violated Bilhah, his father's concubine. (Genesis 35:22.) So he lost his birthright because of adultery, another sin to be avoided if we desire to protect our priesthood heritage.

We are told that the sons of Bilhah and Zilpah were evil. Joseph worked with them tending their father's flocks, and he saw their evil doings. As a seventeen-year-old boy, he was appalled by what he saw and so reported to his father. Israel loved Joseph, not only because he was the firstborn of his beloved Rachel, but also because he was an obedient child and a handsome lad. When his brothers saw that Israel loved Joseph more than they, they became insanely jealous of him and hated Joseph. They would have killed him had it not been for Reuben's intervention. They did take Joseph's clothes and threw him into a pit to die. Unbeknown to Reuben, and under the leadership of Judah, they sold him to a passing caravan of Ishmaelites, who in turn sold him into slavery in Egypt to Potiphar, one of the Pharoah's officials and captain of his guard.

When Reuben came to rescue Joseph, he found him gone, and he despaired, not knowing what he should do. When he went back to his brothers, they advised him to dip in the blood of a kid goat the special coat Jacob had made for Joseph. Then they returned to Jacob and told him that Joseph had been killed and eaten by a beast of prey. Jacob mourned for Joseph and refused to be comforted at the loss of his favorite son.

Not only was Judah vindictive and a liar, but he also lost his birthright because he married one of the daughters of Canaan and committed fornication with his daughter-in-law, Tamar. Through his wickedness and his envy and his disobedience, he lost the birthright that might have been his.

We should not close this chapter on a sour note, for Joseph was a righteous man. Though the ten brothers who preceded him were unrighteous, Joseph remained true and faithful. When Potiphar's wife attempted to seduce him, he fled from her. What a lesson for us to remember! His virtuous act resulted in his being jailed, for Potiphar's wife unjustly accused him of trying to seduce her. Despite this injustice, Joseph remained faithful. As a result, the Spirit of God rested on the righteous young man and he was able to interpret Pharoah's dream. He then rose in stature in Pharoah's realm because of his honesty, his intelligence, and his hard work, and so became second in command to Pharoah and a great power in the land. During a time of famine when Israel and his family were forced to seek assistance from Egypt, Joseph was generous and became a savior to his father's family. Thus he inherited the birthright as head of the family and used it in caring for and preserving his family. The joy of Israel knew no bounds when his favorite son, Joseph, was restored to him again. Joseph established Israel and his family in the land of Goshen in Egypt, which was the most fertile portion of the land. And so we see how the Lord blesses the righteous, both temporally and spiritually, after they have been tried and tested. So Israel was blessed, so Joseph was blessed, and so will each of us be blessed when we have proved our worthiness to receive such blessings.

12

The Importance of Patriarchal Blessings

Through his ability, generosity, and nobility, Joseph was able to save his father's family from famine and establish them safely in the land of Goshen in Egypt. Let it not be forgotten that this was done under the hand of God to fill the promises God had made to the patriarchs. Before Jacob went down to Egypt, God said to him: "I am God, the God of thy father: fear not to go down into Egypt; for I will there make of thee a great nation: I will go down with thee into Egypt; and I will also surely bring thee up again: and Joseph shall put his hand upon thine eyes." (Genesis 46:3-4.) Israel and his family were preserved from famine and became prosperous in the land of Goshen. They were preserved by the hand of the Lord. They were seventy in number, as the total family of Jacob went into the land of Egypt.

When Israel was 147 years old and feeble, he called Joseph to him and reminded him of the promises God had made to him.

And Jacob said unto Joseph, God Almighty appeared unto me at Luz in the land of Canaan, and blessed me,

And said unto me, Behold, I will make thee fruitful, and multiply thee, and I will make of thee a multitude of people; and will give this land to thy seed after thee for an everlasting possession.

And now thy two sons, Ephraim and Manasseh, which were born unto thee in the land of Egypt before I came unto thee into Egypt, are mine; as Reuben and Simeon [that is, just as Reuben and Simeon are mine], they shall be mine.

And thy issue, which thou begettest after them, shall be thine, and shall be called after the name of their brethren in their inheritance. (Genesis 48:4-6.)

So the birthright blessing in the priesthood as head of the family was taken from Reuben and Simeon for reasons already stated and given to Ephraim and Manasseh, who henceforth were to be considered as sons of Israel. Then Israel blessed them with a patriarchal blessing. Manasseh was the older son, so Joseph had him kneel before his father so Jacob's right hand would be upon Manasseh's head, and he placed Ephraim to the right of Manasseh so Jacob's left hand would be upon Ephraim's head. But Jacob crossed his hands knowingly and placed his right hand on the younger Ephraim's head, thus placing the birthright upon him rather than upon Manasseh. The scriptures do not say why this change was made. Subsequent events have proved that Manasseh did become a great nation, but Ephraim has become even greater.

117

Israel subsequently called all his sons to him and gave each of them a patriarchal blessing according to what they had earned and according to the promises given them for the future, particularly for the last days. "And Jacob called unto his sons, and said, Gather yourselves together, that I may tell you that which shall befall you in the last days. Gather yourselves together, and hear, ye sons of Jacob; and hearken unto Israel your father." (Genesis 49:1-2.)

He then blessed each one, defined certain limitations to them, and gave them promises for the future. In other words, he set up divine guidelines to direct them and their descendants in their coming lives. We can quote the blessings of Joseph as an example of these prophetic promises:

Joseph is a fruitful bough, even a fruitful bough by a well; whose branches run over the wall:

The archers have sorely grieved him, and shot at him, and hated him:

But his bow abode in strength, and the arms of his hands were made strong by the hands of the mighty God of Jacob; (from thence is the shepherd, the stone of Israel:)

Even by the God of thy father, who shall help thee; and by the Almighty, who shall bless thee with blessings of heaven above, blessings of the deep that lieth under, blessings of the breasts, and of the womb:

The blessings of thy father prevailed above the blessings of my progenitors unto the utmost bounds of the everlasting hills: they shall be upon the head of Joseph, and on the crown of the head of him that was separate from his brethren. (Genesis 49:22-26.)

From this we learn that the birthright blessings of his progenitors, the patriarchs, were passed on to Joseph and his posterity through Ephraim and Manasseh. Ephraim was to assume the leadership responsibilities for the house of Israel in the last days. This is the heritage responsibility of the tribe of Ephraim in the days in which we live.

We learn from the scriptures that the genealogy of a family may not follow the birthright. This happened in Jacob's family, when the birthright was transferred to Joseph and from him to Ephraim. "Now the sons of Reuben the firstborn of Israel, (for he was the firstborn; but, forasmuch as he defiled his father's bed, his birthright was given unto the sons of Joseph the son of Israel; and the genealogy is not to be reckoned after the birthright." (1 Chronicles 5:1.) These birthright blessings that were given to Ephraim pertain principally to the last days. The dispersion of both the people of Judah and Israel (the ten tribes) is well documented in the Old Testament. The gathering again of the people of the kingdom of Judah and the kingdom of Israel in the last days was given as a covenant promise. This gathering is described in Jeremiah, chapters 30 and 31, and is to be led by Ephraim.

Behold, I will bring them from the north country, and

gather them from the coasts of the earth, and with them the blind and the lame, the woman with child and her that travaileth with child together: a great company shall return thither.

They shall come with weeping, and with supplications will I lead them: I will cause them to walk by the rivers of waters in a straight way, wherein they shall not stumble: for I am a father of Israel, and Ephraim is my firstborn. (Jeremiah 31:8-9.)

This gathering again in the last days is the great hope of all Israel. It will occur when enmity between Judah and Israel shall cease. This is the blessing of Israel and the richer blessing of Ephraim, as is made plain in a revelation given us in Doctrine and Covenants 133:21-35, informing us that the land of Israel and of Judah will be joined together as it was before the earth was divided into the various continents.

Note the futurity of these blessings. The bloodlines of the patriarchs are difficult to trace from the time of these sons of Israel down to the present. As the families became ever larger and were distributed over ever wider areas, it became difficult to maintain records of all these bloodlines. Genealogies undoubtedly were kept, but the very bulk of these records made it impossible to retain them in the form of scriptures, such as is found in the Bible. The genealogies given in the New Testament of the lineage of Jesus through his mother's bloodline or through the line of his legal father, Joseph, are evidence that such records were kept.

We have no record of the faith and obedience of those whose names are recorded. We have already seen how lack of obedience resulted in a change of heritage blessings from one son to another. We know from our own experience that some families remain childless. Adoptions are often made to continue a line by grafting into a family, by the power of the priesthood of God, a person who thus becomes properly qualified to continue the line. Such a person can have sealed upon him all the rights, privileges, and blessings of priesthood heritage and lineage as he would have had he been born into that family. Sometimes the patriarchal right is shifted to a collateral bloodline family, as, for example, when the direct line dies out or a direct-line descendant becomes disqualified through sin or disobedience. Many things can and do happen, but the concept of patriarchal rights and blessings remains and must be accepted. These rights and blessings are of tremendous importance, both to an individual and to a family.

It was pointed out in an earlier chapter that all those who accept the gospel of Jesus Christ become the seed or children of Abraham. (Abraham 2:10-11.) This is specially and more emphatically stated for those who receive the priesthood power. (D&C 103:17; 84:34.) Nearly every member of the Church is undoubtedly a literal blood descendant of Jacob, who gave those patriarchal blessings to his twelve sons. Israel's descendants inherit a right to those blessings, and it is the privilege of each descendant of those children of Israel, as they are gathered out of the nations of the earth into the family of Jesus Christ, to receive a personal patriarchal blessing.

Because genealogical records showing bloodlines have not been kept faithfully, some means must be provided for members of the Church to know what their patriarchal lineage is. For this reason, patriarchs or evangelists are ordained in each stake to bless the people with patriarchal blessings. Such divinely chosen patriarchs are ordained individually by prophets of God. Being ordained with such power, these men, through the power of the Holy Spirit, are qualified to bless the people, declare their lineage, and define their heritage blessings. By means of a patriarchal blessing, each person knows what heritage blessings to anticipate as a member of the house of Israel in the last days. When so moved by the Spirit of God, the patriarch also gives an inspired and prophetic statement of the life mission of that person, together with admonition, counsel, guidance, and precautions that will enable the person to guide his life course according to the promises given. It must be emphasized that all promises are conditioned on the faith and works of the individual.

One thing should be made clear about the lineage declared in a patriarchal blessing. The lineage declared may or may not differ from the genealogical lineage. The fact is that all of us are descended through a mixed lineage. I doubt that anyone can lay claim to a perfect descent from father to son through a single lineage line. The blood of Israel has been thoroughly mixed with the gentile nations. Intermarriage was also common among the various tribes of the children of Israel. The Lord said: "For, lo, I will command, and I will sift the house of Israel among all nations, like as corn is sifted in a sieve, yet shall not the least grain fall upon the earth." (Amos 9:9.) Those who come into the Church today have the blood of perhaps several tribes of Israel flowing in their veins and, in addition, the blood of the gentile nations among whom the people were sifted. Under inspiration, the patriarch gives that lineage which predominates and through which we are to receive the promises made to the fathers. Most of the members in the Church today come from Ephraim, according to Ephraim's leadership promise, but Manasseh's descendants are coming into the Church in ever greater numbers now to fulfill Joseph's promise. As the work grows we will find increasing numbers from other tribes coming into the Church and receiving their patriarchal blessings.

These patriarchal blessings are recorded so that a record is kept in the Church as a testimony for each individual. A copy of his blessing is also given to the individual to serve as a guide and a constant reminder of the treasure awaiting him if he is willing to search for and find it. The highly personal nature of these patriarchal blessings should be emphasized. They should not become common property and be discussed with others as conversational items, nor should they be talked about in order to exhibit pride or superiority. These are sacred personal records to be treasured in the privacy of the home and family. They rightfully belong in a personal book of remembrance, where they can be referred to for inspiration and personal guidance. They are intimate personal blessings to be shared only with one's immediate family. If one prepares himself by prayer and fasting prior to receiving such a blessing, the patriarch may receive greater inspiration from the Holy Spirit as he reaches through the veil in his search for light and knowledge.

122

Patriarchs who realize the divine nature of patriarchal blessings seek earnest and continual guidance from the Holy Ghost in making their prophetic utterances. In effect, patriarchal blessings are individual revelations given for guidance and direction of the individual. We have seen how important this patriarchal lineage is. It must not be regarded lightly. When one takes the responsibilities of a patriarchal lineage seriously and lives worthily to receive the promised priesthood blessings pertaining thereto, the time will come when that patriarchal order within the Melchizedek Priesthood can be sealed upon a man and his wife in the temple of God. Each man then becomes a true patriarch in his own family and each woman so sealed becomes a matriarch in her immediate family. Such unions of worthy patriarchal families chained together in proper sealing order will eventually constitute that family of God which will be rebuilt in the resurrected flesh following the resurrection and final judgment.

Exaltation consists, then, in a continuation of these family units into eternity. The unfortunate thing that causes sorrow to God and to man is that some unworthy mortal links in the patriarchal chain will have to be dropped. It is hard to conceive that every generation in any one blood family line will all prove faithful. Those generations not willing to pay the price will have to be eliminated from the chain. Gaps will have to be closed and new links forged and inserted through an adoptive process, but when it is completed, the patriarchal chain will be intact from us to Adam, from Adam to Christ, and from Christ to God the Eternal Father. What a glorious promise to contemplate and what a treasure to desire! It is worthy of our finest efforts and a personal goal toward which every one of us should strive.

Thus there is a great need to choose wisely in family affairs so that a man makes a wise choice in a wife, and a woman chooses carefully before accepting a man as her husband. So much depends on heritage blessings that marriage becomes perhaps the greatest and most important step a person takes in life. Just as it was important to Abraham, to Isaac, and to Jacob, so it must become to each one of us. We must impress this fact on our children as we teach them of life. We must demonstrate to them our love as parents, not only to each other, but also to them. Family is important and true love and devotion the basis for successful family living. It is really the key to our treasure house in the eternities.

A child born into a patriarchal family or adopted officially into such a covenant line becomes a very precious person. Such children must be taught the value of their priesthood heritage. They should be treasured and loved by their parents and given every advantage to grow up in love and understanding. They should be taught to serve and share that love with others, for this is one of the basic responsibilities of priesthood leadership. It was not in vain that the Lord said: "Remember the worth of souls is great in the sight of God; For, behold, the Lord your Redeemer suffered death in the flesh; wherefore he suffered the pain of all men, that all men might repent and come unto him." (D&C 18:10-11.) These children are his sheep for whom he gave his life. Every one is precious to him. If the sheep are that valuable, think how precious in his sight the shepherds must be. The shepherds are those of the special patriarchal lineage who are foreordained to become the leaders of the flock.

I have spoken of the promises made to the fathers that God would provide faithful descendants for those who would preserve their lineage patriarchal lines. This presents a problem for certain members of the Church, particularly for those who do not fully understand the true nature of this patriarchal lineage. Too often they look only on themselves or on their own immediate families, instead of taking the long view and catching a vision of the eternal nature of the family relationship.

Let us take a typical example. A person joins the Church and then tries to convert parents and other family members. Such efforts are often rejected. Sometimes parents are not only disinterested, but even antagonistic when a son or daughter joins the Church. Existing family problems may be intensified because of these strained relationships, and things may go from bad to worse. Yet one person in that family finds the truth, accepts it, and becomes indeed a faithful son or daughter of God.

124

That faithful person who joins the Church qualifies himself to go to the temple and to receive endowment blessings. To whom should he be sealed? If living, the parents would not qualify. Let us suppose they are deceased. The faithful member in the meantime finds warm, close, personal friends in the Church who are older and who show great love and kindness to the convert. Such friends may be either living or now deceased. The Church member, because of that warm, personal relationship, desires to be sealed to such a couple as their child. This is requested on the basis that his own parents do not qualify, would not want each other, or have been so wicked in life that he would not want them as parents. Hence the request is made to be sealed to a couple outside the family line.

Such a person might believe that not only his parents, but even his grandparents, would fail to qualify themselves by reason of their unrighteous conduct to receive temple ordinances. Such a person overlooks the promises made to the fathers. It may be that the great-grandparents are righteous people who not only would qualify, but would gladly accept temple ordinance work done in their behalf. Perhaps they have had their hearts broken as they have seen the iniquity of their children and grandchildren. How they rejoice when that great-grandchild accepts the gospel and lives a righteous life. Their heritage line can now be preserved through that righteous great-grandchild who now, on accepting the truth and living worthily, is qualified to have the temple ordinance work performed for them. The family lineage and the accompanying blessings can thus be preserved for them through the work of that great-grandchild who can serve as a savior for his worthy progenitors.

People forget that many who live dissolute and even wicked lives on earth sometimes do so because they have never really had an opportunity to hear and understand the truth. The gospel has never been explained to them in such a way that their hearts were touched. We forget the far-reaching power of repentance or the mercy God shows for the soul who does repent. Those parents and grandparents may yet repent when the gospel is explained to them in a manner they can understand. If so, they will then want their families preserved in the patriarchal order. Even if a child in mortality refuses to accept the gospel, righteous great-grandparents have a claim on their progeny.

How tragic, then, it would be for a person to seek to be sealed into another family line and in this manner reject his family responsibilities for his own bloodline ancestors. Family lineage and blood responsibilities are important. We ought to take care of our own direct-line ancestors and leave it to the tender mercies of God to determine when and if some link in that family line will have to be dropped. If one or more generations have to be dropped, the link can still be closed to a previous generation. The final judgment will be a just one, as the prophet Jacob reminds us: "O then, my beloved brethren, come unto the Lord, the Holy One. Remember that his paths are righteous. Behold, the way for man is narrow, but it lieth in a straight course before him, and the keeper of the gate is the Holy One of Israel; and he employeth no servant there; and there is none other way save it be by the gate; for he cannot be deceived, for the Lord God is his name." (2 Nephi 9:41.)

The preservation of one's family heritage is important. We should not seek to make that final judgment ourselves, but should let the judgment of our family members rest with Jesus Christ, who truly is our advocate with the Father.

126

A word ought to be written concerning children of illegitimate parents who are abandoned and given for adoption. In reality there was no marriage and no family and hence no claim may be made of such children as rightful heirs. But there are people who love children. Some childless parents desire children with a love that most people fail to comprehend. Other parents just love children so much that they adopt them into a home already crowded with children in order to provide a blanket of love and affection for that wanted child.

Adopted children are fortunate in most instances in knowing that they are needed, wanted, and loved. When such children are sealed into a family by the power of the Holy Priesthood, they become heirs with all the rights and privileges and blessings that are given to the other children in the family who are born in the covenant. They become heirs to the priesthood and are entitled through righteous living to every priesthood lineage blessing. Their line of genealogical responsibility becomes their sealing line. Their line of inheritance becomes their sealing line. How wonderful it is to know that one is so loved!

13

Elijah, the Tishbite

It has been stated that it is difficult to establish a chronological genealogy of the fathers or patriarchs following the days of Joseph. Just before his death, Joseph made the following statement:

And Joseph said unto his brethren, I die: and God will surely visit you, and bring you out of this land unto the land which he sware to Abraham, to Isaac, and to Jacob.

And Joseph took an oath of the children of Israel, saying, God will surely visit you, and ye shall carry up my bones from hence.

So Joseph died, being an hundred and ten years old: and they embalmed him, and he was put in a coffin in Egypt. (Genesis 50:24-26.)

As time passed and the children of Israel became very numerous, the Egyptians became jealous of their power. Joseph and his work were forgotten, and the Israelites were made slaves. They were mistreated and abused. Terrible burdens were placed on them in an effort to destroy them. Pharoah even gave an edict that all their male children should be destroyed at birth.

When people are placed in slavery, especially as terrible as the slavery the Egyptians imposed on the Israelites for 400 years, they are robbed of growth and development. That kind of slavery even destroys spirituality and faith. Stephen, in speaking of this bondage under the Egyptians, said of the seed of Abraham: "And

God spake on this wise, That his seed should sojourn in a strange land; and that they should bring them into bondage, and entreat them evil four hundred years. And the nation to whom they shall be in bondage will I judge, said God: and after that shall they come forth, and serve me in this place." (Acts 7:6-7.) After terrible oppression and mistreatment, God did raise up a prophet, Moses, who led the children of Israel out of bondage. This was done in accordance with the promises that had been made to the fathers.

128

It is true that the people suffered, as the scriptures indicate: "And God heard their groaning, and God remembered his covenant with Abraham, with Isaac, and with Jacob. And God looked upon the children of Israel, and God had respect unto them." (Exodus 2:24-25.) It is generally believed that these slaves gladly followed Moses' leadership, but the scriptures tell us otherwise. They were unwilling followers of Moses. It is difficult for those who have never lived in slavery to understand the deadening effect slavery has on the spirituality of a people. Even though the Lord reaffirmed his promise to the Israelites, they found it hard to believe: "And I will bring you in unto the land, concerning the which I did swear to give it to Abraham, to Isaac, and to Jacob; and I will give it you for an heritage: I am the Lord. And Moses spake so unto the children of Israel; but *they hearkened not* unto Moses *for anguish of spirit,* and for *cruel bondage.*" (Exodus 6:8-9. Italics added.) The children of Israel had to be brought out of Egypt and their physical bondage with power—the power of God.

Moses, a prophet, was raised up to lead them out of Egypt into another land. To lead them out of spiritual bondage, it was necessary for God to restore to them priesthood power, which power and authority had been lost through those long years of slavery and oppression. The first step was to give them the Ten Commandments and related laws to teach them what to do and to build their faith. Instructions were also given for the construction of a portable temple they were to take with them on their journey. In this tabernacle or portable temple, the ordinances of the priesthood could be performed. This was for the edification, strengthening, and growth of the people. Moses received these instructions in priesthood-related matters during his forty-day period of speaking with the Lord on a high mountain. Then, at the close of this instruction, God prepared two stone tables on which were written on both sides the oath and covenant of the Melchizedek Priesthood. These covenants Moses was to take to the children of Israel to restore to them their covenant rights.

129

When Moses came down from the mountain he found the children of Israel worshiping a golden calf as their Egyptian masters had done. They were spiritually so weak that within just this forty-day period they had already forgotten the miracles done in freeing them. They had forgotten and rejected their priesthood heritage and their covenant rights to these great blessings. Moses, in righteous anger, broke the tablets on the ground; then he destroyed the golden calf and cleansed the people. This cost the lives of 3,000 of the ringleaders who had led the people astray.

After the people had been purified, the Lord prepared another priesthood covenant more suited to their weak faith and their spiritual immaturity.

And the Lord said unto Moses, Hew thee two other tables of stone, like unto the first, and I will write upon them also, the words of the law, according as they were written at the first on the tables which thou brakest; but it shall not be according to the first, for I will take away the priesthood out of their midsts; therefore my holy order, and the ordinances thereof, shall not go before them; for my presence shall not go up in their midst, lest I destroy them.

But I will give unto them the law as at the first, but it shall be after the law of a carnal commandment; for I have sworn in my wrath, that they shall not enter into my presence, into my rest, in the days of their pilgrimage. Therefore do as I have commanded thee, and be ready in the morning, and come up in the morning unto mount Sinai, and present thyself there to me, in the top of the mount. (Inspired Version, Exodus 34:1-2.)

So the keys of the Melchizedek Priesthood were withdrawn. Every elder from now on would have to be specifically and individually approved by the Lord. Only the Levitical, or Aaronic, Priesthood was given the people to direct them. From that time on, each prophet called of God had to be individually called of God and ordained to the Melchizedek Priesthood. The powers and authority given each of these ministers depended on the extent of their calling.

130

About 900 B.C., in the days of the wicked King Ahab of Israel, a special prophet was called of God and ordained to the Melchizedek Priesthood. Not much is known of him except that he came from Gilead and was called Elijah the Tishbite. Elijah appeared suddenly and departed also in a mysterious manner. He only appeared and mingled with the people when the Lord sent him with instructions or commanded him to perform a given task. This prophet, Elijah, was given certain sealing powers and keys of the priesthood by means of which he could seal on earth and have it sealed in heaven, or loose on earth and have it loosed in heaven.

King Ahab was a wicked and idolatrous man and completely under the influence of his wife, Jezebel. "And he reared up an altar for Baal in the house of Baal, which he had built in Samaria. And Ahab made a grove; and Ahab did more to provoke the Lord God of Israel to anger than all the kings of Israel that were before him." (1 Kings 16:32-33.) We then read: "And Elijah the Tishbite, who was of the inhabitants of Gilead, said unto Ahab, As the Lord God of Israel liveth, before whom I stand, there shall not be dew nor rain these years, but according to my word." (1 Kings 17:1.) This demonstrates the sealing power Elijah held, for in accordance with that statement, rain ceased to fall and a famine came into the land. After he made that prediction he suddenly left and made his home on the banks of the brook Cherith, where he was fed by ravens.

As the famine increased in intensity and the brook dried up, Elijah departed and went to the city of Zarephath of Zidon, where the Lord appointed a widow to feed and care for him. When Elijah asked her for food and drink she replied:

As the Lord thy God liveth, I have not a cake, but an handful of meal in a barrel, and a little oil in a cruse: and, behold, I am gathering two sticks, that I may go in and dress it for me and my son, that we may eat it, and die.

And Elijah said unto her, Fear not; go and do as thou hast said: but make me thereof a little cake first, and bring it unto me, and after make for thee and for thy son.

For thus saith the Lord God of Israel, The barrel of meal shall not waste, neither shall the cruse of oil fail, until the day that the Lord sendeth rain upon the earth. (1 Kings 17:12-14.)

This was not selfishness on the part of Elijah. He was a prophet of God and spoke as he was commanded by the Lord. The woman had great faith in the Lord and recognized Elijah as his duly authorized agent. The result of her faith and obedience was that during the famine, the meal in her barrel and the oil in her cruze never failed. Even when her son died, Elijah, as a result of her faith and by the power of the priesthood that he held, restored him to health and strength again.

One of the best-remembered episodes in the life of Elijah was his challenge to the priests of Baal. He challenged King Ahab to gather the priests of Baal for a contest of their powers and the power of Baal as compared to his own power as a prophet and the power of Jehovah. Ahab gathered 450 of these priests for the contest and Elijah made them a proposal. He said, in effect, "Let us take two bullocks. You take one and I will take the other. You build your altar to Baal and take your bullock and sacrifice it to your god. I will sacrifice my bullock to the God of Israel, but we will put no fire under the offering. You pray to Baal and I will pray to Jehovah, the true and living God. If fire comes down and consumes your sacrifice, we will worship Baal. But if fire comes down and consumes my offering, then we will serve the Lord." They accepted the challenge.

The priests of Baal gathered, built their altar, made their sacrifice beginning in the morning, and prayed all day long. Elijah mocked them when no fire consumed their sacrifice. He asked them to call louder, for perhaps their god was asleep. Perhaps he had gone hunting. Perhaps he had gone on a journey. They leaped on the altar; they cried themselves hoarse; and they even cut themselves, as was their custom, to gain Baal's attention, all to no avail. When it was evident that they had failed, it was time for Elijah to act.

Elijah went to a broken-down altar of the Lord and repaired it. He placed twelve stones to form this altar, one for each of the twelve tribes of Israel, and laid thereon the wood and the bullock he had prepared for the sacrifice. He dug a trench around the altar and then had the priests drench the sacrifice, wood, and altar with four barrels of water. This was repeated three times, until the trench was overflowing with water. He then offered a simple prayer at the time of the evening sacrifice.

Then the fire of the Lord fell, and consumed the burnt sacrifice, and the wood, and the stones, and the dust, and licked up the water that was in the trench.

And when all the people saw it, they fell on their faces: and they said, The Lord, he is the God; the Lord, he is the God.

And Elijah said unto them, Take the prophets of Baal; let not one of them escape. And they took them: and Elijah brought them down to the brook Kishon, and slew them there. (1 Kings 18:38-40.)

This slaying of the priests may seem like an ungodlike act, but they were a wicked lot, beyond repentance themselves, and were deliberately destroying the covenant children of God. On another similar occasion, the Lord justified the taking of a life. Such should only be done at the Lord's express command and never at the instance or on command of a man. "Behold the Lord slayeth the wicked to bring forth his righteous purposes. It is better that one man should perish than that a nation should dwindle and perish in unbelief." (1 Nephi 4:13.) Thus there is consistency and reason behind this destruction of the false priests of Baal who had led the people astray.

Following the destruction of the priests of Baal, Elijah removed the command he had given the elements that it did not rain. Just as he had power to seal the heavens shut, he now loosed that sealing, and the heavens opened and the rains came as he commanded. Elijah truly held the keys of the sealing power.

133

But Elijah's problems continued. Jezebel, the wicked queen, sought his life for the slaying of her priests of Baal. Discouraged, he fled for his life, seeking refuge in a cave. He was so hurt at the rejection of his message that he asked the Lord to take his life. Instead, an angel came to comfort him and brought him food and drink. He ate and was filled and went forty days on the strength derived from this food. Then he went up on Mount Horeb, also known as Sinai, the same mountain where Moses had received the covenant of the priesthood. There he sought the Lord and found him, not in the wind nor in the earthquake or fire, but in a still, small voice. The Lord asked him what he was doing there, and in his sorrow at the hardness of the hearts of the people, he explained how they had rejected his message and that only he remained. They had even sought to take his life. The Lord showed him that there were others, still true and faithful, even seven thousand faithful people, and Elijah was comforted.

Elijah was then sent on a mission to anoint Hazael to be king of Syria and Jehu to be king of Israel to take the place of Ahab and Jezebel, who were to be destroyed. Elijah prophesied that the dogs in the street should lick their blood, and so it came to pass. He was told to anoint

Elisha as a prophet in his stead; he did as he was commanded and called Elisha to follow him. When Elisha was given his mantle of priesthood authority, Elijah's work was completed for that period of time and he was translated or taken into heaven without tasting death. "And it came to pass, as they still went on, and talked, that, behold, there appeared a chariot of fire, and horses of fire, and parted them both asunder; and Elijah went up by a whirlwind into heaven." (2 Kings 2:11.) Elijah's life was preserved in a miraculous manner so that he would later be able to continue his mission. The mantle of priesthood authority (but not the *keys* of the sealing power) was given to Elisha so he could continue the work of the ministry of God on earth.

We read in the Book of Mormon how the Lord himself also gave the sealing power to Nephi, the elder son of Helaman the Second. Nephi was a prophet of great faith and courage, and the Lord gave him the sealing power in the temple, as we read from the following account:

Behold, thou art Nephi, and I am God. Behold, I declare it unto thee in the presence of mine angels, that ye shall have power over this people, and shall smite the earth with famine, and with pestilence, and destruction, according to the wickedness of this people.

Behold, I give unto you power, that whatsoever ye shall seal on earth shall be sealed in heaven; and whatsoever ye shall loose on earth shall be loosed in heaven, and thus shall ye have power among this people.

And thus, if ye shall say unto this temple it shall be rent in twain, it shall be done. (Helaman 10:6-8.)

Thus the sealing power was given in the Western Hemisphere as well as in the Eastern Hemisphere. However, the keys were not given to Nephi—only the sealing power. The keys of the sealing power were reserved for Elijah, and therefore he was translated so his life could be preserved for further work in the ministry to which he had been called.

There were reasons why Elijah was translated. We

may well ask, Exactly what is the mission of Elijah? Joseph Smith answered that question in the following words:

The spirit, power, and calling of Elijah is, that ye have power to hold the key of the revelations, ordinances, oracles, powers and endowments of the fullness of the Melchizedek Priesthood and of the kingdom of God on earth; and to receive, obtain, and perform all the ordinances belonging to the kingdom of God, even unto the turning of the hearts of the fathers unto the children, and the hearts of the children unto the fathers, even those who are in heaven. (*History of the Church*, 6:251.)

We will see later on how this mission was filled.

Moses also was translated. The Old Testament account of how he died and was buried by the hand of the Lord in an unknown grave as recorded in Deuteronomy 34:5-7 is simply not accurate. This account has been garbled in the preservation of the record or in its translation. The prophets of the Book of Mormon had in their possession the brass plates, which contained a true account of what actually transpired.

And when Alma had done this he departed out of the land of Zarahemla, as if to go into the land of Melek. And it came to pass that he was never heard of more; as to his death or burial we know not of.

Behold, this we know, that he was a righteous man; and the saying went abroad in the church that he was taken up by the Spirit, or buried by the hand of the Lord, even as Moses.

But behold, *the scriptures saith the Lord took Moses unto himself;* and we suppose that he has also received Alma in the spirit, unto himself; therefore, for this cause we know nothing concerning his death and burial. (Alma 45:18-19. Italics added.)

As in the case of Elijah, Moses also had a further mission to perform.

Enoch and his people were translated a few hundred years after the death of Adam. Except for the few faithful patriarchs who were left on the earth to continue their ministry and to preserve the covenant seed, the rest of

135

the faithful were translated and joined with the city of Enoch. "And Enoch beheld angels descending out of heaven, bearing testimony of the Father and Son; and the Holy Ghost fell on many, and they were caught up by the powers of heaven into Zion." (Moses 7:27.)

We learn that this translation of the faithful continued down to the flood:

And men having this faith, coming up unto this order of God [receiving the Melchizedek Priesthood], were translated and taken up into heaven.

And now, Melchizedek was a priest of this order; therefore he obtained peace in Salem, and was called the Prince of peace.

And his people wrought righteousness, and obtained heaven, and sought for the city of Enoch which God had before taken, separating it from the earth, having reserved it unto the latter days, or the end of the world;

And hath said, and sworn with an oath, that the heavens and the earth should come together; and the sons of God should be tried so as by fire. (Inspired Version, Genesis 14:32-35.)

So the mission and purpose of the translation of the city of Zion and its people is yet to be fulfilled. It must have something to do with the restoration of the earth to its paradisiacal glory before the beginning of the Millennium.

Not much has been revealed about the doctrine of translation, but there is purpose and reason for it. Joseph Smith has given the following explanation:

Now the doctrine of translation is a power which belongs to this Priesthood. There are many things which belong to the powers of the Priesthood and the keys thereof, that have been kept hid from before the foundation of the world; they are hid from the wise and the prudent to be revealed in the last times.

Many have supposed that the doctrine of translation was a doctrine whereby men were taken immediately into the presence of God, and into an eternal fullness, but this is a mistaken idea. Their place of habitation is that of the terrestrial order, and a place prepared for such characters He held in reserve to be ministering angels unto many planets, and who as yet have not entered into so great a fullness as those who are resurrected from the dead. (*History of the Church*, 4:209-10.)

Thus Enoch, Moses, Elijah, Alma, and others were translated and reserved for later missions. Elijah the Tishbite was a great prophet who held the keys of the sealing power of the priesthood and who had a great mission to perform in the future.

137

14

The Atonement

The disobedience of Adam and Eve in the Garden of Eden brought sin into the world. When they partook of the forbidden fruit, a physical change was brought about in their bodies so that eventually death came upon them. That they should become mortal was a necessary part of the plan of salvation. In order for man to grow and develop, it was necessary that he be separated from his heavenly parents; only in this way could he be thoroughly tested and proved. This separation of the children of God from their heavenly parents is referred to as "the fall." The fall which brought about the mortality of Adam and Eve and their posterity was a necessary and fundamental principle in the plan of salvation.

Adam's fall brought not only temporal death into the world, but spiritual death as well. The death of the body with its return to the dust of the earth we can all understand. This death brings about a separation of the spirit from the body. Spiritual death is a separation of the spirit from the presence of God, and is also referred to as the second death. From the very beginning, as the plan of salvation was presented, a provision was made to restore those spirits back into the presence of their heavenly parents.

The atonement is the restoration of those spirits into the presence of God. It is a reconciliation, propitiation, ransom, restoration, or restitution that involves making such sacrifice or payment that the principles of justice can be satisfied and the mercy of God made possible. The atonement also is a fundamental principle in the plan of salvation and was to be brought about by the Firstborn Son of God, whose name was Jehovah. When Adam and Eve were placed in the Garden of Eden, they enjoyed the companionship of both Father and Son. When they were driven from the Garden of Eden, their direct association with the Father was ended. From that point on, direct contact between Elohim and his now mortal children ceased. A veil was drawn between mankind and Elohim, and his appearances on rare occasions were limited to acknowledging Jehovah as his Son. As Jehovah took upon himself a body of flesh and bone, the Father testified of him that he was his Only Begotten Son in whom he was well pleased. Direct communication with man was limited to the Son, the Creator of this world. Jehovah was the "Only God" of the Old Testament, the Savior or Redeemer who was known as Jesus Christ in the New Testament. He is the only God with whom we as mortals have direct communication. The atonement that he made for us brought about our reconciliation with God the Eternal Father. Through this atonement, the veil can be removed that presently separates us from our Father.

Through the reconciliation made by Jesus Christ, the spiritual death of the fall is replaced by the spiritual life of the atonement. The temporal death of the body is replaced by that immortality which comes through the atonement and resurrection. As Paul expressed this thought: "If in this life only we have hope in Christ, we are of all men most miserable. But now is Christ risen from the dead, and become the firstfruits of them that slept. For since by man came death, by man came also the resurrection of the dead. For as in Adam all die, even so in Christ shall all be made alive." (1 Corinthians 15:19-22.) As natural death brought about a separation of the body and the spirit, so the atonement brings about immortality, which is a reconciliation of body and spirit, never again to be separated.

Now, this atonement or reconciliation is a double restoration. There are two parts to the atonement. The first part we may speak of as universal salvation or immortality. Immortality comes as a free gift to all men by the grace of God alone, without any works of righteousness on our part. Jacob gave a beautiful explanation of this grace of God in providing for universal salvation. (See 2 Nephi 9:6-13.) It is by the grace and mercy of God that all mankind is saved: "For we labor diligently to write, to persuade our children, and also our brethren, to believe in Christ, and to be reconciled to God; for we know that it is by grace that we are saved, after all we can do." (2 Nephi 25:23.) When I hear people say, "I am saved by grace" or "I am saved by faith in Jesus Christ," I have a hard time not to say something that might offend them. It is true that they are "saved," but they would be "saved" even if they did not believe in Jesus Christ, since this portion of salvation (immortality) applies to everyone who ever lived on this earth. Universal salvation of this type comes through the grace of Jesus Christ and is a free gift to *all* mankind.

Conditional salvation is the second, or more advanced, part of the atonement and makes exaltation possible. Exaltation is conditioned not only by the atonement of Jesus Christ, but also by our righteousness and willingness to follow Jesus Christ with all our heart, might, mind, and strength. It also requires completing all the ordinances of the gospel necessary to reach perfection.To attain exaltation, we must not only be hearers of the word, but doers also. (See James 1:22.) In explaining about the nature of the atonement, Amulek answered a question as to the work to be accomplished as Jesus Christ came into the world:

And he shall come into the world to redeem his people; and he shall take upon him the transgressions of those who believe on his name; and these are they that shall have eternal life [exaltation is the end result of the conditional atonement], and salvation cometh to none else.

Therefore the wicked remain as though there had been no redemption made, except it be the loosing of the bands of death [immortality is the end result of the unconditional or universal atonement]; for behold, the day cometh that all shall rise from the dead and stand before God, and be judged according to their works.

Now, there is a death which is called a temporal death; and the death of Christ shall loose the bands of this temporal death, that all shall be raised from this temporal death [universal salvation applies to all mankind].

The spirit and the body shall be reunited again in its perfect form; both limb and joint shall be restored to its proper frame, even as we now are at this time; and we shall be brought to stand before God, knowing even as we know now, and have a bright recollection of all our guilt.

Now, this restoration shall come to all, both old and young, both bond and free, both male and female, both the wicked and the righteous; and even there shall not so much as a hair of their heads be lost; but everything shall be restored to its perfect frame, as it is now, or in the body, and shall be brought and be arraigned before the bar of Christ the Son, and God the Father, and the Holy Spirit, which is one Eternal God, to be judged according to their works, whether they be good or whether they be evil. (Alma 11:40-44.)

I have heard it said that the sons of perdition who suffer the second death, which is total banishment into utter darkness without contact with any of the Godhead, will have their bodies dissolved so that the resurrection really does not apply to them. This is not true. All mankind will be resurrected as a result of that universal atonement, and those bodies reunited with the spirit can never die nor see corruption. The spirit will never again be divided from the body. (Alma 11:45.) This will be the true hell of the existence of the sons of perdition—to have a body of flesh and bone and never be able to do anything constructive with it.

The gospel was given so that man could have more than mere immortality. The gospel was given so that man would know what to do to obtain exaltation. It is this latter type of atonement, prepared from the foundation of the earth, that leads to the treasures in heaven to be found in the highest degree of glory. In order to obtain

141

these treasures, we have to meet those conditions which make that existence possible. (Mosiah 4:6-10.) Moroni makes this clear as he gives us the pattern as to how the atonement can result in the salvation of the children of God:

Behold he created Adam, and by Adam came the fall of man. And because of the fall of man came Jesus Christ, even the Father and the Son; and because of Jesus Christ came the redemption of man.

And because of the redemption of man, which came by Jesus Christ, they are brought back into the presence of the Lord; yea, this is wherein all men are redeemed, because the death of Christ bringeth to pass the resurrection, which bringeth to pass a redemption from an endless sleep, from which sleep all men shall be awakened by the power of God when the trump shall sound; and they shall come forth, both small and great, and all shall stand before his bar, being redeemed and loosed from the eternal band of death, which is a temporal death. (Mormon 9:12-13.)

142

Then comes the judgment as to what degree of exaltation we shall receive. This reward depends upon what we have done in this life and how we have prepared ourselves to meet that judgment. The object of this book is to hold ever before our eyes the greatest treasure of all—to have not only immortality, but eternal life. (D&C 29:43-45.)

There is another aspect of the atonement that needs consideration. Let us review the instructions given by Jacob:

For as death hath passed upon all men, to fulfil the merciful plan of the great Creator, there must needs be a power of resurrection, and the resurrection must needs come unto man by reason of the fall; and the fall came by reason of transgression; and because man became fallen, they were cut off from the presence of the Lord.

Wherefore, it must needs be an infinite atonement—save it should be an infinite atonement this corruption could not put on incorruption. Wherefore, the first judgment which came upon man must needs have remained to an endless duration. And if so, the flesh must have laid down to rot and to crumble to its mother earth to rise no more.

O the wisdom of God, his mercy and grace! For behold, if the flesh should rise no more our spirits must become subject to that angel who fell from before the presence of the Eternal God, and became the devil, to rise no more.

And our spirits must have become like unto him [cast out from the presence of God the Father eternally]; and we become devils, angels to a devil, to be shut out from the presence of our God, and to remain with the father of lies, in misery, like unto himself; yea to that being who beguiled our first parents, who transformeth himself nigh unto an angel of light, and stirreth up the children of men unto secret combinations of murder and all manner of secret works of darkness. (2 Nephi 9:6-9.)

143

Through the atonement of Jesus Christ we have been made free, and Satan has no hold on us unless we permit it through disobedience to the commandments of God.

Note that this atonement was to be an infinite atonement. That is, it not only affected this world and its inhabitants, but was valid and operative throughout the universe. The atonement applied not only to this earth, but to all the planets of this universe. We might well ask, Why did Jesus Christ come to this earth instead of to some other planet? The answer to this question is also given in the scriptures. The Lord wept when he saw the wickedness of the people of this world, for these were his children and he loved them as only such a great parent could. When Enoch asked him why he wept, the Lord answered: "Wherefore, I can stretch forth mine hands and hold all the creations which I have made; and mine eye can pierce them also, and among all the workmanship of mine hands there has not been so great wickedness as among thy brethren." (Moses 7:36.) The most frightening thing about this passage of scripture is the prediction Jesus Christ made that in the last days, even as it was in the days of Noah, so shall it be in these last days as wickedness grows in the earth. (Matthew 24:37-40.) In fact, this wickedness will become so great that for the elect's sake these days will be shortened. (Joseph Smith 1:20.) "For in those days there shall also arise false

Christs, and false prophets, and shall show great signs and wonders, insomuch, that, if possible, they shall deceive the very elect, *who are the elect according to the covenant.*" (Joseph Smith 1:22. Italics added.)

This earth is the most wicked of all the creations of God. It is the only world so wicked that its inhabitants would destroy their Creator. Jesus Christ was sent to this earth instead of to some other planet because if he could withstand the pressure, wickedness, and temptations of this world, he could withstand the wickedness of any other world. Man would then be left without excuse. No creature anywhere in the universe could say, "We had it harder than you. If you had been subject to the trials and temptations we had, you would have cracked up also!"

What a blessing in turn it is for us to be sent to this most wicked of all the creations of God. It is true that we are thus tested with the greatest temptations ever given to the children of God, but if we withstand the temptations here, we can, as a result, receive greater rewards than are given to those who have never had to fight and win such battles. As a result, we can either sink farther into sin or rise to a higher degree of glory, depending on what we desire and are willing to do. When Satan was cast out of heaven, he was cast down to *this* earth. "And the great dragon was cast out, that old serpent, called the Devil, and Satan, which deceiveth the whole world: he was cast out into the earth, and his angels were cast out with him." (Revelation 12:9.) Hence the earth is his battleground, and the battles we win here have far-reaching importance to our exaltation.

There was purpose, then, in sending Jehovah to this earth to take upon himself a body of flesh and bone. Jesus Christ was to become our advocate with the Father. To do so, he had to descend below all things, so that he might rise above all things. When Joseph Smith complained about some of the things he had to suffer, the Lord reminded him: "The Son of Man hath descended below them all. Art thou greater than he?" (D&C 122:8.)

144

A more extensive explanation is given in the following scripture: "He that ascended up on high, as also he descended below all things, in that he comprehended all things, that he might be in all and through all things, the light of truth." (D&C 88:6.) Through this atonement, then, he was able to understand the needs of all men and thus be better able to become a true advocate for man.

In Chapter 10 reference was made to the preview of the atonement given as Abraham was tested to see if he would be willing to give his only son, Isaac, as a sacrifice. He was not called upon to make the final offering, for the Lord provided as a sacrifice a ram with his horns caught in a nearby thicket. It was there stated that at the atonement of Jesus Christ, no ram was provided. The actual sacrifice of the Only Begotten of the Father had to be made. This was most difficult for both the Father and the Son. Jesus was frightened by the weight of this responsibility and said to his disciples: "I am come to send fire on the earth; and what will I, if it be already kindled? But I have a baptism to be baptized with; and how am I straitened [worried, pained, concerned] till it be accomplished!" (Luke 12:49-50.) When he went into the Garden of Gethsemane to pray and to prepare himself for the coming ordeal, he expressed his concern to Peter, James, and John, "and began to be sorrowful and very heavy. Then saith he unto them, My soul is exceeding sorrowful, even unto death: tarry ye here, and watch with me." (Matthew 26:37-38.)

What caused him to be frightened and concerned? It wasn't the pain or death that he feared, but the frightful responsibility of knowing that the whole plan of salvation, the fate of the whole universe, rested on his shoulders. It was because of this that he asked the Father if it were possible to let this cup pass from him. He asked, "Isn't there some other way?" This was the man speaking, a man frightened by the crushing weight of the task ahead. Three times he asked, "O my Father, if it be possible, let this cup pass from me!" Three times the godlike nature within him added these words: "Nevertheless, not as I will, but as thou wilt." (Matthew 26:39.) There was no answer from the Father, nor could there be, for there was no other way. This was the most vital part of the whole plan of salvation, which was provided for and agreed upon from before the foundation of the world. Prophets had told of it and the voice of God had spoken it. These predictions could not be changed. And so Jesus Christ committed himself to this action.

This commitment was not made without great suffering. We often think of the pain Jesus suffered on the cross, but this suffering on the cross was not as great as that which he experienced in the Garden of Gethsemane. It was there that he suffered so intensely that the blood vessels broke beneath his skin and great drops of blood formed and fell to the ground. Jesus described his agony in these words: "Which suffering caused myself, even God, the greatest of all, to tremble because of pain, and to bleed at every pore, and to suffer both body and spirit—and would that I might not drink the bitter cup, and shrink—Nevertheless, glory be to the Father, and I partook and finished my preparations unto the children of men." (D&C 19:18-19.) It was there in the garden that he committed himself to action and made up his mind to be willing and obedient.

Jesus was crucified, but so were the thieves on either side of him. They suffered on the cross the same bodily pain that Jesus suffered. The difference was that the thieves had no choice in the matter. They had to die. It was different in the case of Jesus. He could have stepped down at any moment, but had he done so, the plan of salvation would have been destroyed. It was this thought that caused him so much anguish in the Garden of Gethsemane—the thought that he might not have the courage to go through with it. But, having made up his mind and having committed himself, both heart and mind, his suffering was now made relatively easier. The Jews, we ought to mention, did not take his life, but he permitted them to take his life. Jesus said: "Therefore doth my Father love me, because I lay down my life, that I might take it again. No man taketh it from me, but I lay it down of myself. I have power to lay it down, and I have power to take it again. This commandment have I received of my Father." (John 10:17-18.)

As Jesus hung there on the cross, a legion of angels surrounded him to comfort and encourage him. The presence of his Father was also there to give him strength and support. But as the hours wore on and his body became weaker and weaker, the angels began to withdraw until they were all gone. Finally, as the end approached and his agony reached a peak, even his Father withdrew his presence and Jesus was left hanging on the cross just as would any other mortal being, with only his faith to sustain him. What thoughts must have crossed his mind! Had he imagined all these things? Was all this just the idle imaginings of his mind? Why not test it and step down from the cross? No! To do so would destroy everything. It was at this moment of crisis that he cried out in anguish of body and mind: "Eloi, Eloi, lama sabachthani? which means, being interpreted, My God, my God, why hast thou forsaken me?" (Mark 15:34.) We can almost hear the gentle voice of the Father answering:

"My son, my son, you must stoop below all things so that no person can ever say they had it harder than you. Now you know personally how difficult it is to live by faith alone. Now you know how mortals feel who must trust in the justice of God without actually seeing for themselves. Now, having experienced this feeling, you can truly be their advocate and plead their cause before me with greater sympathy, compassion, and full understanding."

Jesus understood this, and through his faith and courage he completed the work to which he had been called. This suffering was made easier for him because he had already come to a decision back there in the Garden of Gethsemane. Having firmly and conclusively made up his mind, he was able to muster the necessary faith and strength to complete his stewardship and thus become the Savior of the world.

147

15

The Father and the Son

There is another aspect of the atonement that needs to be fully understood. The atonement had to be infinite in nature. Jesus Christ had to have that infinite or godly power within himself to be able to take up his body again as the first fruits of the resurrection. He held the keys of this ministry and received them from the Father as he was born into this world. He had the power to lay down his life (to die), which he received from his mortal mother, Mary. He also had the power to live forever, or to take up again that body which he received from his Eternal Father. Jesus was not fathered by Joseph nor by the Holy Ghost, but was the actual begotten child of God the Eternal Father. He was the Only Begotten of God in the flesh. Thus he had the seeds of mortality and the seeds of immortality within his body. Only in this way could he possibly bring about an atonement or a reconciliation of our souls with God, the Father.

Jesus Christ is the only person ever to be born on this earth who had the power to bring to pass the resurrection from the dead. He was the only person who was able to pass this power on to others. This came about because he was the literal son of God the Eternal Father in the flesh. His Father was an immortal personage and his mother a mortal woman. This is a fundamental or basic truth of the gospel that makes possible his atonement for the sins of others. Amulek gave a clear and positive statement to this affect:

And now, behold, I will testify unto you of myself that these things are true. Behold, I say unto you, that I do know that Christ shall come among the children of men, to take upon him the transgressions of his people, and that he shall atone for the sins of the world; for the Lord God hath spoken it.

For it is expedient that an atonement should be made; for according to the great plan of the Eternal God there must be an atonement made, or else all mankind must unavoidably perish; yea, all are hardened; yea, all are fallen and are lost, and must perish except it be through the atonement which it is expedient should be made.

For it is expedient that there should be a great and last sacrifice; yea, not a sacrifice of man, neither of a beast, neither of any manner of fowl; for it shall not be a human sacrifice; but it must be an infinite and eternal sacrifice.

Now there is not any man that can sacrifice his own blood which will atone for the sins of another. Now, if a man murdereth, behold will our law, which is just, take the life of his brother? I say unto you, Nay.

But the law requireth the life of him who hath murdered; therefore there can be nothing which is short of an infinite atonement which will suffice for the sins of the world.

Therefore, it is expedient that there should be a great and last sacrifice; and then shall there be, or it is expedient there should be, a stop to the shedding of blood. . . . (Alma 34:8-13.)

This infinite sacrifice was the Son of God.

Jesus Christ was the God of the Old Testament who was known to the people of that time as Jehovah, or God the Father. It is necessary to explain this last title. Elohim, or God the Eternal Father, is the literal father of Jesus Christ and is the Father of the spirits of the human race. Jehovah, who on earth was known as Jesus Christ, was the Creator and thereby the "Father" of the earth and all things therein. God the Father says of this creative process: "And by the word of my power, have I created them [the things of this earth], which is mine

Only Begotten Son, who is full of grace and truth. And worlds without number have I created; and I also created them for mine own purpose; and by the Son I created them, which is mine Only Begotten." (Moses 1:32-33.) When the scriptures speak of "the very eternal Father of heaven and earth" or "the Everlasting Father," they mean Jesus Christ as Creator, since *eternal* and *everlasting* are synonymous. Jesus Christ is also the Father of those who abide in his gospel.

Centuries before Jesus Christ was born, Abinadi explained how Jesus was the Father of those who accepted the gospel and followed his teachings:

150

> And now I say unto you, who shall declare his generation? Behold, I say unto you, that when his soul has been made an offering for sin he shall see his seed. And now what say ye? And who shall be his seed?
>
> Behold I say unto you that whosoever has heard the words of the prophets, yea, all the holy prophets who have prophesied concerning the coming of the Lord—I say unto you, that all those who have hearkened unto their words, and believed that the Lord would redeem his people, and have looked forward to that day for a remission of their sins, I say unto you, that these are his seed, or they are heirs of the kingdom of God.
>
> For these are they whose sins he has borne; these are they for whom he has died, to redeem them from their transgressions. And now, are they not his seed?
>
> Yea, and are not the prophets, every one that has opened his mouth to prophesy, that has not fallen into transgression, I mean all the holy prophets ever since the world began? I say unto you that they are his seed. (Mosiah 15:10-13.)

Thus members of the Church are the children of Jesus Christ, for he becomes our Father as we take upon ourselves his name. In our own day Jesus Christ himself has explained that he is Alpha and Omega, the First and the Last, and that he has given us power through him to become sons of God. (D&C 45:7-9.) Most of the confusion in people's minds concerning the Father comes through misunderstanding the scriptures. When Jehovah spoke in

Old Testament times or when he as Jesus Christ spoke to the people in New Testament times, he represented Elohim and spoke in the first person as though he were Elohim. He did this by divine right of investiture, having his authority from God the Father. It causes no confusion for us to read in section 36 of the Doctrine and Covenants that Joseph Smith said: "Thus saith the Lord God, the Mighty One of Israel," etc. We all understand that this was Jesus Christ speaking. Yet if Joseph Smith had said this in person, speaking in the first person, and speaking with power and authority, might not some persons have thought that Joseph Smith was Jesus Christ? Because it is written and because we understand that this was a revelation given to Joseph Smith, who gave the revelation to us, there is no confusion. The Lord, in giving a revelation in Old Testament times, spoke also in the first person because his words represented the words of his Father. This is what causes the confusion in some people's minds. If we understand this, then we are not confused.

151

Another example to illustrate this practice is found in Revelation when an angel spoke in the first person, as though he were God, to John the Revelator. He spoke with such power and glory that John fell down to worship him: "And I John saw these things, and heard them. And when I had heard and seen, I fell down to worship before the feet of the angel which shewed me these things. Then saith he unto me, See thou do it not: for I am thy fellowservant, and of thy brethren the prophets, and of them which keep the sayings of this book; worship God." (Revelation 22:8-9.) The angel then went on to give additional instructions as though he were the risen Christ, speaking in the first person. If we understand this principle, we can know that the person we refer to as Jesus Christ is the Everlasting Father of the Old Testament and our Savior, our Redeemer, our Lord, and our Father. Jesus Christ is not the father of our spirits. The father of our spirits and of Jesus Christ is Elohim. Since Jesus Christ is the Only Begotten Son of Elohim in the flesh, the only way we can return to Elohim in the flesh is through his Only Begotten Son, the only son he had in the flesh. That Son is Jesus Christ, and it is in this respect that Jesus Christ becomes our Father by covenant.

There is great significance to the name of Jesus Christ. When the angel Gabriel made his announcement, he told Mary that the child's name should be Jesus. The coming of the Messiah was prophesied by most of the Old Testament prophets. His coming was also prophesied by Book of Mormon prophets. The first mention made in the Book of Mormon of Jesus Christ is found in the following verse: "For according to the words of the prophets, the Messiah cometh in six hundred years from the time that my father left Jerusalem; and according to the words of the prophets, and also the word of the angel of God, his name shall be Jesus Christ, the Son of God." (2 Nephi 25:19.) Thus, six hundred years before he was born in the flesh, his name was known among the early prophets on the American continent.

When I was president of the West German Mission, an investigator wrote me citing this verse and saying that this was proof that the Book of Mormon was false. There is no question but that Old Testament prophets were divinely called and appointed to represent the Lord and to bear witness of him. Therefore, the investigator wrote, "Since the Old Testament prophets never wrote of Jesus Christ, they never were informed of that name. Surely if God had revealed the name of Jesus Christ to the prophets mentioned in the Book of Mormon, he also would have done so to the prophets of the Old Testament. Since he didn't reveal that name to the Old Testament prophets, he wouldn't have revealed that name to the Book of Mormon prophets. Hence the Book of Mormon is false."

I did not know what to answer, so I appealed for aid to my good friend, Dr. Hugh W. Nibley, at Brigham Young University. He sent me some very valuable information, which I summarize in the rest of this chapter.

We do not know the language or the exact words used by the Book of Mormon prophets. Certainly they did not speak English. A good translator translates meanings and not just words. The reader of the translation must be able to understand the thought expressed in the original work and understand the meaning thereof. If Joseph Smith, in translating the words actually used, had written down the original words, no one would have understood what was meant. Even if he had used the English equivalents and had written "the Redeemer, the Anointed," not everyone would have understood whom he referred to. But when he translated those words as *Jesus Christ*, everyone understood, and that very quickly. It is a good translation.

153

It is not generally understood that when ancient writers gave the various titles ascribed to the Son of Man, who was yet to be born, they were using their equivalents of those words which we write in English as *Jesus Christ*. In the English version of the Koran, Sura 3, verse 46, we read: "When the angels said, O Mary, Allah give thee glad tidings of a word from Him; his name [shall be] the Messiah Jesus, son of Mary. . . ." The actual words used for *Messiah Jesus* are *al-Masih 'isa*. The word *isa* is the Moslem rendering of the name Jesus, and its original meaning is either lost in time or intentionally obscured. The Hebrew equivalent, *Yasha*, always means *Savior*. In all other Semitic languages it is merely a name as in modern Spanish, where the name *Jesus* is commonly used.

Al-Masih, on the other hand, is too prominent a root in any Semitic language to be obscured. It always means "anointed." A Moslem would never use the word *Christ* or *Savior* the way Christians now do. However, an Arab Christian would not hesitate to render *al-Masih 'isa* as "Christ the Savior," or "Jesus Christ." Semitic people in referring to Jehovah as the Savior would use their equivalent of our English word *Messiah*, while the Greeks would say *Christ*, though both words mean one and the same thing. So a Moslem reading *al-Masih 'īsa* would render it "the anointed," while the Arabic Christian would translate it as "Jesus Christ." We translate meanings instead of words, and those meanings must represent the culture and the understanding of the people who are to read the translation.

The following table will make the meaning of various words clear. How a word is actually translated will depend upon the audience that will use the translation.

LANGUAGE	WORD
Arabic	Masih
Hebrew	Maschiach
German	Messias
Greek	Cristos
English	Messiah

All of these words mean "the anointed," but the word used in a translation would depend upon the reader to be reached. *Masih* or *Maschiach* is a generic term that can be applied to any individual. The Greek word *Christos* and the English word *Christ* apply only to a specific person, and to that one person only. There have been many Czars, Caesars, and Kaisers, but when we speak of Caesar, we mean Gaius Julius, the Roman conquerer. There are many messiahs, but only one Messiah (Jesus Christ). There are many men, even many living today, who bear the name Jesus, but there is only one Jesus who is the Son of God.

We can compose a similar table for the word *Jesus:*

LANGUAGE	WORD
Arabic	'īsa
Hebrew	yasha (formerly yeshua or yehoshua)
German	Jesus (pronounced "yāsūs")
Greek	Hesus
English	Joshua

All of these words mean *savior* or *redeemer.* Thus again, the word to be used in a given translation depends upon the reader to be reached and the use to which the translation will be put. When the angel spoke to Mary, he used the Aramaic language, which she spoke and understood. As the account was then written as *Yasha al-Maschiach*, it was translated into Greek as *InōoûsXpiōr'os* or *Hesus Christos;* and then when the Greek was translated into English, it was rendered as *Jesus Christ*. In all these languages it means literally "the Savior—the Anointed."

Thus, the ancient Book of Mormon prophets and the prophets of the Old Testament were all speaking of the same person, though they used the words their people would understand. They referred to the same person we refer to as "Jesus Christ, the Son of God." Regardless of the language they used, the meaning is clear. Joseph Smith, in translating the Book of Mormon, used the words "Jesus Christ" because they gave a clear-cut understanding of what was written by the original scribe.

155

There is only one name given and only one person through whom we can be saved. Peter testified: "This is the stone which was set at nought of you builders, which is become the head of the corner. Neither is there salvation in any other: for there is none other name under heaven given among men, whereby we must be saved." (Acts 4:11-12.)

King Benjamin, that great Book of Mormon leader, taught his people:

And under this head ye are made free, and there is no other head whereby ye can be made free. There is no other name given whereby salvation cometh; therefore, I would that ye should take upon you the name of Christ, all you that have entered into the covenant with God that ye should be obedient unto the end of your lives.

And it shall come to pass that whosoever doeth this shall be found at the right hand of God, for he shall know the name by which he is called; for he shall be called by the name of Christ. (Mosiah 5:8-9.)

By taking upon ourselves the name of Jesus Christ, we become his sons and his daughters by covenant and the door is opened to us to lay claim to that treasure which is eternal life.

16

The Principle of Adoption

In the last chapter the statement was made that we become the children of Jesus Christ by covenant. We do
this by taking upon ourselves the name of Jesus Christ.
Remember, the worth of souls is great in the sight of
God. He loves all his children and would like to see every
one of them obtain exaltation. This state of exaltation,
however, can only be obtained by taking upon ourselves
the name of Jesus Christ and keeping his commandments.

Take upon you the name of Christ, and speak the truth in
soberness.

And as many as repent and are baptized in my name,
which is Jesus Christ, and endure to the end, the same shall be
saved.

Behold, Jesus Christ is the name which is given of the
Father, and there is none other name given whereby man can
be saved;

Wherefore, all men must take upon them the name which
is given of the Father, for in that name shall they be called at
the last day;

Wherefore, if they know not the name by which they are
called, they cannot have place in the kingdom of my Father.
(D&C 18:21-25.)

Hence we must take upon us the name of Jesus Christ in
order to obtain exaltation. How is this done? How does
one obtain the name of Jesus Christ?

One obtains the name of Jesus Christ by baptism.
Through baptism we become the children of Jesus Christ,

his sons and daughters, and through Jesus Christ we become the children of God the Eternal Father. Paul explained this to the Galatian saints in the following words:

For ye are all the children of God by faith in Christ Jesus.

For as many of you as have been baptized into Christ have put on Christ.

There is neither Jew nor Greek, there is neither bond nor free, there is neither male nor female: for ye are all one in Christ Jesus.

And if ye be Christ's [seed or children], then are ye Abraham's seed [children of the covenant or promise], and heirs according to the promise. (Galatians 3:26-29.)

157

What Paul was saying is that regardless of what we formerly were—regardless of our nationality, age, or sex, or whether we are slaves or free—when we are baptized we become equal as children of Jesus Christ. As children of Jesus Christ, we become heirs to the promise given to Abraham that in his seed should all the world be blessed.

Paul then goes on to teach that baptism is the official manner of adoption into the family of Jesus Christ:

Now I say, That the heir, as long as he is a child, differeth nothing from a servant, though he be lord of all;

But is under tutors and governors until the time appointed of the father.

Even so we, when we were children, were in bondage under the elements of the world:

But when the fulness of the time was come, God sent forth his Son, made of a woman, made under the law,

To redeem them that were under the law, that we might receive the adoption of sons.

And because ye are sons, God hath sent forth the Spirit of his Son into your hearts, crying, Abba, Father.

Wherefore thou art no more a servant, but a son; and if a son, then an heir of God through Christ. (Galatians 4:1-7.)

What Paul was saying was that these Galatian saints who were children of Israel, even though they were heirs of God's blessings through heredity, could not be exalted by the law of carnal commandments given by Moses, but under the law could only be servants in that kingdom. By baptism they were redeemed from the law as sons and daughters of Jesus Christ, and so they had become sons and daughters of God the Father and heirs to his kingdom.

It was in this same spirit that Paul wrote to the saints in Ephesus:

Blessed be the God and Father of our Lord Jesus Christ, who hath blessed us with all spiritual blessings in heavenly places in Christ:

According as he hath chosen us in him before the foundation of the world, that we should be holy and without blame before him in love:

Having predestinated [foreordained] us unto the adoption of children by Jesus Christ to himself, according to the good pleasure of his will. (Ephesians 1:3-5.)

In the next few verses (6-12) Paul teaches that in this manner God unites into his family both the living and the dead to form his great, eternal family. Paul taught this same doctrine to the Romans:

For as many as are led by the Spirit of God, they are the sons of God.

For ye have not received the spirit of bondage again to fear; but ye have received the Spirit of adoption, whereby we cry, Abba, Father.

The Spirit itself beareth witness with our spirit, that we are the children of God:

And if children, then heirs; heirs of God, and joint-heirs with Christ; if so be that we suffer with him, that we may be also glorified together. (Romans 8:14-17. See also Romans 9:3-5.)

Thus baptism alone cannot save us, but we must also practice the kind of life that Jesus Christ lived, even if it requires sacrifice and suffering on our part.

It was in this same sense that Paul likened baptism to death and the resurrection:

Know ye not, that so many of us as were baptized into Jesus Christ were baptized into his death?

Therefore we are buried with him by baptism into death;

158

that like as Christ was raised up from the dead by the glory of the Father, even so we also should walk in newness of life.

For if we have been planted together in the likeness of his death, we shall be also in the likeness of his resurrection:

Knowing this, that our old man is crucified with him, that the body of sin might be destroyed, that henceforth we should not serve sin. (Romans 6:3-6.)

Paul is explaining to the Romans how baptism by immersion results in the remission of sins. There must be a death to the kind of life we lived before. The suffering of repentance (incidental to making those changes in our life-style to leave sin behind us and never repeat it again) is likened to the crucifixion of Jesus as he suffered for the sins of the world. With the death or cessation of further sinful acts, those deeds and actions now dead are buried and left in the watery grave of baptism. The burial of sins in the water is likened to death, to the burial of our mortal bodies in the earth. As we come up out of the water, we leave behind the sinful life we formerly led and become reborn into the family of Jesus Christ, just as a new child comes into the world innocent and clean of sin. Thus baptism is compared to the resurrection, where the mortal or corruptible part of the body is left behind in the earthly grave and the pure, immortal body is raised in the resurrection. Through this baptismal ordinance we can begin a new life in the family of Jesus Christ, freed from the former sin which so handicapped us in the past.

There is tremendous symbolism to be found in the gospel. This is remarkably illustrated in the ordinance of baptism. We can understand this better as we go back to the instruction given to Father Adam in the very beginning. This is the instruction he was commanded to teach to his children after his own baptism:

Wherefore teach it unto your children, that all men, everywhere, must repent, or they can in nowise inherit the kingdom of God, for no unclean thing can dwell there, or dwell in his presence; for, in the language of Adam, Man of

159

Holiness is his name, and the name of his Only Begotten is the Son of Man, even Jesus Christ a righteous Judge, who shall come in the meridian of time.

Therefore I give unto you a commandment, to teach these things freely unto your children, saying:

That by reason of transgression cometh the fall, which fall bringeth death, and inasmuch as ye were born into the world by water, and blood, and the spirit, which I have made, and so became of dust a living soul, even so ye must be born again into the kingdom of heaven, of water, and of the Spirit, and be cleansed by blood, even the blood of mine Only Begotten; that ye might be sanctified from all sin, and enjoy the words of eternal life in this world, and eternal life in the world to come, even immortal glory;

For by the water ye keep the commandment; by the Spirit are ye justified, and by the blood ye are sanctified;

Therefore it is given to abide in you; the record of heaven; the Comforter; the peaceable things of immortal glory; the truth of all things; that which quickeneth all things, which maketh alive all things; that which knoweth all things, and hath all power according to wisdom, mercy, truth, justice, and judgment. (Moses 6:57-61.)

Before we were born into this world our bodies were completely surrounded by water. They were nourished by the blood of our mothers. Then, just before we were born, the waters burst and we were born into the world, made alive by the spirit which entered our bodies and enabled us to live and breathe. Without that spirit we would have been stillborn and lifeless.

Just as we were born into this world through these three elements of water, blood, and spirit, even so we must be born again into the kingdom or family of heaven symbolically through means of these same three elements of water, blood, and spirit. As part of this baptism or adoption process, we are surrounded again in the waters of baptism just as we were surrounded by water in the womb. We are saved by the blood of Jesus Christ (Ephesians 1:7), whose blood was shed for the remission of our sins (D&C 27:2), and we are therefore sanctified just as we are nourished in the womb by the blood of our mothers. Finally we must receive the Spirit through a confirmation of authority, just as the mortal body must be made alive by the spirit which gives life to the mortal body. Without the Holy Spirit we would be stillborn or lifeless in the kingdom or family of Jesus Christ. All three elements, then, in their proper order characterize this adoption process or baptism whereby we take upon ourselves the holy name of Jesus Christ and become his sons and his daughters.

I never read that previously quoted passage from the Pearl of Great Price without having a renewed testimony of the divine nature of Joseph Smith's calling as a prophet of God. It is true that a similar scripture is found in the Bible, and it confirms that which was revealed through Joseph Smith as a prophet of God. But the biblical account does not have the same force and clarity as does this revelation from God given through the Prophet Joseph Smith. John was speaking of Jesus Christ as the Lord and Savior and then wrote:

This is he that came by water and blood, even Jesus Christ; not by water only, but by water and blood. And it is the Spirit that beareth witness, because the Spirit is truth.

For there are three that bear record in heaven, the Father, the Word, and the Holy Ghost: and these three are one.

And there are three that bear witness in earth, the spirit, and the water, and the blood: and these three agree in one. (1 John 5:6-8.)

Just as the Father, the Son, and the Holy Ghost represent a unity of the Godhead in heaven, so water, blood, and spirit represent a unity of rebirth on earth into the family of God. God Father, God Son and God Holy Ghost are no more one and the same God than water, blood, and spirit are identical on earth. John was speaking of a unity of operation and agreement, and this is sometimes difficult for people to understand. However, if we remember that John was not writing to investigators and friends, but to members of the church of Christ who understood these things, we may better understand what he was writing about. He was writing to members of the church who understood these principles, and he was reminding them of the nature of the covenants they had made. He wrote to strengthen them in their resolve to be faithful. He was reminding them never to do anything that would bring shame or dishonor to the holy name they now bore. Earlier he had reminded them:

Behold, what manner of love the Father hath bestowed upon us, that we should be called the sons of God: therefore the world knoweth us not, because it knew him not.

Beloved, now are we the sons of God, and it doth not yet appear what we shall be [we have not yet proved ourselves]: but we know that, when he shall appear, we shall be like him; for [if we live the godly life he leads we shall be like him;] we shall see him as he is.

And every man that hath this hope in him purifieth himself, even as he is pure. (1 John 3:1-3.)

When we call one another brother and sister in our church, we are not just being polite. There is real meaning in that form of address. We *are* blood brothers and sisters in the family of Jesus Christ. It is true that we have become such by adoption, but it is nevertheless true that in this manner of adoption we have become true children of Jesus Christ and hence true brothers and sisters. We should live righteously with one another to properly demonstrate that exalted condition.

It was this principle that King Benjamin had in mind when he addressed his people on the American continent. They had made a covenant to accept Jesus Christ as their Father and he now so addressed them:

And now, because of the covenant which ye have made *ye shall be called the children of Christ, his sons, and his daughters;* for behold, this day he hath spiritually begotten you; for ye say that your hearts are changed through faith on his name; therefore, ye are born of him and have become his sons and daughters.

And under this head ye are made free, and there is no other head whereby ye can be made free. There is no other name given whereby salvation cometh; therefore, I would that ye should take upon you the name of Christ, all you that have entered into a covenant with God that ye should be obedient unto the end of your lives.

And it shall come to pass that whosoever doeth this shall be found at the right hand of God, for he shall know the name by which he is called; *for he shall be called by the name of Christ.* (Mosiah 5:7-9. Italics added.)

We read, hear, and speak of Christians. Really, the only persons who have a right to that name are those who have been legally and lawfully qualified to use that name. When we become Christians or members of Christ's family, it can only be in the lawfully prescribed manner of baptism or adoption that Jesus prescribed right at the beginning. After Jehovah had explained to Adam the meaning of the adoptive process and had explained the significance of baptism, he explained to Adam that all things have their likeness and that all things are created to bear record of him. So this symbolic adoption was meant to bring his creations to him in his family in their proper relationship to one another and to him, and in this manner to become his children.

163

When Adam understood this principle, he requested baptism, and he was caught up and then baptized. Let the scripture tell the story of that baptism and how afterward Adam was not only born of the Spirit, but was also ordained to the Melchizedek Priesthood after the order of Jehovah:

And it came to pass, when the Lord had spoken with Adam, our father, that Adam cried unto the Lord, and he was caught away by the Spirit of the Lord, and was carried down into the water, and was laid under the water, and was brought forth out of the water.

And thus he was baptized, and the Spirit of God descended upon him, and thus he was born of the Spirit, and became quickened [made alive in the kingdom or family of Jesus Christ] in the inner man.

And he heard a voice out of heaven, saying: Thou art baptized with fire, and with the Holy Ghost. This [Holy Ghost] is the record of the Father, and the Son, from henceforth and forever;

And thou art after the order of him who was without beginning of days or end of years [the Melchizedek Priesthood was being bestowed upon him], from all eternity to all eternity.

Behold, thou art one in me, a son of God; and *thus may all become my sons*. Amen. (Moses 6:64-68. Italics added.)

From this account we see the importance of baptism as an adoptive or saving process by means of which we become members of the family of Jesus Christ. Since Jesus in turn was the Only Begotten of God the Eternal Father in the flesh, the only way we can become members of the eternal, resurrected family of Elohim is through Jesus Christ, the only physical son he ever had.

17

The Importance of Baptism

In the course of teaching the people, Jesus attracted the attention of the rich as well as the poor, both learned and unlearned. Among the learned could be listed Joseph of Arimathea, who provided the tomb and helped at the burial of Jesus. Joseph was a member of the ruling Sanhedrin, as was Nicodemus, another Pharisee who defended Jesus mildly when the Sanhedrin condemned Jesus to death. Three years before the close of Jesus' ministry, Nicodemus came one night to confer with him. Perhaps Nicodemus was too timid to be seen coming to Jesus during the day and, because of his political position, was afraid of being criticized. After all, he was a ruler of the Jews and one of the leading rabbis of the day. It was highly unusual for a master teacher such as he was to go to one unschooled, yet he had a question that demanded an answer.

We do not have a full account of the conversation that took place, but judging from the answer given, Nicodemus must have asked Jesus how a person could join his church and become a member of the family of believers in the kingdom of God. "Jesus answered and said unto him, Verily, verily, I say unto thee, Except a man be born again, he cannot see the kingdom of God." (John 3:3.) When Jesus referred to the second birth, he was referring to baptism, which we have learned is the adoptive process by means of which we take upon ourselves the name of Jesus Christ. Nicodemus was a teacher. He must have known that Jesus was talking about a symbolic birth and not an actual birth. Yet his next question shows that he had not comprehended the answer Jesus had given, so Jesus went on to answer his second question:

Nicodemus saith unto him, How can a man be born when he is old? can he enter the second time into his mother's womb, and be born?

Jesus answered, Verily, verily, I say unto thee, Except a man be born of water and of the Spirit, he cannot enter into the kingdom of God.

That which is born of the flesh is flesh; and that which is born of the spirit is spirit.

Marvel not that I said unto thee, Ye must be born again.

The wind bloweth where it listeth, and thou hearest the sound thereof, but canst not tell whence it cometh, and whither it goeth: so is every one that is born of the Spirit. (John 3:4-8.)

Strangely, this intelligent and learned man failed to understand or comprehend what Jesus was saying.

Nicodemus was a member of the Sanhedrin, the ruling body over the Jews, and was a rabbi or a teacher among them. For hundreds of years, no convert had been made to Judaism without baptism. He was familiar with this doctrine and practice, yet he had not understood the universality of this requirement, nor comprehended its meaning and significance. Perhaps he thought the Israelites, being of the promised seed, were exempt from the requirement. Evidently he knew the letter of the law but not the spirit or meaning of baptism. At any rate, he was confused, as is shown by his next question: "Nicodemus answered and said unto him, How can these things be?" (John 3:9.) Nowhere is the degree of apostasy among Judah made more evident than in this question. Nicodemus was a learned man, a student of the law, one of the leaders and teachers of the people. They had been practicing baptism for hundreds of years, so this method of bringing converts into the fold was a common practice. Yet, because he was not enlightened by the Holy Ghost, he could not understand either the meaning or the purpose of this holy ordinance. This is a good illustration of the blind leading the blind.

Jesus expressed his amazement that this teacher and leader in Israel did not understand such a basic truth: "Jesus answered and said unto him, Art thou a master of Israel, and knowest not these things? Verily, verily, I say unto thee, We speak that we do know, and testify that we have seen; and ye receive not our witness. If I have told you earthly things, and ye believe not, how shall ye believe, if I tell you of heavenly things?" (John 3:10-12.) Jesus was saying: "Here you are a teacher of this people, and yet you cannot even understand the meaning of this basic ordinance. We know the meaning of this ordinance and teach it, and yet you will not accept our instruction. This ordinance must be performed here on earth as a basic temporal ordinance by means of which individuals are adopted into the kingdom or family of God. If you cannot understand this ordinance which pertains to temporal blessings, how can you ever understand the higher spiritual concepts and ordinances which we teach?"

167

Baptism is a basic ordinance. It is a fundamental principle. It is universal in its application. It applies to every person who reaches the age of accountability and is thus able to comprehend what it means and signifies. As Jesus explained to Nicodemus, baptism is so essential to salvation that without it one cannot even *see* the kingdom of heaven, let alone enter or dwell therein.

When Christ gave his apostles instruction to begin proselyting work and to carry the gospel message everywhere, he told them to baptize. "Go ye therefore, and teach all nations, baptizing them in the name of the Father, and of the Son, and of the Holy Ghost: Teaching them to observe all things whatsoever I have commanded you: and, lo, I am with you alway, even unto the end of the world. Amen." (Matthew 28:19.)

Mark, in recording this assignment, adds these words: "He that believeth and is baptized shall be saved; but he that believeth not [and hence is not baptized] shall be damned." (Mark 16:16.) That this is a true statement and not something that crept into the scriptures during the process of translation is confirmed by the following words of the Savior: "And whoso believeth in me, and is baptized, the same shall be saved; and they are they who shall inherit the kingdom of God. And whoso believeth not in me, and is not baptized, shall be damned." (3 Nephi 11:33-34.) Therefore this principle of baptism must apply to everyone, for it is the gateway into the family of God.

168

So universal is this principle that the Savior himself requested baptism:

Then cometh Jesus from Galilee to Jordan unto John, to be baptized of him.

But John forbad him, saying, I have need to be baptized of thee, and comest thou to me?

And Jesus answering said unto him, Suffer it to be so now: for thus it becometh us to fulfil all righteousness. Then he suffered him. (Matthew 3:13-15.)

That this baptism of Jesus was proper and pleasing to God the Eternal Father is evident as Luke records how the Holy Ghost descended on him in the sign of a dove and how the Father then spoke, saying, "Thou art my Beloved Son; in thee I am well pleased." (Luke 3:22.)

If baptism is the method of adoption into the family of Jesus Christ, what did the Savior mean when he said that his own baptism was necessary to fulfill all righteousness? Certainly there was no need for repentance nor for the remission of sin, for Jesus was a sinless being. And what did adoption into his own family have to do with Jesus Christ? The answer is that baptism is all those things just mentioned, but much more also. It is a universal celestial law. Being a celestial law, it is required of all persons born on earth who reach the age of accountability.

We have been taught in the Church that Jesus was baptized in order to set us a good example, and this is true. However, Jesus was baptized not just to set an example for us to follow, but also in order to be obedient to a command of his Father. The prophet Lehi answers this question boldly as follows:

And now, if the Lamb of God, he being holy, should have need to be baptized by water to fulfil all righteousness, O then, how much more need have we, being unholy, to be baptized, yea, even by water!

And now I would ask of you, my beloved brethren, wherein the Lamb of God did fulfil all righteousness in being baptized by water?

Know ye not that he was holy? But notwithstanding he being holy, he showeth unto the children of men that, according to the flesh he humbleth himself before the Father, and witnesseth unto the Father that he would be obedient unto him in keeping his commandments.

Wherefore, after he was baptized with water the Holy Ghost descended upon him in the form of a dove.

And again, it showeth unto the children of men the straightness of the path, and the narrowness of the gate, by which they should enter, he having set the example before them. (2 Nephi 31:5-7.)

Jesus was baptized in obedience to a principle and therefore fulfilled that righteous demand which the Father placed on all of us. The partaking of the sacrament as a renewal of that baptismal covenant reminds us that we pledge not only to be *willing* (with the partaking of the bread) but also that we *do* (by partaking of the water) keep his commandments. Baptism, in addition to all other things, is a witness to God the Eternal Father, in the name of his Son, that we will be obedient and obey the commandments of Jesus Christ and always remember him. Our covenant with God, which we witness by baptism, is to take upon us the name of Jesus Christ under those specified conditions.

Through the example set by Jesus Christ we can better understand the universality of this commandment and the importance of baptism. Without baptism we will be damned, which means we will be held back, restricted, denied those blessings which from the very beginning were promised us *if* we would be obedient. Now if baptism is that important, and it is, we must answer an important question: What of those who have never had an opportunity to even hear of Jesus Christ, let alone be baptized in his name? Such persons have gone to their graves in ignorance, never having had an opportunity to make such covenants. Are they eternally lost? Will they be eternally damned through no fault of their own?

170

In answer, some religious leaders have preached a doctrine of predestination, which in effect states that some of God's children are predestined to damnation and others are predestined to exaltation. They maintain that whether one attains the one or the other condition depends solely upon the will of God. If in connection with this doctrine they would include a doctrine of a premortal life and explain that damnation was the result of some premortal sin and that exaltation was the result of some premortal righteousness,. there might be some justification for the doctrine of predestination. But then a new problem would arise: If damnation or exaltation has already been determined and we have no control over which of these conditions will be ours, what is the purpose of life? If I am to be damned regardless of what I do, you have robbed me of all hope, which is one of the greatest motivating influences there is. In place of hope you have been given me despair, one of the most discouraging conditions under which man must live. No, there must be a better explanation—and there is!

Jesus Christ was ordained of the Father to be a judge of both the quick (the living) and the dead. Peter taught this doctrine to Cornelius and his family who were not Jews. In this explanation Peter informed Cornelius: ". . . God is no respecter of persons: But in every nation he that feareth him, and worketh righteousness, is accepted with him." (Acts 10:34-35.) Then Peter made this statement concerning Jesus Christ:

Him God raised up the third day, and shewed him openly;
Not to all the people, but unto witnesses chosen before of

God, even to us, who did eat and drink with him after he rose from the dead.

And he commanded us to preach unto the people, and to testify that it is he which was ordained of God to be the *Judge of quick and dead.*

To him give all the prophets witness, that .through his name *whosoever believeth in him* shall receive remission of sins. (Acts 10:40-43. Italics added.)

Peter thus informs us of the universality of the saving power of Jesus Christ both for the dead as well as the living. This is the same doctrine taught by Paul, who used almost the same words. (See 2 Timothy 4:1.) Paul also taught the Romans of the saving power of Jesus Christ: "For to this end Christ both died, and rose, and revived, that he might be Lord both of the dead and living." (Romans 14:9.) So the saving power of Jesus Christ extends beyond both sides of the grave to encompass all people who have ever lived on the earth.

We return to the statement made earlier in this book of the promises made to the fathers. The promise was given that every person born on this earth will have an opportunity to hear the gospel preached at a time, under conditions, and in a manner that every person can understand and accept the gospel plan if he desires to do so. In the planning of this earth life, it was known and understood from the beginning that injustices would occur. Sickness, accidents, diseases, disasters of every kind and description, wars, natural catastrophes, dictatorial compulsion, imprisonment (often most unjust), and every other condition that robs mankind of full agency were all known and anticipated. It was known that times of apostasy would occur when truth would not be found on the earth. It was known that in peopling the earth some individuals would be born at a time and place when they would not be able to hear the gospel message in the flesh. Therefore, ways and means were provided that they could hear the gospel in the spirit world and be able to profit from its promised blessings before the final resurrection and judgment take place.

171

A promise was given in that premortal life to all the children of God that each person would have an opportunity to determine for himself whether to accept Jesus Christ as his Lord and King or whether to reject him. It was on the basis of this promise that the spirit children of God consented to come into mortality during those periods of time when the gospel was not to be found on earth. The promise was given them that the doors of their spirit prison would in time be opened for them. The dead are those who have lived upon the earth as mortal beings, and the living are mortals who sooner or later will pass through that same condition of death. Both the living and the dead are children of the same Father and are to be rewarded with blessings or punished by the withholding of those blessings by the same unerring justice of a perfect God who is loving, merciful, and kind. Jesus died on the cross for the dead as well as for the living, past, present, and future.

The children of God are part of an eternal family whether living or dead. Jesus taught this doctrine by referring to what happened when the Lord spoke to Moses out of the burning bush: "Now that the dead are raised, even Moses shewed at the bush, when he calleth the Lord, the God of Abraham, and the God of Isaac, and the God of Jacob [they being long since dead]. For he is not a God of the dead, but of the living: *for all live unto him.*" (Luke 20:37-38. Italics added.) It is evident that just as he preached his doctrine to the living, so Jesus must also preach the gospel to those in the spirit world. This is made abundantly clear in the scriptures. Let us examine some of the early prophecies made concerning this mission of Jesus.

The mission of Jesus Christ to those beings in the spirit world following death was not to further condemn and torture them in their spirit prison. His mission was a mission of relief and mercy. He went to open the prison doors and to free those who had been restricted during

172

that long period of confinement. His mission was one of deliverance that the captives might go free.

And it shall come to pass in that day, that the Lord shall punish the host of the high ones that are on high, and the kings of the earth upon the earth.

And they [the spirits of those who are dead] shall be gathered together, as prisoners are gathered in the pit, and shall be shut up in the prison, and *after many days shall they be visited.* (Isaiah 24:21-22. Italics added.)

Centuries before this visit was made, Isaiah had prophesied that these spirits would have the gospel taught to them. For what purpose? Isaiah explains: "I the Lord have called thee in righteousness, and will hold thine hand, and will keep thee, and give thee for a covenant of the people, for a light of the Gentiles; To open the blind eyes, to bring out the prisoners from the prison, and them that sit in darkness out of the prison house." (Isaiah 42:6-7.) So we see that the gospel was to be taught to those who had not accepted the gospel or heard it on earth.

This preaching to the spirits of the dead was done not only to teach them the gospel message of salvation, but to actually free them from their confinement. "The spirit of the Lord God is upon me; because the Lord hath anointed me to preach good tidings unto the meek; he hath sent me to bind up the brokenhearted, to proclaim liberty to the captives, and the opening of the prison to them that are bound." (Isaiah 61:1.)

This preaching and opening of the prison doors applied not only to the wicked spirits who had been confined there because of their disobedience, but also to the meek and humble who were there as a result of circumstances over which they had no control. Jesus referred to this passage of scripture from Isaiah, as recorded in Luke 4:18-19, to define his earthly mission. His mission to the dead is exactly the same. He teaches the way toward freedom. If we are obedient, we can es-

173

cape imprisonment of every kind. This applies not only to the living, but also to the dead. We are all children of the same God and subject to the same rules and regulations regardless of our present condition. Thus Jesus becomes the hope of the world, not only for those of us who are living, but also for our ancestors and progenitors who are dead.

174

18

The Gospel Taught to the Dead

Actually there is no such thing as the dead unless one refers to the mortal body, which returns again to the earth. The spirit lives on, and in the resurrection all of us will be made alive again as each body and spirit unite to form an immortal whole. The gospel had to be taught to the living spirits of those whose bodies lie in the grave but who had lived before the meridian of time. But before this could be done, certain preparations had to be made on earth that would make that teaching of the spirits effective and beneficial. Only if this were done could those spirits who were restricted in that spirit existence be freed. In other words, not only was the teaching of those spirits necessary, but a key would actually have to be put into the lock of those prison doors and the key turned so the doors could be opened and the spirits could go free.

One day as Jesus walked along the coasts of Caesarea Philippi, he asked his disciples a question:

Whom do men say that I the Son of man am?

And they said, Some say that thou art John the Baptist: some, Elias; and others, Jeremias, or one of the prophets.

He saith unto them, But whom say ye that I am?

And Simon Peter answered and said, Thou art the Christ, the Son of the living God.

And Jesus answered and said unto him, Blessed art thou, Simon Barjona: for flesh and blood hath not revealed it unto thee, but my Father which is in heaven. (Matthew 16:13-17.)

In other words, this knowledge that Peter had was not received in any of man's ways. He did not hear it from someone else, nor did he read it in a book. Peter had not been taught this concept in the school of the law, nor had he obtained it by sight or experienced it in any normal way. He received this knowledge by revelation from God. Jesus then went on to explain that he would build his church upon that principle, or upon that rock of revelation by means of which Peter had obtained his knowledge of the divinity of the Savior.

176

Jesus went on to make Peter a remarkable promise for the future. He said: "And I will give unto thee the keys of the kingdom of heaven: and whatsoever thou shalt bind on earth shall be bound in heaven: and whatsoever thou shalt loose on earth shall be loosed in heaven." (Matthew 16:19.) Not only did Jesus promise Peter the sealing power that had been given to many of the great prophets, but he said he would give him the *keys* of this power. Thus Peter would not only have the power himself to seal, but, possessing the keys of this power, he would be able to give that power to others as he was directed by the Holy Spirit to do so. This was the same power that was held by Elijah the prophet.

Six days later, Jesus took Peter, James, and John with him to the top of a high mountain. (Matthew 17:1-3.) There he was transfigured as were they also, or they would never have been able to participate in the marvelous experience that followed. After these apostles were transfigured, under the direction of Jesus Christ, Moses appeared to them and gave them the keys of the gathering of Israel through the preaching of the gospel to every nation, kindred, tongue, and people. Also, Elijah appeared and gave them the keys of the sealing power by means of which these gathered people could be sealed in proper family order. Remember that the name *Elias* is the Greek name for Elijah. It was Elijah who was the last prophet who held the keys of the sealing power. We can see why both Moses and Elijah had been transfigured (or translated, as it is sometimes called) so that they did not taste of death. They had a further work to do in mortality, and that was to pass on those keys which they held in an unbroken chain to the apostles at the time of Jesus Christ's earthly ministry. Had they been resurrected, it would have been possible to pass on those keys with their resurrected bodies, but the resurrection had not yet come to pass. Hence transfiguration was the only way to preserve their lives for this momentous occasion. The transfer of authority under the direction of Jesus Christ shows the great order that exists in the priesthood. That such action was pleasing to the Father is noted from the following verse: "While he yet spake, behold, a bright cloud overshadowed them: and behold a voice out of the cloud, which said, This is my Beloved Son, in whom I am well pleased; hear ye him." (Matthew 17:5.) So the Father gave his blessing to what had occurred with this transfer of authority.

177

There is considerable confusion in the minds of students of the scriptures concerning the power of Elias and the power of Elijah. There was a prophet Elias; that prophet's name was Noah, and his office was that of Elias, which is that of a precurser or forerunner. Those who hold this power prepare the way for great things to follow. Such prophets are given the title of an Elias, the office originally held by Noah. For instance, we know that the angel who announced the birth of a son to Zacharias and who announced the coming of a son to Mary was named Gabriel. Joseph Smith stated that Gabriel was known on earth as Noah. Noah stands next in authority to Adam or Michael in the priesthood and was called to that authority and to this office by God. (*History of the Church*, 3:386.) The title of Elias was also given to John the Baptist by Gabriel, or Elias: "And also John the son of Zacharias, which Zacharias he (Elias) visited and gave promise that he should have a son, and his name should be John, and he should be filled with the spirit of

Elias." (D&C 27:7.) Such forerunners of great things to follow are given the title of Elias.

As they were coming down from the mountain, Peter, James, and John were not completely sure of what had occurred. Elijah had come first (as they thought), and so they asked:

Why then say the scribes that Elias must first come?

And Jesus answered and said unto them, Elias truly shall first come, and restore all things.

But I say unto you, *that* Elias is come already [it was, of course, John the Baptist], and they knew him not, but have done unto him whatsoever they listed. Likewise shall also the Son of man suffer of them.

Then the disciples understood that he spoke unto them of John the Baptist. (Matthew 17:10-13. Italics added.)

So we see that John the Baptist was the Elias who was to come in the meridian of time to prepare the way for Jesus Christ, the Savior. The order of appearance of power is illustrated by what occurred. First came the forerunner Elias; then followed the sealing power of Elijah, who held the power to place the seals of the Melchizedek Priesthood upon the house of Israel. Finally the culmination came in the Messiah or Anointed One, who is the Savior or Redeemer with the greatest power of all. This has been carefully explained by Joseph Smith. (*History of the Church*, 6:254.)

Following this experience, Jesus completed giving the sealing power to all the Twelve so that all preparations for a transfer of power could be effected prior to his crucifixion. He told them: "Whatsoever ye shall bind on earth shall be bound in heaven: and whatsoever ye shall loose on earth shall be loosed in heaven." (Matthew 18:18.) When this sealing power was given to the Twelve, what was it to be used for? In Chapter 2 of this book it was pointed out that God used his own sealing power in binding Adam and Eve together in an eternal marriage union. Every prophet appointed by God to hold this special power in the Melchizedek Priesthood was authorized to use it for that same purpose. So it was to be used by these disciples of Jesus Christ.

The Pharisees one day came tempting Jesus with a related question on marriage. However, they confused man's method—marriage for this life only—with God's method of an eternal marriage relationship.

The Pharisees also came unto him, tempting him, and saying unto him, Is it lawful for a man to put away his wife for every cause?

And he answered and said unto them, Have ye not read, that he which made them at the beginning made them male and female,

And said, For this cause shall a man leave father and mother, and shall cleave to his wife: and they twain shall be one flesh?

Wherefore they are no more twain, but one flesh. What God hath joined together [by means of this sealing power which was able to bind or seal on earth and have that union valid in heaven], *let no man put asunder.* (Matthew 19:3-6. Italics added.)

This quotation shows how sacredly Jesus regarded the sealing power that was able to bind a couple together by the power of God in God's own way.

The Pharisees then tried to trap him with a further question, which is also one very applicable in our day when marriage has lost much of its sacredness and vitality.

They say unto him, Why did Moses then command to give a writing of divorcement, and to put her away?

He saith unto them, Moses because of the *hardness of your hearts* suffered you to put away your wives: but *from the beginning* it was not so.

And I say unto you, Whosoever shall put away his wife, except it be for fornication, and shall marry another, committeth adultery: and whoso marrieth her which is put away doth commit adultery. (Matthew 19:7-9. Italics added.)

I have taken the liberty of italicizing parts of the above verses to emphasize the eternal and the sacred na-

179

ture of the marriage covenants when such covenants are sealed by the power of the priesthood such as Elijah restored again to the earth at his coming. All too frequently people enter into these eternal marriage covenants in a light-hearted manner, not realizing the condemnation they bring upon themselves by their seeming disregard of these sacred obligations.

I do not fully understand the meaning of this teaching of Jesus on divorce, for the above account is very fragmentary. I discussed this matter with one of my brethren, who called my attention to a scholarly thesis by one legal authority which stated that under Jewish law there was really no legal action for divorce. Divorce as we know it was not provided for in Jewish law, but it was possible for a man to separate from his wife for cause. For instance, if she were not a virgin on entering marriage, having committed fornication before marriage, she thus married fraudulently. For this reason, he could eject her from his house or tent, thus "putting her away." He was then free to marry another woman, because for him the marriage, being fraudulent, was not valid. The wife, on the other hand, was still married and therefore could not marry another man without now committing adultery. Nor could another man marry her without committing adultery, since she was already married to the first husband. The full instruction as given by Jesus and referred to in the above-quoted scripture was not given by him to the Pharisees, or pronounced openly, but was given privately to his disciples "in the house," as explained by Mark (Mark 10:10-12).

In reading this scripture I get the feeling that when Jesus condemned divorce for trivial reasons, he was particularly emphatic in stressing that divorce comes about because of wickedness on the part of the husband, on the part of the wife, or because both are at fault. As I read these lines I get a feeling that divorce most frequently comes as a result of neglect in following the admonition of the Lord to keep his commandments and to practice love. How could sufficient dislike or hate develop within a marriage that would result in divorce if each of the marriage partners were living close to the Lord and were kind, gentle, considerate, and thoughtful of each other?

Usually sin results not from some sudden evil on the part of one or the other partner. It develops as a result of lack of consideration or carelessness on the part of the marriage partners. Neglect resulting in a decrease of love can ruin any marriage. It is not proper to say that one should "work" continually at the marriage relationship. The word *work* carries with it a connotation of an unwilling task or of being forced into an unwanted or difficult action. A better word would be to *cultivate* marriage by daily expressing one's love and showing that love by thoughtful consideration of the marriage partner. Love occurs when we do something for someone else because we put that person's well-being above our own convenience or well-being. It goes even beyond the command to "do unto others as you would have them do unto you." Love would appear to say, "Do unto others even more than you would expect them to do unto you." If marriage were entered into with this thought in mind, with this desire in one's heart, and with this love made manifest by daily action, probably no divorce would ever take place. If such a marriage, based on eternal love, were sealed by the power of God by one having authority, we would begin to catch a vision of what a great impact the coming of Elijah had in that generation. It had a greater impact than just for that generation, for the same principle extends before and beyond that generation, even to the present.

Now that the necessary preparation and groundwork had been laid for a transfer of authority, Jesus was able to complete his mission on earth. He atoned for the sins of mankind. He made that great and marvelous sacrifice which brought an end to the shedding of sacrificial blood, and brought into the world the beginning of a new type

181

of sacrifice, that of a broken heart and a contrite spirit.

As I read the New Testament I am impressed by the stories and the doctrine given in the four Gospels concerning the mortal ministry of Jesus Christ. One thing, however, is puzzling. There is very little written about what Jesus taught his disciples *following* his resurrection. Luke speaks of the following instruction given to the apostles after the resurrection: "To whom also he shewed himself alive after his passion by many infallible proofs, being seen of them forty days, and speaking of the things pertaining to the kingdom of God." (Acts 1:3.) Surely those things he taught his disciples following his resurrection were as important as the things he taught them before his death. I think they were even more important. Where is the record of these teachings? Such instructions evidently *were* most important, but they were so sacred that they were not to be reduced to writing. They were not to be revealed except to those who were willing to accept them and hold them equally sacred. Such teachings must have been transmitted orally, being too sacred to reveal in writing where anyone by accident might have gained access to them.

The philosophy of such action was explained by Alma in the Book of Mormon:

And now Alma began to expound these things . . . , saying: It is given unto many to know the mysteries of God; nevertheless they are laid under a strict command that they shall not impart only according to the portion of his word which he doth grant unto the children of men, according to the heed and diligence which they give unto him.

And therefore, he that will harden his heart, the same receiveth the lesser portion of the word; and he that will not harden his heart, to him is given the greater portion of the word, until it is given unto him to know the mysteries of God until he know them in full.

And they that will harden their hearts, to them is given the lesser portion of the word until they know nothing concerning his mysteries; and then they are taken captive by the devil, and led by his will down to destruction. Now this is what is meant by the chains of hell. (Alma 12:9-11.)

At one time in writing the record of the Book of Mormon the prophet Mormon wanted to write down all that had been revealed to him, but the Lord forbade him, saying, "I will try the faith of my people." (3 Nephi 26:11.) So Jesus must have told his apostles, as he taught them, that the revelations now given them were so sacred that they should not be reduced to writing.

However, as we read the New Testament there are items to be found therein concerning the teachings given during that period to the apostles. Those who have received greater light and knowledge can recognize these truths as the apostles referred to them in writing to the saints who had previously received this information. The saints of that day knew and understood what the apostles wrote to them, though such items are obscure or cryptic to those who have not received enlightenment. John, for example, wrote: "But ye have an unction [or anointing] from the Holy One, and ye know all things." (1 John 2:20.) He then went on to say: "But the anointing which ye have received of him abideth in you, and ye need not that any man teach you: but as the same anointing teacheth you of all things, and is truth, and is no lie, and even as it has taught you, ye shall abide in him." (1 John 2:27.) Many churches teach of an anointing for the healing of the sick, but this reference is to an anointing given for a special purpose to teach and instruct. It is a mystery known only to those to whom this anointing had been given. The saints of that day knew what John was referring to and could profit thereby.

When Paul wrote to the saints in Corinth he said: "Now he which stablisheth us with you in Christ, and hath anointed us is God; Who hath also sealed us, and given us the earnest of the Spirit in our hearts." (2 Corinthians 1:21-22.)

Though this anointing and sealing is unintelligible to the world generally, it was understood by those who had received such teachings from the apostles. They also knew how to put such teachings to use. In another letter to the saints Paul mentioned resurrected bodies, which

183

were to be entirely different in nature from those bodies found on the earth. He referred to such matters as he taught about the resurrection:

But some man will say, How are the dead raised up? and with what body do they come?

Thou fool, that which thou sowest is not quickened, except it die:

And that which thou sowest, thou sowest not that body that shall be, but bare grain, it may chance of wheat, or of some other grain:

184 But God giveth it a body as it hath pleased him, and to every seed his own body.

All flesh [on the earth] is not the same flesh: but there is one kind of flesh of men, another flesh of beasts, another of fishes, and another of birds.

There are also [in heaven in the resurrection] celestial bodies, and bodies terrestrial: but the glory of the celestial is one, and the glory of the terrestrial is another.

There is [in the heavens] one glory of the sun, and another glory of the moon, and another glory of the stars: for one star differeth from another star in glory.

So also is the resurrection of the dead. It is sown in corruption; it is raised in incorruption. (1 Corinthians 15:35-42.)

Here Paul likened the body to a seed that will produce other seeds in the exalted state in the resurrection. He is also talking of three different heavens or degress of glory. Was this what Paul had in mind when he again wrote to the Corinthians: "I knew a man in Christ above fourteen years ago, (whether in the body, I cannot tell; or whether out of the body I cannot tell; God knoweth;) such an one caught up to the third heaven"? (2 Corinthians 12:2.)

How different this concept of differing degrees of heavenly glory is from that which is now commonly accepted in Christianity. This again I believe was part of that body of knowledge which was revealed to the apostles during those forty days of instruction following the resurrection of Jesus.

Even some of the practices resulting from such instruction are mentioned as Paul wrote in emphasizing the truth of the resurrection. "Else what shall they do which are baptized for the dead, if the dead rise not at all? Why are they then baptized for the dead?" (1 Corinthians 15:29.) Though neither understood nor practiced by modern Christianity, this concept of vicarious work for the dead was understood and practiced by the saints of that day as a result of Christ's forty-day ministry. I believe such practices came from that body of knowledge which the Savior taught, but which was lost during the long years of darkness that followed the death of the apostles.

A foretaste of the instructions that would follow his death was given by Jesus as he hung on the cross. He told of his approaching mission into the spirit world:

185

And one of the malefactors which were hanged railed on him, saying, If thou be Christ, save thyself and us.

But the other answering rebuked him, saying, Dost not thou fear God, seeing thou art in the same condemnation?

And we indeed justly; for we receive the due reward of our deeds: but this man hath done nothing amiss.

And he said unto Jesus, Lord, remember me when thou comest into thy kingdom.

And Jesus said unto him, Verily I say unto thee, *To day shalt thou be with me in paradise* [referring to the spirit world]. (Luke 23:39-43. Italics added.)

We know Jesus went into the spirit world and spent time there, for on his resurrection when Mary was about to embrace him in a show of grateful love that he was alive, he said: "Touch me not; for I am not yet ascended to my Father: but go to my brethren, and say unto them, I ascend unto my Father, and your Father; and to my God, and your God." (John 20:17.) Where had he been during that interval? He had been in the spirit world as he had predicted while on the cross. He went to paradise, or the spirit world, to open the work of the ministry there.

Peter informs us that Jesus did go into the spirit world during that interval before his resurrection:

For Christ also hath once suffered for sins, the just for the unjust, that he might bring us to God, being put to death in the flesh, but quickened by the Spirit [in other words, as a living spirit]:

By which [in this spirit condition] also he went and preached unto the spirits in prison;

Which sometime were disobedient, when once the long-suffering of God waited in the days of Noah, while the ark was a preparing, wherein few, that is, eight souls were saved by water [that is, saved by the ordinance of baptism].

The like figure whereunto even baptism doth also now save us (not the putting away of the filth of the flesh, but the answer of a good conscience toward God,) by the resurrection of Jesus Christ. (1 Peter 3:18-21.)

Peter also explained *why* Jesus taught those spirits the gospel in the spirit world:

For for this cause was the gospel preached also to them that are dead, that they might be judged according to men in the flesh [have the same right to make decisions as to whether or not to accept the gospel and the ordinances performed in their behalf], but live according to God in the spirit [but having accepted these truths, be able to be released from their restrictions in the spirit world and obtain the presence of God]. (1 Peter 4:6.)

Even while Jesus was alive and working with his disciples during his mortal ministry, he taught them the concept of work for the dead. It is doubtful, however, that they fully understood those principles. After his resurrection he was better able to explain these concepts to their comprehension. It is plain that he taught them in mortality that his mission was to the dead as well as to the living.

Verily, verily, I say unto you, He that heareth my word, and believeth on him that sent me, hath everlasting life, and shall not come into condemnation; but is passed from death into life.

Verily, verily, I say unto you, *The hour is coming, and now is, when the dead shall hear the voice of the Son of God: and they that hear shall live.*

For as the Father hath life in himself; so hath he given to

the Son to have life in himself [to live forever, or to have the power of immortality]:

And hath given him authority to execute judgment also, because he is the Son of man.

Marvel not at this: for the hour is coming, in the which *all that are in the graves shall hear his voice,*

And shall come forth; they that have done good, unto the resurrection of life; and they that have done evil, unto the resurrection of damnation. (John 5:24-29. Italics added.)

It is abundantly clear, then, that the mission of Jesus was plainly stated from the very beginning of his earthly ministry. That mission included the dead as well as the living.

187

In a revelation given to Joseph F. Smith, this ministry of Jesus in the spirit world is further explained. Jesus himself did not go among the spirits of the wicked in the spirit world. He went to the spirits of the righteous in paradise and organized the work of the ministry among them. As a result, these righteous spirits were able to do missionary work among those spirits in prison until all had received an opportunity to hear the truth and to accept or reject it. Jesus Christ does not go personally to the various peoples of the earth to proclaim the gospel today. He could only do so in power and glory. The truth would then be so obvious that it would be practically impossible for an individual to exercise his own free agency. In order to properly test us and to determine our faith and willingness to recognize and accept the truth, those truths must not be too obvious, or our free agency to choose would be taken from us. Thus it was explained to President Smith that the carrying of the gospel to the spirits must be done in the same way as it is done on earth, through missionary effort. (Pearl of Great Price, Joseph F. Smith—Vision of the Redemption of the Dead.)

As the gospel is taught to the spirits in prison, they have an opportunity to accept or reject those teachings. If they accept, there still remains the problem of the necessary ordinance work that has to follow belief. If we accept the gospel, we must be baptized; and if we marry

in the Lord's way, it must be done on earth, for these ordinances must be performed on earth and not in heaven.
There is no marriage in heaven and there is no baptism in
heaven. Such ordinances are temporal ordinances of
eternal application and effectiveness and must be
performed on earth by proxy as a vicarious work for the
dead.

The validity of vicarious service for others is a
recognized element in our present legal system. It is also
acceptable before God. The record of history is replete
with instances of vicarious service for others. Even the
horror of human sacrifices to false gods is a vicarious type
of ordinance. It is an apostate application of a universally
accepted practice. The greatest of all vicarious ordinances was the atonement of Jesus Christ. This sacrifice
was vicarious in that Jesus did for us that which we were
unable to do for ourselves. His voluntary sacrifice for us
made propitiation possible and freed us from the claims
of justice through the mercy of God, if we would only
repent. His atonement made possible our attaining that
promised treasure for which we should ever strive.

Our responsibility to perform vicarious service for
our kindred dead is as necessary for us to take care of as it
was necessary for Jesus Christ to atone for our sins. Paul
explained this to the Hebrews. He referred to those saints
who through their faith had withstood all the powers of
the adversary. Through faith they had conquered evil
and had proved their worthiness by their lives. These
were the ancestors and progenitors of those who had received the blessings of the gospel. Paul then wrote: "And
these all, having obtained a good report through faith, received not the promise [in other words, had been deprived of the necessary ordinance work through no fault
of their own, which kept them from receiving a fulness of
promised blessings]: God having provided some better
thing for us [having given us the power to become saviors
for them] that they without us should not be made
perfect." (Hebrews 11:39-40.) What Paul was saying is

188

that just as our ancestors cannot receive a fulness of blessings without our aid to them, so we cannot receive a fulness of blessings unless they receive those blessings through us. We have a vicarious responsibility to aid them, for our lives are possible only through them. From them we receive our bodies. The blood that flows in our veins comes to us from them. We owe them our very lives, and the responsibility for vicarious work and service to our kindred dead is as much our responsibility to them as working out our own salvation and exaltation is to us.

189

19

The Restoration

With the death of the apostles the predicted apostasy from the doctrine and the organization of the Church of Jesus Christ became real. The gospel was taken from the earth and the priesthood with its sealing power was taken from mortal man. The words of the prophet Amos came into fulfillment: "Behold, the days come, saith the Lord God, that I will send a famine in the land, not a famine of bread, nor a thirst for water, but of hearing the words of the Lord: And they shall wander from sea to sea, and from the north even to the east, they shall run to and fro to seek the word of the Lord, and shall not find it." (Amos 8:11-12.) Thus ended for a time the work of salvation, not only for the living but also for the dead. The dark ages crept over the earth.

I think the most discouraging part of the apostasy is that it came from within the church, from false teachers among the flock just as Peter predicted it would come:

But there were false prophets also among the people, even as there shall be false teachers among you, who privily shall bring in damnable heresies, even denying the Lord that bought them, and bring upon themselves swift destruction.

And many shall follow their pernicious ways; by reason of whom the way of truth shall be evil spoken of.

And through covetousness shall they with feigned words make merchandise of you: whose judgment now of a long time lingereth not, and their damnation slumbereth not. (2 Peter 2:1-3.)

In spite of many such warnings that Jesus himself had given, and due to conditions that the apostles had worked hard to prevent, these apostasies began. They started in the days of the apostles and resulted finally in complete and total apostasy.

One cannot read the Book of Mormon without seeing how apostasy crept into the church in the new world in exactly the same way it did in the old world. The trouble came from within the church. The Lamanites did not destroy the Nephites by attacks from without; the Nephites destroyed themselves from within. As I read account after account of their alternate rise and fall, it seems incredible that the destruction of the people of God should have come so rapidly from within the church. As people lust for power, for wealth, for position or fame, they soon find things to criticize. God promises us blessings if we follow his teachings. These blessings are temporal as well as spiritual in nature. As we live the precepts of the gospel we prosper in life. That very prosperity, which results in increased strength, wealth, good food, clothing, housing, etc., causes us to be proud, then forgetful, then downright negligent even to the point of opposition. We feel independent in our own great strength. As we depart from our dependence on and our obedience to God, we lose everything we have gained. This happened with the original Church of Jesus Christ and also with the Nephites. Along with this boring from within came wickedness and oppression from without the church, on both the eastern and the western hemispheres, and gross darkness settled over the earth. Apostasy crept in and overcame the saints of God.

In modern Christianity it is claimed that God ceased to speak to his people because it was no longer necessary, Jesus having revealed everything requisite for salvation. It is true that God ceased to speak, but there was a

191

reason for this closing of the lines of communication. There was no prophet left with whom God could speak. It is just not consistent with reason to believe that as long as there was a divine church upon the earth, God would ever cease to speak to his people. Why should he favor one dispensation with his voice and counsel and deny another? As long as there are divine prophets, God will speak to them if they ask for wisdom and for further light and knowledge. Where there are no prophets, however, God cannot speak.

192

With no prophet to guide the people, wickedness crept into the church. Those entrusted with the sacred records became careless in their preservation. Some scriptures were lost; others were carelessly copied so that errors were made and deletions were carelessly or purposely made. Other scriptures were changed to support the philosophies of men who failed to understand the truths of the gospel. It is truly a miracle that we have as much of the Bible as is available to us today. With all these changes, many of those truths which Christ taught his disciples were lost or changed. That is why continual revelation from God is so necessary.

The golden promise that brought hope to the world, even in times of darkness, was that there would be a restoration of all things, and that in the latter days prophets again would be called. When prophets are divinely called, God speaks with them. Isaiah expresses clearly this promise:

Wherefore the Lord said, Forasmuch as this people draw near me with their mouth, and with their lips do honour me, but have removed their heart far from me, and their fear toward me is taught by the precept of men:

Therefore, behold, I will proceed to do a marvelous work among this people, even a marvelous work and a wonder: for the wisdom of their wise men shall perish, and the understanding of their prudent men shall be hid. (Isaiah 29:13-14.)

Similarly Peter spoke of a restoration to come. His prophecy of this future restoration was that when that time did come, it would result in a full restoration of every blessing and power ever promised to man.

Repent ye therefore, and be converted, that your sins may be blotted out, when the times of refreshing shall come from the presence of the Lord;

And he shall send Jesus Christ, which before was preached unto you;

Whom the heavens must receive until the times of *restitution of all things*, which God hath spoken by the mouth of all his holy prophets since the world began. (Acts 3:19-21. Italics added.)

When Joseph Smith asked for wisdom, the time was ripe for this prophecy to be fulfilled. That sincere young man was called as a prophet, given authority to act, and the full power of the priesthood was restored again to the earth just as Peter promised would be done.

One scripture is so important that it was used in closing the Old Testament, preparatory to the coming of Jesus Christ in the meridian of time. That same scripture was used to usher in the new dispensation when the gospel of Jesus Christ was restored following the great apostasy. It is the only scripture I know of that is so important that it is given in all four standard works, almost word for word. Following that glorious vision when Joseph Smith was taught the true nature of God, a resting period came to give him time to mature and to test his faith. As a result of that first vision, he knew that Jesus Christ was the resurrected Lord and Savior, for the Father himself had borne witness that Jesus Christ was his Beloved Son. Thus Joseph Smith saw and spoke with the Father and the Son and heard the Son instruct him as to the role he would be called to play in the future.

The first scriptural instruction Joseph Smith received was given during the night of September 21, 1823, when the angel Moroni appeared to him in answer to fervent prayer and instructed him in his duties. Note how carefully this instruction was given. The Lord had Moroni repeat his instructions four times word-for-word to impress carefully on Joseph's mind the importance of what was said. The last time the instruction was given was in broad daylight, so Joseph would know this was no uncertain dream of the night. The first scriptural quotation given by Moroni was from the book of Malachi, though with a little variation from the wording of the King James Version. We are not told exactly what Moroni gave from the third chapter, though verses one through three would appear to be most appropriate in opening a new dispensation of the fulness of times:

194

Behold, I will send my messenger, and he shall prepare the way before me: and the Lord, whom ye seek, shall suddenly come to his temple, even the messenger of the covenant, whom ye delight in: behold, he shall come, saith the Lord of hosts.

But who may abide the day of his coming? and who shall stand when he appeareth? for he is like a refiner's fire, and like fuller's soap:

And he shall sit as a refiner and purifier of silver: and he shall purify the sons of Levi, and purge them as gold and silver, that they may offer unto the Lord an offering in righteousness. (Malachi 3:1-3.)

Undoubtedly the angel Moroni explained to Joseph Smith that Joseph was to be that messenger, to assist in the restoration and to prepare the way for the Lord's second coming. Before Christ could come in all his glory, priesthood power and authority would have to be restored and that power would need to be used to accomplish many things in preparation for his second coming.

Then Moroni quoted from the fourth chapter of Malachi: "For, behold, the day cometh, that shall burn as an oven; and all the proud, yea, and all that do wickedly, shall be stubble: and the day that cometh shall burn them up, saith the Lord of hosts, that it shall leave them neither root nor branch." (Malachi 4:1.) It would be well to consider this verse carefully to see what Malachi wrote under inspiration from the Lord. He meant that if we do not do things in the Lord's way, we act wickedly and hence would be destroyed. What is meant by the word *root*? I could well ask, What are my roots? Why, my roots are where I came from. My roots are my parents, my progenitors or ancestors in a direct bloodline. The blood that runs in my veins came to me through my father and my mother, through my grandmothers and my grandfathers, and so on back through the direct lineage of my father and mother. What then is meant by the word *branch*? If I consider myself as the trunk of the tree, nourished and supported by my roots, then the branches constitute that which comes from me. My branches are my children and my grandchildren, etc. In other words, my branches are the posterity that comes from me as branches spring from the trunk of a tree.

195

This same passage is quoted in the Book of Mormon. When the Savior came to the Western Hemisphere following his resurrection, he examined the records the people had kept. He found they were incomplete. He then said to them:

Verily, I say unto you, I commanded my servant Samuel, the Lamanite, that he should testify unto this people, that at the day that the Father should glorify his name in me that there are many Saints who should arise from the dead, and should appear unto many, and should minister unto them. And he said unto them: Was it not so?

And his disciples answered him and said: Yea, Lord, Samuel did prophesy according to thy words, and they were all fulfilled.

And Jesus said unto them: How be it that ye have not written this thing, that many saints did arise and appear unto many and did minister unto them?

And it came to pass that Nephi remembered that this thing had not been written.

And it came to pass that Jesus commanded that it should be written; therefore it was written according as he commanded. (3 Nephi 23:9-13.)

Then the Savior also gave a significant commandment that they should write the words that the Father had given to Malachi. In his translation of the Book of Mormon Joseph Smith gave the words as they are printed in the third and fourth chapters of Malachi, copying them from the King James Version of the Bible in order to save time. I have wondered why the Prophet Joseph did not proceed to write in the corrections in these chapters, as he did in other quotations in the Book of Mormon that were taken from Isaiah. I suppose he did not bother to do so because they were sufficiently clear as they were written in the Bible. In fact, in quoting from Malachi in section 128 of the Doctrine and Covenants, the Prophet actually said so in so many words. He had quoted Malachi 4:5-6 and then said: "I might have rendered a plainer translation to this, but it is sufficiently plain to suit my purpose as it stands. . . ." (D&C 128:18.) What is significant to me, however, is that the Savior asked the ancient Nephites to write down the words of Malachi (3 Nephi 25) so that they might know of these promises just as did the people of the Eastern Hemisphere. If it was that significant to them, surely it ought to be just as significant to us also.

I quote from the Pearl of Great Price the following words as they were given by the angel Moroni in quoting this verse to Joseph Smith on that September evening: "For behold, the day cometh that shall burn as an oven, and all the proud, yea, and all that do wickedly shall burn as stubble; for they that come shall burn them, saith the Lord of Hosts, that it shall leave them neither root nor branch." (Joseph Smith 2:37.) What this scripture means is that we do wickedly unless we follow the set course of the Lord. Unless we do things in the Lord's way, both our roots and our branches will be cut off. We will have neither progenitors nor progeny, but will remain single persons, devoid of family. That was not the plan of the Lord.

If my roots and branches are cut off, then I am left just a dead log. What is a log used for? It is fit for nothing but to be burned for heat, or to be cut up into lumber to be used for making something else, such as a barn, a shed, or a fence. I don't want to be a log fit only for burning, nor do I want to be cut up and made into something else.

I want to live as does a living tree, to provide fruit, shade, and beauty. I want to have joy and to prosper in the love of the Lord in my own proper person with my own personal family around me to share that love and joy with me. What heaven could there be without the close association of those I love the most?

We read on as the angel Moroni quotes the last two verses of the fourth chapter of Malachi, which close the Old Testament. Mighty as these verses are, Moroni quoted them differently, undoubtedly the way they were given and written in the original Nephite record as mentioned in 3 Nephi 24:1:

197

> Behold, I will reveal unto you the Priesthood, by the hand of Elijah the prophet, before the coming of the great and dreadful day of the Lord.
>
> And he shall plant in the hearts of the children the promises made to the fathers, and the hearts of the children shall turn to their fathers.
>
> If it were not so, the whole earth would be utterly wasted at his coming. (D&C 2.)

In this section of the Doctrine and Covenants the scripture is again written which is found in the Bible in Malachi 4:5-6; in the Book of Mormon in 3 Nephi 25:5-6; in the Pearl of Great Price in Joseph Smith 2:38-39; and in the Doctrine and Covenants in the verses above quoted and in 128:17.

In citing these verses, I am reminded of a concept President Harold B. Lee taught the General Authorities one day when we were assembled in our monthly meeting on the fourth floor of the Salt Lake Temple. He warned us not to place our trust nor to build our sermons or personal philosophy on any one single verse of scripture. He said that God is the greatest of all teachers and understands the value of repetition. He instructed us that if an idea is true, we would find that concept repeated again and again throughout the scriptures. Instructions are not confined to any one generation, but are given repeatedly, often in other words so that no one can miss their true meaning. However, such ideas and quotations must not be taken out of context. Since these concepts concerning the work and spirit of Elijah are repeated so many times and are found in all four standard works, they must be very important and should stand a closer analysis.

These verses quoted by Moroni comprise only a few lines on a printed page, but they are loaded with information. The changes he made in the verses given in the Bible, though rather few in number, are of great significance. For instance, when Elijah comes he is to restore the priesthood. When this revelation was first presented to Joseph Smith, he knew nothing of the magnitude of priesthood power, nor did he understand the meaning of the keys of the priesthood by means of which man is authorized, by virtue of holding such keys, to administer powers of the priesthood for others to use. Had Moroni attempted to explain all of these things at that time, it would only have hopelessly befuddled and confused Joseph. I suppose that prophets never do receive a complete revelation at one time. Concepts are revealed piece by piece as rapidly as the prophet can assimilate the information. When one principle has been revealed and been accepted, then the idea or concept is expanded and enlarged. Further details are given until eventually a full understanding is reached. That is why one of our Articles of Faith stresses continuing revelation. In a later revelation, the Lord explained the workings of the Spirit in the following words, revealing how those who hold various keys of priesthood power each reveal their portion from "Adam down to the present time, all declaring their dispensation, their rights, their keys, their honors, their majesty and glory, and the power of their priesthood; giving line upon line, precept upon precept; here a little, and there a little; giving us consolation by holding forth that which is to come, confirming our hope!" (D&C 128:21.)

In another section of the Doctrine and Covenants God revealed an additional truth connected with this piecemeal method of revealing truth, which strengthens

198

my faith and understanding: "And I give unto you a commandment, that ye shall forsake all evil and cleave unto all good, that ye shall live by every word which proceedeth forth out of the mouth of God. For he will give unto the faithful line upon line, precept upon precept; and I will try you and prove you herewith." (D&C 98:11-12.) In other words, when teachings are given us, God will test us to see if we have comprehended the instruction given. If we stand the test, he will then reveal more, but if we fail to understand, he will wait until we find sufficient courage and faith to apply that information to our good that we already have, before he reveals any more to us. If we fail to respond, we will lose all that has been revealed, as the Lord made plain in his instruction to the prophet Nephi:

199

For behold, thus saith the Lord God: I will give unto the children of men line upon line, precept upon precept, here a little and there a little; and blessed are those who hearken unto my precepts, and lend an ear unto my counsel, for they shall learn wisdom; for unto him that receiveth I will give more; and from them that shall say, we have enough, from them shall be taken away even that which they have. (2 Nephi 28:30.)

Thus we see that instructions are given in part to try our faith and to see if we have comprehended those first truths before we are given additional truth to work with. Only if these truths are understood and practiced can we expect to receive more.

And when they shall have received this, which is expedient that they should have first, to try their faith, and if it shall so be that they shall believe these things then shall the greater things be made manifest unto them.

And if it so be that they will not believe these things, then shall the greater things be withheld from them, unto their condemnation. (3 Nephi 26:9-10.)

In this spirit, then, let us examine this matter of the roots and branches and their relationship to the role of the priesthood that Elijah was to bring upon the earth before the second coming of Christ.

20

The Spirit of Elijah

It is evident that the prophecy given by Malachi and quoted by Moroni must be fulfilled in this generation. The coming of Elijah had to take place before the second coming of Jesus Christ, which is spoken of as the great and dreadful day of the Lord. It will be a great day for those who look forward with joy and anticipation to his second advent, but a terrible and dreadful day of realization for those who deny him or this future appearance. The prophet Elijah, who held the keys of the sealing power, did come just as predicted, so we know that the second coming of Jesus Christ is near.

On April 3, 1836, Oliver Cowdery and Joseph Smith were in attendance at a sacrament meeting held in the temple at Kirtland, Ohio. As the sacrament was completed, these two men retired behind the veil of the temple and gave themselves to prayer. They had previously received the Melchizedek Priesthood at the hands of Peter, James, and John, and thus could receive those gifts of the Spirit which belong to this higher order of the priesthood. The Prophet records the following:

The veil was taken from our minds, and the eyes of our understanding were opened.

We saw the Lord standing upon the breastwork of the pulpit, before us; and under his feet was a paved work of pure gold, in color like amber.

His eyes were as a flame of fire; the hair of his head was white like the pure snow; his countenance shone above the brightness of the sun; and his voice was as the sound of the rushing of great waters, even the voice of Jehovah, saying:

I am the first and the last; I am he who liveth, I am he who was slain; I am your advocate with the Father. (D&C 110:1-4.)

Then, under the direction of the Savior under conditions much like those on the Mount of Transfiguration, another series of visions opened before their eyes, and the powers and keys given to Peter, James, and John on the Mount of Transfiguration were restored to Joseph Smith and Oliver Cowdery in the dispensation of the fulness of times.

Moses appeared and conferred his keys of authority on them to gather Israel from all quarters of the earth. Before anything else could be done, the missionary work had to proceed in order to gather the people into the church or kingdom of God. Only by completing the work of salvation for the living could a beginning be made in the work of saving the dead. Moses was followed by Elias, who gave them the keys of the gospel, including the patriarchal order that had been given to Abraham. This power had to be given because the living so gathered would have to be organized in their proper family order in the family of God in true patriarchal order. This is, of course, the end purpose of the gathering of both the living and the dead. Following the restoration of these important keys of authority, the following occurred, as the Prophet reported:

After this vision had closed, another great and glorious vision burst upon us; for Elijah the prophet, who was taken to heaven without tasting death, stood before us, and said:

Behold, the time has fully come, which was spoken of by the mouth of Malachi—testifying that he [Elijah] should be sent, before the great and dreadful day of the Lord come—

To turn the hearts of the fathers to the children, and the children to the fathers, lest the whole earth be smitten with a curse—

Therefore, the keys of this dispensation are committed into your hands; and by this ye may know that the great and dreadful day of the Lord is near, even at the doors. (D&C 110:13-16.)

Elijah restored the keys of the sealing or binding power both for the living, as the hearts of the fathers are turned to their children, and for the dead, as the hearts of the children are turned to their fathers. We should keep in mind that when the full measure of Elijah's mission is understood, his assignment applies just as much to this side of the veil as it does to the other side of the veil. It is not just happenstance that our Church presidents have placed such great emphasis on strengthening living families. The increasing emphasis that has been placed on encouraging fathers to take their rightful place in the home as the head or patriarch of the family; the necessity of mothers to remain at home to teach and care for their children; the establishment and maintenance of the family home evening program; the increased emphasis being given continually to family home teaching—all are evidence of an increased understanding of the spirit and mission of Elijah.

This mission to strengthen the home for the living must be coupled with the turning of the hearts of the children to the fathers. What kind of a heaven would it be if we lost some of those we love on earth through our own carelessness or neglect? The blessings of heaven can't come to us until we have done everything we can on earth to save our own posterity given us by God. In the same way, we owe a great obligation to save those of our lineage who went before us. As we perform our genealogical searches and complete their temple work, we bring joy to those who made our lives possible. We are as important to them as our children are to us. The spirit and work of Elijah extends on both sides of the veil. It is no wonder that the day of Elijah's coming has been so anxiously anticipated by those who know and understand this scripture. Truly that day of the Lord's second coming will be a great and glorious day for those who have looked forward and prepared themselves for the coming of the Lord in all his glory. It will truly be a dreadful day for those who are not prepared and are not worthy to abide that day of judgment.

I know of no minister, other than Joseph Smith, who ever claimed to have had Elijah come to him. I know of no church, other than The Church of Jesus Christ of Latter-day Saints, that claims the appearance of Elijah. I know of no minister or person who can testify that Elijah came and bestowed keys of authority to him to save the earth from being cursed, except Joseph Smith and Oliver Cowdery. Yet in the last hundred and fifty years there has been a sudden upturn of genealogical interest, which, instead of diminishing, is increasing in intensity as the years go by. Since that appearance of Elijah, genealogical societies and associations have been organized by the hundreds, and many thousands of people have become interested in genealogical research and family history. This indicates that something has already happened that is turning the hearts of the children to their fathers.

With this strong evidence and the power of this prophecy of things to come, it appears to me that we must look to the keys of this authority and to the awakening of the spirit of Elijah given to Joseph Smith and to Oliver Cowdery for the fulfillment of this prediction, just as they claimed. Another thing that adds credence to their claim is the orderly manner in which the restoration came about in combination with the restoration of the other priesthood keys related to this power. It is in harmony with the way the transfer of authority was made in New Testament times when like authority was given to Peter, James, and John, as has been cited in previous scriptural quotations. With the fulfillment of this prophecy, all former priesthood powers were again restored to earth and the work of preparing for the second coming of the Savior could begin in earnest. What great significance does the coming of Elijah have for us as individuals? For one thing it alerts us to the fact that the prophecies given in times of old are now at our doors.

In Chapter 17 we learned the importance of baptism and that everyone who reaches the age of accountability has to conform to that ordinance and accept it in order to fulfill all righteousness. Thus baptism becomes as important for our ancestors as it is for us who are living. As the keys of the gathering of the living were exercised as a blessing for the living, so also the keys for the gathering of the dead must be exercised for them.

A revelation was given to Joseph Smith to this effect, which he wrote up in the form of a letter, dated September 1, 1842. Before the keys of the priesthood were restored by Moses, Elias, and Elijah, a temple had to be built in which those keys could be given. Out of the poverty of the people and as a sacrifice to the Lord, that temple was constructed in Kirtland, Ohio. A house had to be constructed where the oracles of the Lord could be heard. Temples of God had been constructed in Old Testament times. As part of the restoration of all things, they had to be built in modern times also. It was not just as a whim that God commanded Moses to build that portable temple called the tabernacle for the use of the children of Israel. It was part of the life of the people and the vitality of their faith. It served a useful purpose in building strength in the priesthood through the performance therein of sacred priesthood ordinances. It was also a place where revelations and directions could be given the prophets for the blessing and guidance of the Lord's people.

During the time of Solomon and afterward, temples of a more permanent nature were built in which sacred ordinances were performed and revelations given. We read also of temples being built on the American continent for use by the Nephites in performing sacred priesthood ordinances and for receiving instruction from the Lord. One early instance can be cited to prove that a temple was constructed soon after Lehi and his people came to the American continent. One of Lehi's sons wrote:

Wherefore I, Jacob, gave unto them these words as I

taught them in the temple, having first obtained mine errand from the Lord.

For I, Jacob, and my brother Joseph had been consecrated priests and teachers of this people, by the hand of Nephi.

And we did magnify our office unto the Lord, taking upon us the responsibility, answering the sins of the people upon our own heads if we did not teach them the word of God with all diligence; wherefore, by laboring with our might their blood might not come upon our garments; otherwise their blood would come upon our garments, and we would not be found spotless at the last day. (Jacob 1:17-19. Italics added.)

So these temples performed a sacred and necessary function for the use of the people.

There was one great difference between the work done in the early temples before the earth ministry of Jesus Christ and the work done after his atonement. Before the time of Jesus Christ there had been no resurrection, for the atonement had not yet been made. Baptisms performed before that time had been made in anticipation of the atonement and had been confined to the living. No work for the dead was possible until after the atonement had been made. Until Jesus Christ opened those prison doors, no vicarious work for the dead could begin. Similarly, when the Kirtland (Ohio) Temple was built, no provision was made for the work for the dead, for the keys of that priesthood had not yet been revealed. Once those keys had been restored, the way was clear for the work of exaltation to begin, not only for the living, but also for the dead.

With the coming of Elijah and the gift of the proper keys and authority, all preliminary preparations were made and the time was now ripe to begin the construction of a new type of temple. The first of these new temples was planned for Nauvoo, Illinois, a temple in which sacred priesthood ordinances authorized by the restoration of the keys of authority of Elijah could be performed. These applied not only to the living, but also to the dead. (D&C 124:28-41.) Accordingly the Lord revealed instructions for opening this new era and gave directions for the baptism of the dead.

And again I give unto you a word in relation to the baptism for your dead.

Verily, thus saith the Lord unto you concerning your dead: When any of you are baptized for your dead, let there be a recorder, and let him be eye-witness of your baptisms; let him hear with his ears, that he may testify of a truth, saith the Lord;

That in all your recordings it may be recorded in heaven; whatsoever you bind on earth, may be bound in heaven; whatsoever you loose on earth, may be loosed in heaven;

For I am about to restore many things to the earth, pertaining to the priesthood, saith the Lord of Hosts.

And again, let all the records be had in order, that they may be put in the archives of my holy temple, to be held in remembrance from generation to generation, saith the Lord of Hosts. (D&C 127:5-9.)

Note the care that must be given in preparing and preserving the records of this sacred work. It stands to reason that if such records are necessary for the dead, they are equally important for the living. I often shudder to see the carelessness with which clerks keep the records of the living members of the Church. I am equally amazed that the living do not check up to see that the data containing a record of their works in the flesh are properly maintained. The next time you attend tithing settlement, or earlier, go to the records to see what is recorded for you and your family. Check them for accuracy of the data so recorded.

Further information was given concerning the sacredness of these records involved with temple work. It was pointed out that there are to be two sets of books kept. One set is the book of life, recording our acts and deeds in life. Another set is to be one in which is recorded our conformance to the earthly ordinances performed in accordance with the requirements of the commandments of God. These are the temple records and the records of the living maintained in the various wards and branches of the Church. The dead are to be judged out of the temple records that we are to keep. (D&C 128:6-7.)

The Prophet Joseph Smith then writes:

Now, the nature of this ordinance consists in the power of the priesthood, by the revelation of Jesus Christ, wherein it is granted that whatsoever you bind on earth shall be bound in heaven, and whatsoever you loose on earth shall be loosed in heaven. Or, in other words, taking a different· view of the translation, whatsoever you record on earth shall be recorded in heaven, and whatsoever you do not record on earth·shall not be recorded in heaven; for out of the books shall your dead be judged, according to their own works, whether they themselves have attended to the ordinances in their own *propria persona* [themselves], or by the means of their own agents [vicariously], according to the ordinance which God has prepared for their salvation from before the foundation of the world, according to the records which they have kept concerning their dead. (D&C 128:8.)

As I said before, when I see the carelessness with which some people regard their own church records, I shudder for them. It is our responsibility to see that our own works and ordinances are properly and accurately reported. We should not just blindly hope that the clerk has made a proper record of our works. We should check to see that the record is accurate and true. This applies as much to the records of the ordinances performed for the dead as it does to the ordinances performed for the living.

The summation of this work may be expressed in a statement that the power of the priesthood is found in the sealing keys that were restored by Elijah in this dispensation:

Now the great and grand secret of the whole matter, and the *summum bonum* of the whole subject that is lying before us, consists in obtaining the powers of the Holy Priesthood. For him to whom these keys are given there is no difficulty in obtaining a knowledge of facts in relation to the salvation of the children of men, both as well for the dead as for the living. (D&C 128:11.)

Thus the keys of the kingdom, which consist of the keys of knowledge, include this sealing and binding power.

The spirit of Elijah is nothing more nor less than the application of this sealing power to build and reconstitute the final, completed family of God in a resurrected condition in the celestial order of exaltation.

After commenting on Paul's statement to the Hebrews, following the death of the Savior, on the practice of baptizing for the dead, and then citing Malachi's promise of the coming of Elijah, Joseph Smith wrote:

208

. . . It is sufficient to know, in this case, that the earth will be smitten with a curse [in other words, the whole purpose of earth life will have failed in its purpose in exalting the children of God] unless there is a welding link of some kind or other between the fathers and the children, upon some subject or other—and behold what is that subject? It is the baptism for the dead. For we without them cannot be made perfect; neither can they without us be made perfect; neither can they nor we be made perfect without those who have died in the gospel also; for it is necessary in the ushering in of the dispensation of the fulness of times, which dispensation is now beginning to usher in, that a whole and complete and perfect union, and welding together of dispensations, and keys, and powers, and glories should take place, and be revealed from the days of Adam even to the present time. And not only this, but those things which never have been revealed from the foundation of the world, but have been kept hid from the wise and prudent, shall be revealed unto babes and sucklings in this, the dispensation of the fulness of times. (D&C 128:18.)

What a revelation of promise is given to us! What treasures has God placed in our hands!

In summation the Prophet then concludes:

Behold, the great day of the Lord is at hand; and who can abide the day of his coming, and who can stand when he appeareth? For he is like a refiner's fire, and like fuller's soap; and he shall sit as a refiner and purifier of silver, and he *shall purify the sons of Levi*, and purge them as gold and silver, *that they may offer unto the Lord an offering in righteousness*. Let us, therefore, as a church and a people, and as Latter-day Saints, offer unto the Lord an offering in righteousness; and let us present in his holy temple, when it is finished, a book containing the records of our dead, which shall be worthy of all acceptation. (D&C 128:24. Italics added.)

There is one other question that should be answered before we close this matter of the spirit of Elijah. Who are the sons of Levi mentioned in the above verse, and what is this offering in righteousness which they are to make? When the children of Israel came out of Egypt after four hundred years of captivity, they were spiritually weak. While Moses was on Mount Sinai receiving instructions from the Lord, the people became impatient. They required Aaron to make them a golden calf to worship such as the Egyptians worshiped while the Israelites lived among them. Isn't it singular that it was the very riches of the people that caused them to sin? Had the Lord not blessed them with golden earrings, rings, ornaments, and jewels, they would not have had the precious gold and jewels with which to make that image to worship. The very blessings from God turn into a curse when the love of money and riches corrupt this prosperity in the hands of men. So, as a result of having been blessed, they had their riches that God gave them from the Egyptians. It was from this wealth that they made their golden calf and so sinned before the Lord.

209

When Moses came down from the mount with Joshua, he destroyed the golden calf, ground up the gold, and forced the people to drink it. He also punished the people who had been the leaders of that wicked rebellion against the Lord. When he called for volunteers to aid him in this purification of the people, the sons of Levi gathered to his support. Moses used them to destroy the ringleaders and to purify the people. Under the Aaronic Priesthood, then, the Levites became a special task force, using their portion of that priesthood for purification purposes in handling those sacrifices in the temple which atoned for the sins committed by the children of Israel.

We read in Ezekiel 43:18-27 how the sons of Levi were chosen originally to make a blood offering that would not only purify themselves, but would also purify the people so the Lord could accept them. They served in the temple dressed in their clean linen garments, representing purity and righteousness before the Lord. The ordinances of blood sacrifice that they performed were cleansing or purifying ordinances. Ezekiel, speaking for the Lord, said of them: "And they shall teach my people the difference between the holy and profane, and cause them to discern between the unclean and the clean." (Ezekiel 44:23.) So these lesser priests had a duty to perform that was important for the remission of the sins of the people whom they served.

210

The atoning sacrifice of Jesus Christ ended blood sacrifice among the people of God and substituted a new sacrifice that was superior and more difficult to give. The new sacrifice was that of a broken heart and a contrite spirit. The outward manifestation of this sacrificial ordinance is that of baptism. (D&C 20:37.) The Lord informs us that the greater, or Melchizedek, priesthood holds the keys of the mysteries of the kingdom, even the key of the knowledge of God. Without this priesthood, no man can see the face of God the Father and live. (D&C 84:22.) When the children of Israel hardened their hearts and rebelled, the higher priesthood was taken from them and they were left with the lesser priesthood.

Now this Moses plainly taught to the children of Israel in the wilderness, and sought diligently to sanctify his people that they might behold the face of God;

But they hardened their hearts and could not endure his presence; therefore, the Lord in his wrath, for his anger was kindled against them, swore that they should not enter into his rest while in the wilderness, which rest is the fulness of his glory.

Therefore, he took Moses out of their midst, *and the Holy Priesthood also;*

And the lesser priesthood continued, which priesthood holdeth the key of the ministering angels and preparatory gospel;

Which gospel is the *gospel of repentance and baptism, and the remission of sins,* and the law of carnal commandments, which the Lord in his wrath caused to continue with the house of Aaron among the children of Israel until John, whom God raised up, being filled with the Holy Ghost from his mother's womb. (D&C 84:23-27. Italics added.)

This baptism for the remission of sins is a cleansing ordinance for the people even today.

As I interpret this scripture, the offering to be made by the sons of Levi in righteousness today is that members of the Aaronic Priesthood are to prepare themselves and purify themselves to go into the temples and there perform an offering in righteousness by being baptized for the dead. In performing this ordinance, they purify the dead so they can be released from their spirit prison and can stand before the Lord to be judged according to their deeds and according to the purifying temple ordinance work done for them in the flesh. Since males can only officiate for males, sisters of corresponding age and virtue should likewise make an offering in righteousness for the spirits of females who are dead, so those spirits may likewise have their sins remitted and stand purified before the Lord to receive their final judgment.

211

Unless this interpretation of this scripture is correct, I cannot understand the meaning of the following word of the Lord:

Therefore, as I said concerning the sons of Moses—for the sons of Moses *and also the sons of Aaron* shall offer an acceptable offering and sacrifice in the house of the Lord, which house shall be built unto the Lord in this generation, upon the consecrated spot as I have appointed—

And the sons of Moses *and Aaron* shall be filled with the glory of the Lord, upon Mount Zion in the Lord's house, *whose sons are ye;* and also many whom I have called and sent forth to build up my church. (D&C 84:31-32. Italics added.)

Not only are those of the Levitical, or Aaronic, Priesthood to be engaged in the purifying ordinance of baptism in the house of the Lord as they make their sacrifices, but those who hold the higher priesthood (cited as sons of Moses) are likewise to make their sacrifice of time and effort and love not only to purify, but also, through those higher ordinances of the Lord's house, to exalt the souls of the children of God who have died. We speak of sons, but the daughters are included also. Without them the work could only be half-done.

We might well go back to that quotation from Doctrine and Covenants 128:24, which states that the "sons of Levi—may offer unto the Lord an offering in righteousness." If the sons of Moses (the Melchizedek Priesthood) must participate in temple service, why did the Lord, speaking through Joseph Smith, just refer to the sons of Levi? That question can be answered with another question. What was the subject of that revelation? It was a revelation on baptism for the dead. It was a revelation concerning a purification ordinance for the dead. Therefore, since baptism is a particular ordinance for the remission of sins, it applies to the sons of Levi, and they are the ones mentioned then in that revelation. To me this is another testimony that Joseph Smith was inspired of God. He could not have known all these things right from the beginning. Revelation was given step by step. Joseph was a true prophet of God. The later revelations included higher temple ordinances to be performed by the higher priesthood, referred to as the sons of Moses.

Note the pattern of the restoration. Just as John came as a forerunner for Jesus Christ in the meridian of time, so he came again in the last days. The forerunner of the restoration of the priesthood was the return of John the Baptist as an Elias, to restore the Aaronic Priesthood. This enabled the people to be purified. Then came Peter, James, and John to restore the greater or Melchizedek Priesthood by means of which the people could be exalted. Since our day is the generation of the fulness of times spoken of by Peter, there must be a "restitution of *all* things which God hath spoken by the mouth of all his holy prophets since the world began." (Acts 3:21. Italics added.) Following this pattern, then, before Jesus can come a second time there must be a restoration of the sealing power at the hands of Elijah, as was predicted. Everything had to be prepared beforehand in proper order before Jesus Christ can appear in power and glory. The work of the ministry at present is to use these powers and keys in preparation for that coming day.

21

Building the Eternal Family

Jesus Christ, during his forty-day ministry to his disciples following his resurrection, was able to explain many concepts in greater detail than he could during his earthly ministry. While he was still with them in the flesh he had taught them the sacredness of the marriage covenant. That original marriage of Adam and Eve in the Garden of Eden had been sealed by the priesthood power of God the Father and was designed to last forever. Only by the use of the priesthood power of God can marriages be performed that will last eternally. God gave such priesthood power to various prophets through the ages, and it was this same sealing power that he gave to Elijah. Under the direction of Jesus Christ, Elijah conferred the keys of that power to Peter, James, and John, and from them the sealing power was given to the others of the Twelve.

So important is the coming of Elijah in the minds of the Jewish people that, as they celebrate the Feast of the Passover in their homes, they set an extra setting on the table and prepare an extra chair at the table in preparation for his coming. It is regrettable that they do not know that Elijah has already come and restored that power, first in the days of Jesus Christ and now in the last days as the gospel with all its power and authority has been restored. It is strange that this tradition which is so strong among the Jews and is given so plainly in the Bible should be so completely ignored by the Christian churches of today. They also look forward to the second coming of the Lord in power and glory and, like the Jews, look forward to some time in the future when Elijah shall come, not realizing this has already come to pass.

Before his death, Jesus told his disciples that heaven was not just a single place:

Let not your heart be troubled: ye believe in God, believe also in me.

In my Father's house are many mansions: if it were not so, I would have told you. I go to prepare a place for you.

And if I go and prepare a place for you, I will come again, and receive you unto myself; that where I am, there ye may be also. (John 14:1-3.)

When Jesus did come again, during those forty days following his resurrection, he explained more about these mansions and the kingdoms of heaven. Thus, when Paul wrote to the Corinthians, he was able to explain how the dead are raised and what kind of bodies they will possess. He likened the most exalted state of the resurrection to the planting of a seed and indicated that in that resurrected state one could have offspring just as one seed produces other seed of the same kind. But he pointed out that there would be differences in the resurrection and that all bodies would not have that same power. There are different kinds of bodies in the resurrection, depending upon the kingdom in which those bodies exist. Just as there are different kinds of bodies here on the earth, so there will be different kinds of bodies in the kingdoms in heaven. He compares those bodies with the kinds of bodies there are on the earth:

All flesh is not the same flesh: but there is one kind of flesh of men, another flesh of beasts, another of fishes, and another of birds.

There are also celestial bodies, and bodies terrestrial: but the glory of the celestial is one, and the glory of the terrestrial is another.

There is one glory of the sun, and another glory of the

moon, and another glory of the stars: for one star differeth from another star in glory.

So also is the resurrection of the dead. It is sown in corruption; it is raised in incorruption. (1 Corinthians 15:39-42.)

In these few verses Paul indicated some of the instructions Jesus gave his disciples following his resurrection.

From this short account of Paul, it is not possible to understand much about the various kingdoms of heaven. For this reason it was necessary that God reveal more about them, a knowledge of which was given to Joseph Smith and Sidney Rigdon. Since we should be searching for and striving for the greatest of God's promised treasures, I will confine myself principally to the celestial degree of glory. All kingdoms of heaven, however, are kingdoms of glory. The glory of the lowest, or telestial, kingdom is greater than we now enjoy on earth. Beautiful as the earth is and as wonderful as earth life can be at present, it cannot compare with the beauty and tranquillity of the telestial kingdom, which is the lowest degree of glory. There will be, of course, a wide variety of blessings in that kingdom in reward for what those who will inhabit it have earned during their earth life. We are told that as one star differs in brightness from another, so will the degree of blessings differ in this kingdom. Those who will inherit that degree of glory will enjoy the teachings and presence of the Holy Ghost and they shall be heirs of salvation.

And also the telestial receive it [administration of those blessings] of the administering of angels who are appointed to minister for them, or who are appointed to be ministering spirits for them; for they shall be heirs of salvation.

And thus we saw, in the heavenly vision, the glory of the telestial [kingdom], *which surpasses all understanding;*

And no man knows it except him to whom God has revealed it. (D&C 76:88-90. Italics added.)

This lowest kingdom, then, is a higher degree of glory than we can imagine from our earthly experience.

Nothing is said about divisions in the next higher

216

kingdom, known as the terrestrial kingdom. We are told that this kingdom is inherited by good men and women who have been blinded by the craftiness of men and who have allowed themselves to be deceived. We should understand that these are good people of good hearts and minds. However, they have allowed others to do their thinking for them and have obeyed others instead of thinking for themselves and obeying the commandments of God. They have not been valiant in searching for the truth, or if they have found it they have not been willing to sacrifice for it. These are well-meaning people, but they have been somewhat indifferent to spiritual things. They have not wanted to be bothered by religion, nor have they been willing to give up the pleasures of earthly experiences that they so much enjoyed while living on earth. They have been more interested in sports, fishing, hunting, or teas, dances, theater, etc., than in the service of God or in spending a portion of their time in church. They just have not sacrificed time and money and effort in searching for the best. They are content with what they have on earth at present and will be blessed accordingly. They will enjoy the presence and the teachings of the Holy Ghost and Jesus Christ, but they can never see the Father. The scripture says of this glory: "And thus we saw the glory of the terrestrial [kingdom] which excels in all things the glory of the telestial, even in glory, and in power, and in might, and in dominion." (D&C 76:91.) This glory is so great that unless it were hidden from our minds with a veil, we might be tempted to go there now and not complete our lives on earth. We would be tempted beyond our ability to resist in order to obtain this glory with all its blessings. It is much better and more glorious than anything we can imagine from the experiences we have had here on the earth.

The highest degree of glory is the celestial kingdom, where God the Eternal Father lives and where those who inhabit this glory enjoy the presence and the teachings of all three members of the Godhead. Those who inhabit this degree of glory include the Church of the Firstborn

217

who have overcome by faith. They have been washed clean in the waters of baptism, have received the higher priesthood after the order of the Only Begotten Son, and have been sealed by the Holy Spirit of promise which the Father sheds forth upon all who are just and true in the faith. "And thus we saw the glory of the celestial [kingdom], which excels in all things—where God, even the Father, reigns upon his throne forever and ever." (D&C 76:92.) This glory is so bright that eye has not seen nor ear heard, neither has it entered into the hearts of men the beauty, the tranquillity, the peace, the happiness, or the joy of those who reach this exalted state. This is the greatest of all the promised treasures of God.

We are told that there are three grand divisions in this celestial kingdom:

In the celestial glory there are three heavens or degrees;
And in order to obtain the highest, a man must enter this order of the priesthood [meaning the new and everlasting covenant of marriage];
And if he does not, he cannot obtain it.
He may enter into the other, but that is the end of his kingdom; he cannot have an increase. (D&C 131:1-4.)

I am comforted to read that this limitation applies to men who hold the priesthood and therefore can take positive action. Because women cannot take the initiative in marriage, this restriction does not apply with the same rigor to women, as explained in an earlier chapter. We need, therefore, to know more about that highest degree of the celestial kingdom, for if there are treasures to obtain, we ought to search for the ultimate. Even if we fall short of the highest goal, we will at least have risen higher than we otherwise would, were we content to strive for a lesser goal.

The law of the new and everlasting covenant was instituted for the perfection of man. Through this covenant man could receive a fulness of glory or blessings from the Lord. The philosophy of the reasoning behind covenants can be obtained from the following scripture:

218

And verily I say unto you, that the conditions of this law are these: All covenants, contracts, bonds, obligations, oaths, vows, performances, connections, associations, or expectations, that are not made and entered into and sealed by the Holy Spirit of promise, of him who is anointed, both as well for time and for all eternity, and that too most holy, by revelation and commandment through the medium of my anointed, whom I have appointed on the earth to hold this power (and I have appointed unto my servant Joseph to hold this power in the last days, and there is never but one on the earth at a time on whom this power and the keys of the priesthood are conferred), are of no efficacy, virtue, or force in and after the resurrection from the dead; for all contracts that are not made unto this end have an end when men are dead. (D&C 132:7.)

219

Thus the marriage referred to in the previous paragraph, which qualifies one for the highest degree of the celestial kingdom, must be one that conforms to the above requirement or it is ineffective after death. Any marriage covenant made in the world and authorized by worldly authority has no force or validity when man is dead. The family ceases to exist and parents and children become individuals without any further relationship or family ties one to another.

In order for a family to be formed with lasting force to bring to pass a continuing patriarchal order from father to son and from mother to daughter, that marriage must meet the following condition:

And again, verily I say unto you, if a man marry a wife by my word, which is my law, and by the new and everlasting covenant, and it is sealed unto them by the Holy Spirit of promise, by him who is anointed, unto whom I have appointed this power and the keys of this priesthood; and it shall be said unto them—Ye shall come forth in the first resurrection; and if it be after the first resurrection, in the next resurrection; and shall inherit thrones, kingdoms, principalities, and power, dominions, all heights and depths—then shall it be written in the Lamb's Book of Life, that he shall commit no murder whereby to shed innocent blood, and if ye abide in my covenant, and commit no murder whereby to shed innocent blood, it shall be done unto them in all things whatsoever my servant hath put upon them, in time, and through all eternity; and shall be of full force when they are out of the world; and they shall pass by the angels, and the gods, which are set there, to their exaltation and glory in all things, as hath been sealed upon their heads, which glory shall be a fulness and a continuation of the seeds forever and ever. (D&C 132:19.)

What a promise of glory these words reveal to those who are willing to pay the price to obtain such blessings!

Marriage is a beautiful experience and is a time in the lives of people when they are very tender toward one another. I have seen many young people radiantly happy as they were married by civil or church authority. As a bishop it was touching for me to see the joy of a couple in love as I performed a marriage for them and pronounced them man and wife. How happy a couple is when children come and they find the joy of that close family association! Now I almost weep when I compare those promises made in civil marriages with the promised blessings that accompany a sealing ceremony in the temple. Now as I perform such a sealing of man and wife in the temple, I sometimes have difficulty in controlling my voice as the promises of exaltation and eternal blessings roll forth and are sealed upon the couple kneeling at the altar of the Lord. The only true basis for such an eternal marriage is that of love. If people will only listen to the promises given in that sealing ceremony and cultivate their love for each other, that marriage will grow to infinite power. That is the final treasure God promises his children who will be obedient and follow his doctrines and procedures rather than man's.

Our prophets and leaders have stressed the need for us to cultivate the marriage relationship and to become more cognizant of our obligations in marriage. Too often people just don't think. They rush into marriage without the necessary preparation for it. Many times parents are to blame for unsuccessful marriages by stressing the importance of a temple marriage without also stressing the obligations that go along with that kind of marriage. We live in the world and are subject to the mores and customs of those around us. We are daily exposed to the temptations of Satan as he tries to destroy the souls of men and women with immorality and sensuousness of all kinds. When we marry in the temple, it should be with the idea that our marriage is to last forever, regardless of what may happen physically or emotionally to one or the other in that marriage relationship. We must learn to serve one another and to meet the needs of one another in a kind, warm, and gentle relationship. We must prepare ourselves financially, mentally, and physically to meet the requirements of a lasting marriage. That takes planning, preparation, and maturity.

221

The temple is a holy place, a house of God. We must prepare ourselves before we enter by living lives that are clean and moral. We cannot degrade ourselves or our bodies by unclean or immoral actions and then expect to receive those spiritual blessings to be obtained in the temple. Sometimes through the pleading of parents, young people enter the temple when they know they are unworthy to enter that sacred place. They are not truthful in their interviews with bishops and stake presidents. It is true that they can receive recommends through deception, but one must also remember that these sealings are performed by the Holy Spirit of promise, and there no deception is possible. An ordinance performed in good faith by one having authority is valid, but it cannot become effective until all prerequisites are met. If people understood this, they would realize that they make a mockery of most sacred things when they go into the temple unworthily. God will not be mocked. If people go unworthily to the temple, they only bring added condemnation upon their heads over and above the sins they have already committed.

In this mortal life we have procreative powers. By virtue of the power given our mortal bodies, we can create. Exaltation, in the sense of receiving this sealing power in our behalf, leads to perfection. In other words, we reach up and obtain a status above and beyond that which we already have. We have power in mortality to procreate on earth for a limited time. When exaltation is attained, that power must lead to perfection above and beyond any power that we already possess. Hence exaltation results in unlimited power to procreate through all eternity. We can enjoy the warmth and companionship of those we love, not for just a few short years, but forever. In addition, we will be freed of all those limiting conditions of health, stress, finances, etc., that at times worry us so much in our married lives on earth. To enjoy eternal bliss and happiness without those earthly or temporal limitations is exciting to contemplate.

222

If we are to obtain such blessings for the eternities, we should do everything in our power to try to live as close as we can to a celestial life on earth. It hurts me as I work and talk with our Church members, even with leaders of our people, to see how they sometimes speak and act toward their companions. I have seen men in very important positions pay little or no attention to their wives and families. I have heard them belittle their wives on occasion, making fun of them for some little deed or error. I have seen children rush up to a father to greet him or just to be with him, only to see him push them away or ignore them completely. When I see the disappointment of these children, sometimes with tears at being rejected, my heart breaks for them. It hurts me to see neglect from those who should know better. I thrill to see our Church presidents and other leaders as they show tender care and consideration for their companions. The gentleness and solicitude they have for their companions shows they have caught the vision of the eternities with respect to the marriage relationship.

Paul caught the vision of this solicitude for wife and family as he wrote: "But if any provide not for his own, and especially for those of his own house [kindred], he hath denied the faith, and is worse than an infidel." (1 Timothy 5:8.) Paul was referring to more than just providing one's family with housing, food, and clothing. He was referring also to love, companionship, and understanding. That love and consideration, that kindness and thoughtfulness, must be of an eternal nature, being constantly nourished, cultivated, and expanded as we gain knowledge and understanding of the eternal nature of these family covenants.

When a couple are sealed by the Holy Spirit of promise, they have a right to call forth into their family as children of the promise the finest, most special spirit children of God. Such children are "born in the covenant" and are heirs to the blessings of the priesthood. Such children are born with the seals of God already placed upon them. Through carelessness or wickedness, sometimes divorce occurs and parents may request a cancellation of sealing. Should such a cancellation of sealing be granted, it does not have any effect on the child born in the covenant or sealed to that couple. That cancellation does not affect the child, for he is now sealed with inherent priesthood rights that can only be taken from him through his own wickedness. Should a parent remarry, that child is never sealed to the new couple, for he has been already sealed and need never be sealed to a parent again. What happens to his sealing and his right to noble parentage if his parents separate? His sealing follows the sealing of the more righteous parent. If neither parent were righteous, his sealing would be automatically transferred to a righteous ancestor to protect his lineage and priesthood rights. God is a just God, and no child of the covenant will ever be denied any right to which he is entitled and worthy.

Parents have an obligation then to teach their children concerning the gospel, as the Lord makes clear: "Wherefore, ye shall remember your children, how that ye have grieved their hearts because of the example that ye have set before them; and also, remember that ye may, because of your filthiness, bring your children unto destruction, and their sins be heaped upon your heads at

223

the last day." (Jacob 3:10.) The prophet speaks of filthiness, but I would stress plain carelessness and indifference. When we are selfish and think only in terms of our own convenience and comfort instead of considering others in our family, we cannot help but offend our wives and our children. The same obligation of unselfishness rests upon the wife. One of the consequences of a temple marriage is that we carry with us at all times, both day and night, a constant reminder of our sacred obligation to so conduct our lives that we rise above the common run of married men and women. We are reminded that we must prove our rights to these special priesthood blessings by an attitude of special love and tenderness toward our marriage partners and to our families.

224

If I were to give counsel both before marriage and within that marriage relationship, I would refer you to God. What would our Father do under such conditions? If you have any question about what you should do within the marriage covenant, ask yourself this question: What would our heavenly father and mother do? There are those who claim that there are no limitations regarding sexual activity within the marriage covenant. Should such situations arise, ask this question: Can I imagine Heavenly Father doing this? When you are thoughtless or careless in being polite or considerate of a wife or children, just ask: Would Heavenly Father be so indifferent of those *he* loves? The answer is obvious. There are rules by which we must live: "For if you will that I give unto you a place in the celestial world, you must prepare yourselves by doing the things which I have commanded you and required of you." (D&C 78:7.) This is the key to assuring ourselves a place in the celestial kingdom.

22

A Missionary Work

When Moses appeared to Joseph Smith and Oliver Cowdery to restore the keys of the gathering of Israel in the last days, missionary work took on new significance. Missionary work began even before the Church was founded, but when the keys of the gathering were restored, new significance and importance were given to this work. The revelation given through the Prophet to his father, Joseph Smith, Sr., applies not only to missionary work on the earth, but also to missionary work among the spirits in prison.

Now behold, a marvelous work is about to come forth among the children of men.

Therefore, O ye that embark in the service of God, see that ye serve him with all your heart, might, mind and strength, that ye may stand blameless before God at the last day.

Therefore, if ye have desires to serve God [that is, a passionate intensity to participate] ye are called to the work;

For behold the field is white already to harvest; and lo, he that thrusteth in his sickle with his might, the same layeth up in store [pays off his past indebtedness] that he perisheth not, but bringeth salvation to his soul;

And faith, hope, charity and love, with an eye single to the glory of God, qualify him for the work.

Remember faith, virtue, knowledge, temperance, patience, brotherly kindness, godliness, humility, diligence.

Ask, and ye shall receive; knock, and it shall be opened unto you. Amen. (D&C 4.)

These qualifications for missionary service on earth are the same qualifications we need for missionary service to our kindred dead. Surely if the field is white and ready to harvest on earth, it must be equally white and ready to harvest on the other side of the veil. In our genealogical and temple activity we are trying to prepare a place for ourselves in the celestial kingdom. God said that if we are to obtain such a place in that kingdom, we must prepare ourselves by doing the things he has commanded us to do. (D&C 78:7.)

226

A great promise of missionary work has been given the youth of the Church as recorded in the Doctrine and Covenants. This also applies to the dead as well as to the living. "Therefore, thus saith the Lord unto you, with whom the priesthood hath continued through the lineage of your fathers." (D&C 86:8.) "Oh," I can hear someone say, "there must be something wrong with that passage of scripture! I am the only member of my family in the Church. None of my people are members. How could I have received my priesthood through the lineage of my father or my mother when they are not even members of the Church?" All I can answer is that the Lord said it, so it must be true. It can be explained, I believe, as follows: The blood that runs in my veins runs in the veins of my parents, grandparents, and other progenitors. If I have received the priesthood, it must be that a promise was given my ancestors that I would receive an heirship to obtain such priesthood powers and blessings if I made myself worthy. The promise given me was also a promise given them. The blessings given me, if I exercise that power as I should, would also result in priesthood blessings for them. These priesthood promises are therefore family promises, all part of the patriarchal order of life on earth and in heaven. We must understand that with God all life is a perfect whole, with past, present, and future all a part of the total plan. If God gave such a promise to my ancestors that the priesthood would

continue in their seed, then that becomes a lineage blessing and I *do* receive my priesthood through them.

The Lord further emphasizes these lineage rights, as
the revelation goes on to state: "For ye are lawful heirs,
according to the flesh, and have been hid from the world
with Christ in God." (D&C 86:9.) This means we receive
a right to priesthood blessings from our parents, grandparents, and great-grandparents, that is, through our
blood ancestry. I hope you understand that heirship to
the priesthood with its accompanying blessings is not au-
tomatic, but it is dependent to a great degree on a family
blood relationship, since, having a right to receive those
blessings, we are much more likely to listen when the
voice of God calls us. Possessing this knowledge, we can
begin to appreciate our earthly families more than we
have ever done before.

What does the Lord mean by the expression "hid
from the world with Christ in God"? He means that according to the plan of salvation, we were reserved or held
back in the heavens as spirit children of God to be born
in a time and at a place in which we could perform a special mission in life. This concept of being foreordained
for a special mission is not new. Reference has already
been made to such a foreordination in the appointment
of a special group of mortals who are known as the
children of the covenant or the chosen people. It is referred to many times in the scriptures. Paul in teaching
the Ephesians said of this foreordination: "Blessed be the
God and Father of our Lord Jesus Christ, who hath
blessed us with all spiritual blessings in heavenly places
in Christ. According as he hath chosen us in him before
the foundation of the world, that we should be holy and
without blame before him in love." (Ephesians 1:3-4.)
Paul then further explained to the Ephesian saints:

Having made known unto us the mystery of his will, according to his good pleasure which he hath purposed in
himself:

That in the dispensation of the fulness of times he might
gather together in one all things in Christ both which are in

227

heaven [in other words, those children of God in the spirit world both past and present], and which are in earth [his children in mortality]; even in him:

In whom also we have obtained an inheritance, being predestinated [this should have been translated as foreordained] according to the purpose of him who worketh all things after the counsel of his own will:

That we should be to the praise of his glory, who first trusted in Christ. (Ephesians 1:9-12.)

Thus this foreordination was for a purpose: so that we could participate in the work of the ministry in the due time of the Lord.

228

From the time the earth was originally planned, God the Eternal Father knew that in the last days as time became ever shorter, Satan would become desperate in his efforts to destroy the plan of salvation. As the second coming of Jesus Christ draws ever nearer, Satan is doing everything in his power to destroy the work of God. He is using every artifice he has available to destroy the plan of salvation and make it inoperative. He is now raging on the earth in blood and horror. But God knew in advance what Satan would attempt to do in these last days, and he devised a plan to counteract that challenge. He reserved for these last days some of his most valiant spirit sons and daughters. He held back for our day some of his most proved and trusted children, who he knew from their premortal behavior would hear the voice of the Shepherd and would accept the gospel of Jesus Christ. He knew they would live so valiantly that they would qualify themselves to receive the holy priesthood and could then use this power as a buffer against all the powers of Satan. Through the exercise of the priesthood of God they could thus limit Satan's destructiveness and make it possible for God to complete the work he had planned for saving his children.

Young people on the earth today (especially those who are members of the Church) represent some of the finest men and women ever to be born on the earth. In connection therewith we could also say that God would not dare entrust these precious souls to just any parents. These special spirits have to be protected and taught, and so we have a right to say that they have the finest parents of any generation ever born. Both children and parents have a special responsibility to each other. We can use the words of Peter to describe this generation as he wrote:

. . . ye are a chosen generation, a royal priesthood, an holy nation, a peculiar people; that ye should shew forth the praises of him who hath called you out of darkness into his marvellous light:

Which in time past were not a people, but are now the people of God: which had not obtained mercy, but now have obtained mercy. (1 Peter 2:9-10.)

229

The Lord, in speaking of priesthood leaders, said of those ordained to the High Priesthood:

And this is the manner after which they were ordained— *being called and prepared from the foundation of the world* according to the foreknowledge of God, on account of their exceeding faith and good works [remember that this faith and good works were demonstrated and proved in the premortal world]; in the first place being left to choose good or evil; therefore they having chosen good, and exercising exceeding great faith [here on the earth], are called with a holy calling, yea, with that holy calling which was prepared with, and according to a preparatory redemption for such. (Alma 13:3. Italics added.)

Thus we and our parents were reserved to be born at a time and in a place where we could not fail to hear the gospel preached. We were reserved for a special time when we could exercise our right to know and accept the gospel and receive the holy priesthood. Thus a preparatory redemption was made for us as children of the covenant through the priesthood heritage we received by lineage from our fathers, mothers, and ancestors.

Now we might well ask: What does God expect us to do with this priesthood power? The Lord himself answers that question: "Therefore your life and the priesthood have remained, and must needs remain through you and your lineage until the restoration of all things spoken by the mouths of all the holy prophets since the world began." (D&C 86:10.) What were those things spoken by the mouths of all the holy prophets since the world began? Why, they were those promises made to the fathers or patriarchal leaders of the Church of God from the very beginning of man's life on the earth. This promise was that ways and means would be provided to bring back into the presence of God the Eternal Father every soul who desired that blessing and who would make the effort to attain it, that they might share his family treasure. This is a clue for missionaries to turn to members of the Church for their finest referrals. They will know that members of the Church in whose blood these priesthood promises have continued as a priesthood lineage blessing can be the entry point for missionary work to whole families of people. If a person joins the Church, then he has the assurance that his parents and other blood relatives will eventually join the Church also. Every one of his blood relatives is a prospective member of the kingdom of God.

The whole secret of bringing our relatives into the Church is in demonstrating how our membership has benefited us and improved our own life. We need not preach the gospel to our relatives. All we need to do is to express our love for them. We must never drop them and think that it is useless and that they will never join the Church. We must never criticize them, neglect them, nor threaten them. We must take every opportunity to show them by our actions that we love them. We must express that love by word and by deed. If we practice our religion, it will help us to be healthier, happier, more considerate of others, more kind, more forgiving, more lovable, even wealthier than we were before. They cannot help but notice the change in us and will then want to know what caused such a change for the better in our life.

One of my missionaries came to me one day weeping

because he was so discouraged. He said that he was the
only member of his family in the Church. When he
joined the Church he was disowned, and now he was on a
mission on his own. The other elders received mail
regularly from their folks and letters of encouragement,
but he had nobody to write to him or to encourage him.
He felt rejected and all alone and was just about ready to
give up his mission. He said, "I don't know if I can take it
any longer. I love my family so much I am homesick and
want to quit." I asked him before he took that step to do
me a favor and write a letter home to his family every
week without fail. "They won't read my letters,
President. They just return them unopened." "Do you
really love them?" I asked. "With all my heart," he replied. Then I told him to write a short note every week
to his mother. "Don't preach to her; don't try to convert
her. Just tell her you love her and the rest of the family
and miss them, but write every week without fail." I told
him also to write a short personal note to his father telling him how much he loved him and how proud he was
to bear his name. "They'll never read them," he replied.
"Then write them a postcard and just tell them you love
them," I answered. "They will read the postcard."

He did this and was constant with his writing. He
followed my advice and did not preach to his family or
try to convert them. He just kept emphasizing how much
he loved them. Within a few months he was receiving
mail from home, and I advised him again to write nothing but love and appreciation and to express pride in his
family and in his family name. The family became more
and more interested. His father even sent him a little
money occasionally, and before long his parents asked
him what he was doing as he went about in his
missionary calling. One of his companions, after being
released, visited the family to bring them their son's love.
The family asked him about what their son was doing,
and he taught them. By the time the elder was ready to
be released, his family was awaiting his return so he

231

could come home and baptize them! We must remember that the blood that runs in our veins runs in the veins of our blood relatives. With patient and kind teaching, they will eventually join the Church, for they possess the same priesthood heritage we do.

Because Jeremiah the prophet understood that blood lineage is more important than other factors in bringing people to a knowledge of the truth, he wrote the following revelation: "Turn, O backsliding children, saith the Lord; for I am married unto you [you are part of my family]: and I will take you one of a city, and two of a family, and I will bring you to Zion: And I will give you pastors according to mine heart, which shall feed you with knowledge and understanding." (Jeremiah 3:14-15.) Everyone knows that more people live in a city than live in a family. Why didn't the Lord say two of a city and one of a family? It was because of that promise of a priesthood heritage blessing given to the children of the covenant. The family to which we belong is more important than where we live. Blood relationship constitutes a family treasure of promise right here on this earth that we must never overlook nor minimize. We must recognize this blessing and use it to help ourselves and others attain greater knowledge and blessings.

We can now conclude the revelation from which I have quoted so extensively with these challenging words of instruction and promise from the Lord: "Therefore, blessed are ye if ye continue in my goodness, a light unto the Gentiles, and through this priesthood a savior unto my people Israel. The Lord hath said it. Amen." (D&C 86:11.) In this final verse the Lord reminds us of two things. First he reminds us of our responsibility to do missionary work here on the earth. Second, he informs us that we are not only to be messengers of salvation to the living, but also saviors for our ancestors who went before us and who, though now dead, have paved the way whereby we might receive our present blessings. It is through the lineage rights promised them that we have

232

received our priesthood. The promise was made them that, even if they were born at a time and place where they could not hear the gospel preached in life, God would provide saviors for them from among their descendants so they could eventually receive all the blessings promised them. We are those saviors God promised through whom they can have every priesthood blessing as children of the promise.

In great measure those who enjoy present priesthood blessings have failed to realize their obligation to save their kindred dead. This is as much a priesthood responsibility as is our missionary obligation here in mortality. Only through us can they receive these blessings. They are totally dependent upon us to open the doors of exaltation for them. We must use the sealing power God has given us to unite into a complete family unit all the children of God who desire that blessing. If we neglect this priesthood responsibility, we do so at the peril of our own salvation. It was for this reason that Elijah restored the keys of the sealing power to the earth so that we could accomplish this work of salvation for our dead.

Thus, although the revelation to save the dead as well as the living was given right at the opening of this dispensation, it was not fully understood at that time. A full knowledge of the gospel developed slowly as it was revealed by the Lord line on line and precept by precept. Timing was important. First things had to be developed first. The Church of Jesus Christ had to be reestablished and church administration had to be organized. Then a people had to be gathered and the Church developed and strengthened. It took time to build and strengthen a people and to teach and prepare them for their future work.

Temples had to be built in which these sacred principles could be revealed and in which keys of authority could be obtained. That took people and time and peace and wealth. Now the Church is strong enough to build temples and to staff and use them. The time has come for

233

God to hasten this aspect of priesthood growth and development. Salvation and exaltation for the whole eternal family of God is the goal toward which everything has been pointed and toward which we have been working and preparing ourselves from the beginning. We must continue to gather the children of God now living on the earth. We must continue to strengthen them physically, mentally, morally, and spiritually so they will be prepared to go into the temples and there receive power with which to strengthen their earthly families. As this is done, they can thus be prepared to become saviors on Mount Zion to save not only their living relatives, but their kindred dead as well.

234

The total plan of God is to save *all* his children, where possible, in a family relationship. We must reconstruct our lineage eventually back to Adam, who made his covenant to become a son of Jesus Christ, who is the Only Begotten Son of God in the flesh. Gaps caused by unfaithful or disobedient ancestors will have to be closed through revelation from God. The end result will be that the family of God will be reconstituted or reorganized so that in the resurrection, all his *faithful children* will be sealed together in perfect family order.

God requires that we do this work. Joseph Smith explained the basis of how this was to be done:

. . . It is sufficient to know . . . that the earth will be smitten with a curse unless there is a welding link of some kind or other between the fathers and the children. . . . For we without them cannot be made perfect; neither can they without us be made perfect. . . . for it is necessary in the ushering in of the dispensation of the fulness of time . . . that a whole and complete and perfect union, and welding together of dispensations, and keys, and powers, and glories should take place, and be revealed from the days of Adam even to the present time. . . . (D&C 128:18.)

Do you see the urgency, as the second coming of Jesus Christ approaches, for us to become more actively engaged in this type of missionary work? We have spoken from time to time of salvation for the dead, but in great measure the family priesthood responsibility God has given us has been overlooked and neglected. We cannot neglect it any longer, for it is a vital part of God's overall missionary program. The need is real and increases in importance with each passing day. As children of the covenant, let us realize what a treasure God has reserved for us in his presence if we will only take seriously those lineage rights, blessings, and responsibilities which have come down to us through the ages. Let us listen to the voice of the Shepherd and respond with that willing service by means of which we can share in his glory by becoming saviors on Mount Zion, not only for the living but also for the dead.

235

23

Lines of Responsibility

In connection with our personal responsibilities to do genealogical and temple work, we should reflect on the magnitude of the task God has set before us. Consider the billions of people who have lived and died on this earth without an opportunity of hearing the gospel taught or of having the keys of priesthood administration. They were not prepared for celestial glory while they lived on the earth, for there was no power that could prepare them for celestial glory without those keys of the priesthood.

Accordingly they must go to a spirit prison where they will be confined, both good and bad, both righteous and unrighteous. All must go to paradise or the spirit world. It was to them that Jesus went to open the gates of the prison for their release. Ever since that time, worthy spirits of those who held the priesthood here on earth take that power with them into the spirit world to minister to those spirits, teaching them the gospel. Missionary work in the spirit world has to proceed under the direction of those who held the keys of the priesthood here on earth. These leaders are continually calling one person after another from the earth to aid them in this mighty task. Just as we must lengthen our stride and quicken the pace of missionary effort on the earth, so that missionary work in the spirit world must be expedited as the end approaches.

Those billions of spirits must be taught. Opportunity

must be given them to hear the gospel taught in a manner and under such conditions that they can understand and comprehend it. If through carelessness or indifference on earth we have failed our missionary responsibility here, then that lack must be filled there. God is a just God and will not condemn or punish one of his children for something over which that child had no control. Nevertheless, though the gospel is taught and explained to those in the spirit world, there are bounds set beyond which they cannot pass. The necessary ordinance work for salvation is a mortal work that must be done in the flesh. Baptisms, washings, anointings, endowment covenants, commitments, and sealings must all be completed on earth. It takes as much work and effort to save a dead person as it does to save a living person. Just as that ordinance work must be done individually by a person living on the earth, so it must be done individually for a person who is dead.

237

Billions of spirits are thus looking to us to perform the necessary ordinance work on earth that will release them, after they have accepted the gospel, from their present confinement. Not all those spirits are willing or ready yet to accept this vicarious work done in their behalf, but I am certain that there are so many millions of spirits now waiting on us to release them that it would shock us if we only knew the extent of the work waiting for us to do on earth. At the time of this writing, about 50,000,000 people die annually. We perform slightly more than three million endowments for the dead annually at present, so we are not even keeping up with those who die, let alone reducing the backlog of previous years and generations. It takes little imagination to see why this work for the dead must increase in volume and in rapidity.

How can we ever accomplish so great a task? It can be done only by breaking the work down into manageable portions. In attempting to arrive at a decision as to the responsibilities of individual Church members for genealogical and temple work, we must restudy what has already been revealed and explained concerning this responsibility. The opening revelation of the coming of Elijah gives us a clue:

Behold, I will reveal unto you the Priesthood, by the hand of Elijah the prophet, before the coming of the great and dreadful day of the Lord.

And he shall plant in the hearts of the children the promises made to the fathers, and the hearts of the children shall turn to their fathers.

If it were not so, the whole earth would be utterly wasted at his coming. (D&C 2.)

238

Those promises made to the family of God as a whole apply particularly to the individual, as do all of God's promises. Exaltation is an individual and not a group achievement. While group action can and does aid in the overall organization of the work, it is the individual action of a person for his own family members that determines his or her final judgment. Note that the hearts of the children then are to turn to *their* fathers and mothers, and not to the ancestors belonging to someone else.

When the next statement was given on December 6, 1832, it again emphasized the individual nature of the responsibility for those of one's own lineage.

Therefore, thus saith the Lord unto you, with whom the priesthood hath continued through the lineage of *your* fathers—

For ye are lawful heirs, according to the flesh, and have been hid from the world with Christ in God—

Therefore your life and the priesthood have remained, and must needs remain *through you and your lineage* until the restoration of all things spoken by the mouths of all the holy prophets since the world began.

Therefore, blessed are ye if ye continue in my goodness, a light unto the Gentiles, and through this priesthood a savior unto my people Israel. The Lord hath said it. Amen. (D&C 86:8-11. Italics added.)

Again we can see that although the principle applies to all the covenant children of God, it is the individual's particular lineage and not his general lineage as a child of God that determines his responsibility as a savior for his family.

On March 28, 1835, further information was given concerning the patriarchal order of the priesthood that is the culminating work within the temple as families are sealed together.

The order of this [patriarchal] priesthood was confirmed to be handed down from father to son, and rightly *belongs to the literal descendants* of the chosen seed, to whom the promises were made.

This order was instituted in the days of Adam, and came down *by lineage* in the following manner:

239

From Adam to Seth, who was ordained by Adam at the age of sixty-nine years, and was blessed by him three years prior to his (Adam's) death, and received the promise of God by his father, that his posterity should be the chosen of the Lord, and that they *should be preserved unto the end of the earth.* (D&C 107:40-42. Italics added.)

This revelation limits the rights to those priesthood promises in the patriarchal order to one lineage and not to all the children of God.

On April 3, 1836, the promise of the right to share in this priesthood order within the Melchizedek Priesthood was fulfilled when Elias restored the keys of the Abrahamic order and Elijah restored the sealing power. (D&C 110:12-16). Almost two years later, in March 1838, the statement was again made that the priesthood belongs to Zion as a lineage right. (D&C 113:8.) Then, on September 1 and 16, 1842, Joseph Smith revealed in letters to the Church, recorded in sections 127 and 128 of the Doctrine and Covenants, the doctrine of baptism for the dead. Therein he explained that the welding or binding link which joins together the family of God involves the sealing ordinances for individual families. After quoting Paul in Hebrews 11:40 concerning the dead, he wrote:

. . . For we without them [referring to our own family members] cannot be made perfect, neither can they without us be made perfect. Neither can they nor we be made perfect without those who have died in the gospel also [showing our general obligation to all members of the Church]; for it is necessary in the ushering in of the dispensation of the fulness of times, which dispensation is now beginning to usher in, that a whole and complete and perfect union, and welding together of dispensations, and keys, and powers, and glories should take place, and be revealed from Adam even to the present time. (D&C 128:18.)

In closing this second letter the Prophet wrote:

240

. . . Let us, therefore, as a church and a people [taking care of the general aspects of the work], and as Latter-day Saints [working individually for our own families], offer unto the Lord an offering in righteousness [performing this work of salvation in the temples]; and let us present in his holy temple, when it is finished, a book containing the records of *our* dead, which shall be worthy of all acceptation. (D&C 128:24. Italics added.)

Thus there appear to be separate responsibilities implicit in the Church working cooperatively together as a whole, and as individual Latter-day Saints working separately within our own families, to prepare a written record of completed temple ordinance work that makes possible the exaltation of "our" dead, which I take to mean those of our own lineage.

The significance of the new and everlasting covenant of marriage was given in Doctrine and Covenants 131:1-4 on May 6 and 17, 1843. On July 12 of that same year the great revelation on the sealing power was given as it pertains to marriage for eternity. The eternal nature of that ordinance was explained and instructions were given to faithful Church members regarding the promise made to Abraham: "This promise [originally given to Abraham] is yours also, because ye are of Abraham, and the promise was made unto Abraham; and by this law is the continuation of the works of my Father, wherein he glorifieth himself. Go ye, therefore, and do the works of Abraham; enter ye into my law and ye shall be saved." (D&C 132:31-32.) The fulfillment of this promise was

made possible by the restoration of the keys of the patriarchal dispensation of the gospel of Abraham by Elias,
as noted in Doctrine and Covenants 110:12.

We should remember how Abraham sought for his
personal patriarchal rights according to his lineage
(Abraham 1:2-4), and how the Lord promised Abraham
that as many as receive the gospel would be called after
his name, be accepted as his seed (Abraham 2:10), and receive his priesthood blessing:

. . . and in thy seed (that is, thy Priesthood), for I give unto
thee a promise that this right shall continue in thee, and in thy
seed after thee (that is to say, the literal seed, or the seed of
the body) shall all the families of the earth be blessed, even
with the blessings of the Gospel, which are the blessings of salvation, even of life eternal. (Abraham 2:11.)

Seed can be singular, referring to "the Seed," or Jesus
Christ, but it is also plural and refers to the posterity of
Abraham, as is clear from the above scripture. So important is this work of salvation for our own kindred
ancestors who are dead that Joseph Smith declared:
"This doctrine was the burden of the scriptures. Those
Saints who neglect it in behalf of their deceased relatives,
do it at the peril of their own salvation." (*History of the
Church*, 4:426.) The Prophet again emphasized the personal or family obligation we have to do this work for our
own kindred dead.

The Prophet Joseph Smith explained how this work
was to be done, in the following words:

But how are they to become saviors on Mount Zion? By
building their temples, erecting their baptismal fonts, and going forth and receiving all the ordinances, baptisms, confirma-
tions, washings, anointings, ordinations and sealing powers
upon their heads in behalf of all *their* progenitors who are
dead, and redeem *them* that *they* may come forth in the first
resurrection and be exalted to thrones of glory with them; and
herein is the chain that binds the hearts of the fathers to the
children, and the children to the fathers, which fulfills the
mission of Elijah. (*History of the Church*, 6:184. Italics added.)

This chaining effect plainly defines the family nature of

this responsibility, and the above statement makes clear that it is our personal responsibility to take care of members of our own individual family lineage.

Brigham Young, who followed Joseph Smith, was even more outspoken about our personal responsibility for our own deceased ancestors. People so often speak of a generalized responsibility for genealogical and temple work that it is refreshing to see how Brigham Young pins this work down as a personal responsibility.

242

We have a work to do just as important in its sphere as the Savior's work was in its sphere. Our fathers cannot be made perfect without us; we cannot be made perfect without them. They have done their work and now sleep. We are now called upon to do ours; which is to be the greatest work [I think he means the largest task] man ever performed in the earth. . . .

. . . There must be this chain in the holy Priesthood; it must be welded together from the latest generation that lives on the earth back to Father Adam, to bring back all that can be saved and placed where they can receive salvation and a glory in some kingdom. This Priesthood has to do it; this Priesthood is for this purpose. . . .

The ordinance of sealing must be performed here man to man, and woman to man, and children to parents, etc., *until the chain of generation is made perfect* in the sealing ordinances back to Father Adam. . . .

. . . Now, all you children, are you looking to the salvation of *your* fathers? Are you seeking diligently to redeem those who have died without the Gospel, inasmuch as *they* sought the Lord Almighty to obtain promises for *you?* For *our* fathers did obtain promises that *their* seed should not be forgotten. O ye children of the fathers, look at these things. *You are to enter into the temples of the Lord and officiate for your forefathers.* (*Discourses of Brigham Young,* comp. John A. Widtsoe, Deseret Book Co., 1946, pp. 406-8.)

Despite the clarity of this exposition, the doctrine was not followed by members of the Church. Church members in the early days, not understanding such matters, wanted to assure themselves of a faithful family ancestry. Accordingly they had themselves sealed to prominent men and women in the Church who had proved their faithfulness during their lives. People thought that in this manner they could assure themselves of a righteous family association in the celestial kingdom.

This practice became very disturbing to President Wilford Woodruff, for it appeared to violate the instructions given as to the patriarchal nature of the welding or sealing link. He sought the Lord in prayer to receive an answer as to what should be done in the matter of such sealings. The Lord told him that to go outside of one's patriarchal lineage was wrong. Now along with presenting the matter to the people, President Woodruff took action. First he stated the principle; then he explained how progression comes through implementing this principle and promise. Following this, he explained what future action should be taken by Church members in regard to such sealings, and finally he stated how united the leaders of the Church were in support of this action.

Joseph Smith . . . told us that there must be a welding link of all dispensations and of the work of God from one generation to another. This was upon his mind more than most any other subject that was given to him.

In my prayer the Lord revealed to me that it was my duty to say to all Israel to carry this principle out, and in fulfilment of that revelation I lay it before this people.

I say to all men who are laboring in these temples, carry out this principle and then we will make one step in advance of what we have had before.

Myself and counselors conversed upon this and were agreed upon it, and afterwards we laid it before all the apostles who were here . . . and the Lord revealed to every one of these men . . . that that was the word of the Lord to them. I never met with anything in my life in this Church that there was more unity upon than there was upon that principle. They all feel right about it, and that it is our duty. That is one principle that should be carried out from this time henceforth. . . .

We want the Latter-day Saints from this time to trace *their* genealogies as far as they can, and to be sealed *to their fathers and mothers*. Have children sealed to *their* parents and *run this chain through as far as you can get it*. . . . This is the will of the Lord to his people, and I think when you come to reflect upon it you will find it to be true. (*The Discourses of Wilford Woodruff*, Bookcraft, 1946, pp. 156-57. Italics added.)

This doctrine and definition of personal responsibility to the progenitors of our own lineage is so clear that no one could misunderstand it. Yet, if there is one major problem we have in the Genealogical Department of the Church even today, it is the desire of some people to build a huge book of remembrance of names they have gathered and for whom they have done temple work. They have gathered names wherever they could instead of turning their hearts to their own fathers and mothers. They have interfered with the rights of others to do this work for their own kindred dead. By so doing they have sometimes sown dissension and resentment among the members of the Church and have often brought confusion and disorder into the compiling of our records for the dead. We need to emphasize again these principles taught so clearly by these prophets concerning the personal nature of our responsibilities to save *our* kindred dead.

Each prophet of the Church since the time of Wilford Woodruff has expressed himself in a like manner, pointing out the personal responsibility we have of doing work for our own ancestry. This same doctrine is taught today by our present leaders. Recent instructions were given by Elder Mark E. Petersen of the Council of the Twelve, who quoted Joseph Smith as follows:

. . . as soon as the Temple and baptismal font are prepared [Joseph Smith was referring to the construction of the Nauvoo Temple], we calculate to give the Elders of Israel their washings and anointings, and attend to those last and more impressive ordinances, without which we cannot obtain celestial thrones. But there must be a holy place prepared for that purpose. . . . for every man who wishes to save his father, mother, brothers, sisters and friends, must go through all the ordinances for each one of them separately, the same as for himself, from baptism to ordination, washings and anointings,

and receive all the keys and powers of the Priesthood. . . .
(*History of the Church*, 6:319.)

Elder Petersen then commented on the personal nature of this work as given in this quotation from Joseph Smith.

Do you see how personalized this work must be? Do you see how personalized it must always remain? For each one of them personally, he says. We must go through all of the ordinances for each one of them separately, the same as for himself, from baptism to ordination, washings and anointings, and receive all the keys and power of the priesthood, for it is a personalized work for us. It's a personalized work for our ancestors, and we individually are personally charged with the responsibility of saving our own particular dead. I am not charged with saving your dead and you are not charged with saving my dead. But I *am* charged with saving *my* own, and *you* are charged with saving *your* own. Therefore we must personally take an individual interest in our own ancestors.

We have this individual personalized responsibility for our own ancestors. Inasmuch as we have that, no matter what the developments are in the world, no matter what the developments may be with respect to electronics or computers, or men in orbits around the earth, no matter what may happen in the world, God will not change this responsibility for us. We are personally and individually held accountable, and just as baptism will never change, so our responsibility for our dead will never change, and everyone is charged with that responsibility, and it's personalized. (Address delivered at the Genealogical Association Conference, October 4, 1962.)

In October 1975 when Elder Petersen was giving genealogical instruction to the Regional Representatives of the Twelve, he again emphasized the personal nature of our responsibilities toward our own ancestors. These are powerful and moving words and leave no doubts as to our personal responsibility to control and supervise genealogical and temple work for our direct ancestors.

It is astounding to hear so many people tell me their genealogical work is all completed. They say: "We have exhausted all the record sources and there is nothing left for us to do. Others in our family have taken care of our

245

responsibility." I hear this often and am reminded of the following words from a modern prophet:

Those who thoughtfully consider the work inquire about those names that cannot be collected. "What about those for whom no record was ever kept? Surely you will fail there. There is no way you can search out those names."

To this I simply observe, "You have forgotten revelation." Already we have been directed to many records through that process. Revelation comes to individual members as they are led to discover their family records in ways that are miraculous indeed. And there is a feeling of inspiration attending this work that can be found in no other. When we have done all that we can do we will be given the rest. *The way will be opened up.* (Boyd K. Packer, general conference address, October 1975, in *Ensign*, November 1975, p. 99.)

The Genealogical Department is gathering records daily in many ways from all over the earth. There is a constant flood of new and important information pouring into the genealogical library in the form of books, pamphlets, maps, pictures, records, film, and even tapes and oral genealogies that we did not know existed in the past. New procedures and new methods of research are being developed that now enable us to compile genealogies with greater accuracy. We can now use genealogical records more effectively some of which were not even known about ten years ago. As research methods and procedures have improved and as new information has become available, we have discovered errors in previous genealogical research that have resulted in incorrect sealings. We have sealed the wrong people together, and such errors need to be corrected. Often such errors have resulted in overlooking some members of our own families who are thus left without the necessary ordinance work done in their behalf.

President Woodruff was appalled at the magnitude of the work to be done for his ancestry. He realized that he personally could not do all this work himself. When he enquired of the Lord, it was explained to him that he could secure help from other Church members. In the revelation in section 128 the way is pointed out that we are not only to work individually, but also as a church and as a people. As Latter-day Saints, we are to help each other. We can assist one another in the temples by doing ordinance work not only for our own lineage, but for the lineage of others. It is true that our personal responsibility is to see that the work is done for our own ancestry, but there is nothing in the scriptures that prohibits us from obtaining aid from others or from giving aid to our brothers and sisters to speed this work.

Some people are physically handicapped, some lack language abilities, and others find themselves involved with complex research problems that require the help of specialists. Some may be so heavily involved with Church leadership and administrative responsibilities that it becomes difficult to find the extended time necessary to do personal genealogical research in complex areas. Such persons can seek and obtain aid from experts who can perform such service for them. However, the responsibility for such work still rests with the individual. He must maintain control and assume the responsibility to see that such work is done accurately and carefully. Paid research by experts working in the field of genealogy is one of the ways we have of gathering information about our ancestors for temple ordinance work. Such genealogical research must never be left as a blanket responsibility of the researcher. The control must always remain in the hands of the person who requests that work to be done for him. If I were to hire an accredited researcher to do my work for me, I would request a monthly report from the researcher as to what was done, what records were searched, and what were the results. I would not only insist on a financial and record accounting, but I would require that all names so found be properly entered on entry forms and given to me so that I could personally examine them and so that I could report them to my high priest group leader and then submit them to the Genealogical Department myself for processing. I would not just leave these important matters in the hands of another person, no matter how much I trusted and respected him. This is my personal responsibility and I would act accordingly.

The Church itself, in order to keep the work moving through the temples, gathers names of individuals and prepares them for temple ordinance work. Such work is usually concentrated on records where there is a high rate of duplication, with resulting increased costs both to the individual and to the Church in processing the records. This work is an assistance to the Saints, for it is carefully indexed as it is completed. Individual Latter-day Saints can search this indexed record to see if the work done for any given individual fits into their family lineage. If so, a proper notation can be made on that person's individual record and research can then be directed to other individuals to complete the lineage line. The work done by the Church as a whole in submitting records for temple ordinance work can be done only for a portion of the children of Israel. It is done for individuals as an aid to Church members in general in speeding the process of handling the bulk of temple work that has to be done in this generation. It can never take the place of lineage research in building the patriarchal order. The work done by the Genealogical Department has to be limited to readily available records where bulk input is possible and needed.

In the Genealogical Department we speak of collateral lines, which are different from direct lines of ancestry. Collateral lines involve cousin relationships and similar branches from our main or direct lines of ancestry. Because such persons are relatives or relatives-in-law, there is a strong desire of Church members to gather these collateral names and perform temple ordinance work for them. Church leaders are sympathetic and understanding in such matters. For this reason certain privileges have been extended Church members whereby they may do work of this nature on a limited basis. It should be pointed out that our collateral relatives are someone else's direct ancestors. Carried too far, we begin to intrude on the rights of others. It is for this reason that the Genealogical Department discourages collateral research and name submission for temple ordinance work. It is just not logical to state that if we do not do this work it will never be done. This statement is incorrect. It is the personal responsibility of our relatives to do genealogical research and temple ordinance work for their direct ancestors, just as it is our responsibility to perform this service for our direct ancestors. God will not hold us responsible for someone else's duties. He will hold us responsible for our own lineage lines. Let us be orderly then, and perform our own labors and permit others to perform theirs. It is not only their responsibility—it is their right of precedence that entitles them to have this privilege.

249

At the beginning of this chapter a statement was made concerning the magnitude of this work. That huge task becomes manageable if each family would perform the work for its particular family line. When we try to do everything for everyone all at once, the task becomes impossible. If I try to do someone else's work, not only will I not succeed because of my interference in their work, but I will also neglect my own. As we cross lines of responsibility, confusion results and the tremendous duplication of time and effort and money spent in this manner causes waste and inefficiency. If we follow the direction of the prophets and assume our own individual responsibility for the work in our own family, the task can and will be accomplished in an orderly fashion.

24

The Family Organization

In any discussion of genealogical research, the first question asked is: How do I get started? A general rule in learning any subject is to start with what we already know and proceed from there. Several years ago the Genealogical Department began to organize what is known as the four-generation program. This was designed as a teaching program to familiarize Church members with the kind of information needed for genealogical and temple work and to acquaint them with the various forms used in compiling and organizing this information for use.

To understand this program, we need a "road map" leading into the family to show us where we fit into the overall family organization. The four-generation program thus begins with a pedigree chart, which demonstrates visually our immediate family lineage lines. It can be diagrammed in a simple manner as follows.

We have two parents, four grandparents, and eight great-grandparents, the number of ancestors doubling with each generation. In order to keep the work simple, the program was limited to these first four generations. By the use of this diagram, one can see that we have many lineage lines, but to begin with we can first concentrate our efforts on only one of these lines, in order to become familiar with it and to simplify the learning process. That line can be our surname, which we inherit

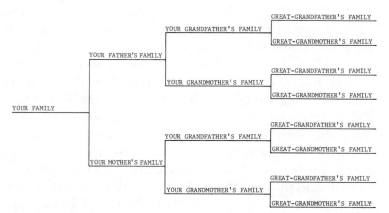

		GREAT-GRANDFATHER'S FAMILY
	YOUR GRANDFATHER'S FAMILY	
		GREAT-GRANDMOTHER'S FAMILY
YOUR FATHER'S FAMILY		
		GREAT-GRANDFATHER'S FAMILY
	YOUR GRANDMOTHER'S FAMILY	
		GREAT-GRANDMOTHER'S FAMILY
YOUR FAMILY		
		GREAT-GRANDFATHER'S FAMILY
	YOUR GRANDFATHER'S FAMILY	
		GREAT-GRANDMOTHER'S FAMILY
YOUR MOTHER'S FAMILY		
		GREAT-GRANDFATHER'S FAMILY
	YOUR GRANDMOTHER'S FAMILY	
		GREAT-GRANDMOTHER'S FAMILY

from our father. Or, if we desire, we can choose the surname that is the maiden name of our mother for our own particular field of genealogical interest as we begin the learning process.

Each line on the family pedigree chart represents a complete family unit. As we go back into each line of our ancestry for each surname, we open up a new direct surname line with each new generation. The information about the individual members who constitute each particular family unit can be compiled on a family group record form as shown by the sample reproduced here.

It is felt that if a person were to hold one of these family group record forms in his hands and complete the form for his own immediate family by filling in the necessary information, he would become familiar with the simple type of information needed and would lose all fear of the unknown. Beginning genealogy is not a complicated task. The information required is simple and usually it is easily obtained, since most of it is already known and can be written down from memory. One need not look up information from any other source than from information to be found in or around the home. After that first family group sheet has been completed, the others follow logically as we gather information from living relatives or from sources readily available to most Latter-day Saints.

There were several reasons for inaugurating this familiarization program. The main reason was that it begins with one's own family and, if used, removes fear of the unknown and proves to the Saints that the beginning of this work is neither difficult nor too time-consuming. It was felt this four-generation program would:

1. Stimulate and encourage Church members to become actively engaged in the work of family exaltation.

2. Provide research training through actual experience in searching for genealogical records within the immediate family.

3. Provide a basis for assembling these records into a personal book of remembrance and so develop a visual representation of our close affinity with immediate and near ancestors and their families.

4. Give Church members an opportunity to verify the accuracy and completeness of existing family and church genealogical and temple records.

5. Provide necessary information so temple ordinance work not already performed could be completed for eligible families.

6. Assist in building a reference file (as copies of these records are sent to the Genealogical Department for filing and microfilming) to aid future generations and recent converts in compiling their genealogies.

7. Motivate Latter-day Saints to catch the spirit of priest-

hood genealogical work and qualify themselves to complete their own temple ordinances and so be able to become saviors for their own kindred dead.

This program has helped many people to get started in genealogical work and has been well worth the time and effort to collect this information.

Another effective way to get started in genealogical and temple work is to begin writing a personal history of one's own life. Such a simple assignment becomes an interesting and absorbing hobby. Once started, it is amazing how much we can remember of our own life history. One may not think that his life is very interesting to others, but rest assured it will be. This writing will become more interesting as we begin to recall and write down those things that have happened to us during our lifetime. It will also become a treasure chest of information for our children and grandchildren. They are more interested in us than we imagine and want to know more about us and what we did when we were their age. What problems did we have and how did we solve them? They will refer to it often, and in years to come it will recall fond memories to them as they read it to their children and remember their own experiences shared with us. We ourselves will want to use that history, or tell a particular story from it, in family home evening as we share experiences with members of our family. This becomes extremely important if we write in our life story some of the spiritual experiences we have had, or thoughts as they came to us in quiet moments as we thought about life and its meaning to us. One cannot write such a book without questions coming to one's mind: Where do I come from? Who are my progenitors? What did they do? This leads automatically to a desire to know more about our family and forebears.

Such a life history is one that *every* person can write. With tape recorders so readily available, all we have to do is to talk into the machine and one of our family can transcribe it for us. We know our own life story better than anyone else does. This book, simple as it may be,

253

will lead one into the four-generation program and then into compiling a personal book of remembrance for himself and his family. This is how one gets started in genealogical work. It begins with curiosity and develops into an interesting and absorbing hobby. In our case as a member of the Church, this activity becomes more than an interesting hobby. It becomes a valuable tool in preserving for ourselves and for our posterity that information which leads to that tremendous treasure of eternal life for which we should all be seeking.

254

President Spencer W. Kimball has long recognized the importance of maintaining a personal journal that can serve as a basis for compiling such a personal history.

Your journal is your autobiography, so it should be kept carefully. You are unique, and there may be incidents in your experience that are more noble and praiseworthy in their way than those recorded in any other life. There may be a flash of illumination here and a story of faithfulness there; you should truthfully record your real self and not what other people may see in you.

Your story should be written now while it is fresh and while the true details are available. . . .

What could you do better for your children and your children's children than to record the story of your life, your triumphs over adversity, your recovery after a fall, your progress when all seemed black, your rejoicing when you had finally achieved? ("The Angels May Quote from it," *New Era*, October 1975, p. 5.)

We need to remember how the Savior, when he appeared on the American continent, reprimanded those who kept the records because they had not recorded some of the very important things that had transpired. Family records are important, or those genealogies already preserved in the scriptures would not have been recorded therein and preserved as we now have them. Some may think the "begats" are not very interesting, but they must be important or God would not have had them preserved in the scripture the way they are. Someday we will understand why they are there preserved. If we begin with either or both of these simple programs mentioned above, we will be led to compile our own family records, which can be the basis for the work of exalting our fathers and mothers through temple service.

Genealogical and temple work is a family-centered activity. There is good reason for the ever-increasing emphasis being placed on the family by our Church officials. The family is the prime foundation upon which the Church is built. The gospel of Jesus Christ is a family plan. The only way this work of exaltation of God's children can be achieved is by strengthening the family in the home. Fathers and mothers must "come back home" from those many activities into which our modern society has taken them. Outside activities and interests have taken parents out of the home and have left children on their own to fend for themselves as best they can. This is wrong. It is one of the tools Satan is using to attempt to destroy the plan of salvation. It is done so gradually and insidiously that we do not realize what is happening until it is too late and the damage has already been done. We should be eternally grateful for wise prophets of God who recognize the dangers involved. They are trying to get us to return to the way of the Lord. We must listen and obey these warning voices, for God will not be mocked.

Priesthood leadership begins in the home with the father as the patriarch or head of the family. If the father abdicates this position of leadership, his home can never be truly happy and successful. Fatherhood is leadership—the most important kind of leadership there is. Fatherhood based on sacred covenants is the only job assignment a priesthood holder has from which he will not be eventually released. Patriarchal leadership based on love and kindness has been important in the past and will continue to be so in the future. The father, assisted and counseled and encouraged by the mother standing by his side, must preside in the home. It is not a question of ability, worthiness, or strength. It is simply a matter of order, appointment, and responsibility. The father is to

255

preside at family prayer, at the table as grace is spoken, in the family home evening as he is guided by the Holy Spirit to give direction. He is to see that his children are taught correct principles and that they are given directions and counsel to guide them in their daily lives. He is to take an active part in establishing family rules and discipline, in teaching children the principles of salvation and respect for righteous authority. He must plan how to cultivate love, consideration, and service among family members. That is what the patriarchal order is all about.

256

Genealogical work begins within this immediate family. As we work with the records close to us, individual family members can cooperate in compiling a family book of remembrance. The four-generation program is an excellent guide for this activity. The basic family gathering for the immediate family is the weekly family home evening. Some of these meetings can be devoted to gathering and recording genealogical information and in teaching children about family goals and objectives. The genealogy of the children differs from that of either parent, since it is a combination of the two. As a result of work done in a consistent manner in some of the family home evenings, each child before he leaves the home will have his or her own personal book of remembrance. This book will contain a personal record, a pedigree chart of the first four generations, and the fifteen family group sheets that constitute the four-generation program. Each child will thus be firmly anchored in the family and will begin to have a concept of his or her responsibility to "turn their hearts to their fathers." They will also have begun their own life story and will be prepared to understand the meaning of the gospel message as it affects their own personal lives.

It is in this immediate family unit that the basic programs of the Church have their beginning. It is in the basic family that money is saved and boys and young men are trained for missionary service. It is in the immediate family that food and clothing are stored and prepared for welfare emergencies. It is in the immediate family that the children are taught the gospel, family prayers are said, social activity within the Church begins, and family members are encouraged and taken to Church meetings, socials, conferences, and assemblies. It is in this intimate circle that the book of remembrance is initiated and the groundwork for genealogical activity is laid. Within these first few generations there is practically no duplication of effort, and accurate information is most readily obtained and recorded. In this circle there is no waste of time or effort in pursuing this activity.

257

The next level of family activity we might call the "living family association." It is on the grandfather-grandmother level, where several immediate families bind themselves together in a closely knit family association. Instead of meeting together every week, this larger family meets together only for special occasions, such as holidays, birthdays, or other family anniversaries. The missionary effort on this level is less intimate, but family members do assist one another to see that no worthy son within any of these families is deprived of an opportunity to serve on a mission. Welfare service is less detailed and is usually confined to assisting an individual family when some emergency occurs, or to help this or that family member in a special time of crisis. The genealogical activity at this level becomes a little more difficult. Usually one of the immediate families will be assigned research on one limited family surname and another family to another surname to avoid duplication of effort, time, and money. In such larger family associations there must be more carefully organized genealogical work and some specialization begins to take place, usually under the direction of the grandfather or other specially appointed person who is chosen to direct the total family genealogical effort. In this type of family organization, as genealogical work is done, that information is shared; and as pedigree charts and family group sheets are prepared, they are duplicated and distributed to individual families to place in their family books of remembrance. Excursions to do temple work are done in groups more than on an individual basis. We might speak of this as a "living family organization" because all members know each other well, have close associations, and can work well together as a team.

The traditional family organization with which we are most familiar when we speak of a family organization is usually a surname organization. In the Church this type of organization is found principally among those of pioneer ancestry. This type of organization holds the typical family reunion. One of the biggest problems with this organization is that we try to get too many generations together at the same time. We try to include all family members back to the third and fourth great-grandparents and to treat them as though they were members of an intimate family. We forget that they are strangers to each other and usually have little in common to bind them together other than a common name and heritage. Such an organization is just too cumbersome to work effectively for gospel instruction, nor is it very well suited for missionary or for welfare purposes. It is simply too large and the problems to be handled are much too complex. Such a family, however, does have a definite purpose for controlling and directing family genealogical searches.

In the traditional family association just described, there is much duplication of ancestry within the family. Unless genealogical work in such a family is well organized, genealogists working within such family lineage lines waste an enormous amount of time, money, and effort in duplicating work already done by others. When such duplicate names are submitted to the Church for processing, it is very expensive to check them through the Genealogical Department to prepare them for temple ordinance work. The larger the Church becomes and the more temples we build, the more expensive this duplicative effort becomes. However, with proper organization, such traditional family associations can make a

258

great contribution to order in performing genealogical research.

By pooling together the financial resources of the surname organization, sizable sums can be accumulated for genealogical research. By appointing genealogists to control research along given family lineage lines, duplication can be reduced and family funds channeled where they will accomplish effective results. Usually on this level of genealogical research, we go back in time to the point where records are not so plentiful. What records do exist are more difficult to read and interpret because of writing differences and the ravages of time. Often language problems are found in the study of these records that require the services of persons who know and understand those languages and are skilled in genealogical research methods in those particular geographical areas. If each member of the family would contribute regularly a given sum of money to the organization for combined family genealogical research, rather rapid progress could be made on one line after another. Gaps could be closed and pedigree lineage lines extended, resulting in additional opportunities for temple ordinance work.

As these records are completed, the family genealogists can submit them to the Genealogical Department for clearance for ordinance work. These names can be reserved at the temple in the family file for use of the family members as they go to the temples. Members of the family can simply request such names and have the satisfaction of doing temple work for their own kindred dead. Family pedigree charts and family group record sheets can then be printed and furnished to individual family members at reasonable costs. Family members can then see how the work for their own family lineage is being extended and thus avoid personal duplication of genealogical research efforts already done.

Another thing the traditional family can do with its size and resources is to gather, print, and publish biographies and histories of the family and its members.

259

Publication of such books becomes too time-consuming and much too expensive for the "living family" organization or for the immediate family organization. But with bulk printing and the ability to print, bind, and distribute such books on a larger scale, such activity is made possible on terms most family members can well afford. There are advantages for each one of these different types of family organization. Each has its important place to fill in genealogical research.

260

It would appear, then, that our personal responsibility to see that the genealogical and temple work done for our direct ancestors is one principally of organization and control. We first have to identify our own place in the family lineage so we know where to begin our own work. The next step is to gather our own immediate family into the Church. If they are living, our duty and obligation is to bring them into the Church through love, kindness, and patient, long-continuous striving. That will fill our duty in assisting to exalt the living. They in turn will also be able to assist us in the remainder of our duties. Our next responsibility is to our immediate ancestors who are dead. These we usually know, or we are close enough to them in time that we can obtain information about them sufficient to identify them for temple ordinance work. Thus our duty and privilege appears to be self-evident—to go to the temples and there, as saviors, to redeem our kindred dead, particularly those we know either through personal knowledge or from family tradition.

Our next responsibility is to organize our living families so that by working cooperatively together we can gather the information for those more distant, direct ancestors for whom we have a joint responsibility. The whole spirit of the gospel is to learn how to work together in love. Nowhere is this cooperative spirit more necessary than within a family relationship. As far as we are able to make these sacrifices of providing the means and the personnel to search out our ancestry in a joint effort, we are fulfilling our personal responsibility toward our family. It should be the desire and the effort of all family members who are qualified to do so to go to the temples and there perform, as far as possible, the temple work for their own ancestry. We thus fulfill our personal obligations as saviors for our own progenitors and our hearts have been certainly "turned to our fathers." There are limits, however, as to how far this work can be done by us as individuals. I think the Lord expects us to do all we can. If one of us has a shovel and another has a bull-dozer to work with, the Lord will not expect us to perform the same amount of work. Some people have more time, money, and ability to do genealogical research than others. The Lord understands this and so should we. When there are limits to what we can accomplish, we should know that as long as we do our best, the Lord will be pleased with us.

261

25

The Church as a Family

There are limits in genealogical research and temple activity beyond which we cannot presently go. No matter how large, strong, or wealthy a family organization becomes, it does not have the resources nor the authority to build temples for the redemption of the dead. No family organization is strong enough to found a genealogical library large enough to meet all the possible needs of the large family. No family could afford to spend the millions of dollars it takes to find, collect, microfilm, index, and store the needed genealogical records for extended genealogical research. At the time of this writing the microfilming effort of the Church results annually in the production of enough feet of primary genealogical information on microfilm to reach from San Francisco, California, to Halifax, Nova Scotia. Not only must the raw film be purchased, but it must also be exposed, developed, printed, examined for quality and completeness, indexed for use, and stored for safekeeping. The genealogical library of the Church is the largest genealogical library in the world. It has the capability of establishing branch genealogical libraries anywhere in the world where stake leaders request such service for their people. More than two hundred such branch libraries have been established and accredited.

Temples are being constructed at an ever-increasing

rate. Predictions have been made by prophets of God that they shall eventually dot the earth. This presupposes a magnitude of genealogical work and temple activity far greater than any of us can now comprehend. Yet the work must be done. Certainly the Lord implements his work in different ways at different times. As the kingdom of God grows, the work progresses. As circumstances change, the Lord will give the Church further guidance and direction in this work. Ways and means will be provided so that temple ordinances can be performed for those hundreds of millions of worthy dead who will request that these exalting ordinances be done in their behalf. New answers to our genealogical research endeavors seem essential, and new means of implementation of the Lord's commandment to his people to "save their kindred dead" will be revealed.

263

One of the objectives of this book has been to point out that members of the Church are members of the family of Jesus Christ. Those who join the Church make their covenant to become brothers and sisters as children of Jesus Christ. The Church therefore becomes a family organization with family responsibilities as a church to "save their kindred dead." There are certain general responsibilities the Church has in regard to genealogical and temple ordinance work that extend beyond the possibilities of the traditional family, the living family, or the immediate family organization discussed in the last chapter. By covenant we become by adoption the literal seed of Jesus Christ and children of Abraham with lineage responsibilities. We find this emphasized as we do genealogical research and observe how the genealogies of Church members merge as we go back in time. The concept of having the blood of Israel in our veins is a very real thing. In effect, we are all heirs through ultimately the same lineage of the same fathers.

For this reason there must be certain work expected of the Church as a whole that extends beyond that which we can do as individuals or as members of family organizations. I believe this is what the Lord had reference to as Joseph Smith wrote:

. . . Let us, therefore, as a church and a people [speaking to us collectively, to the family of God as a whole], and as Latter-day Saints [speaking to us individually], offer unto the Lord an offering in righteousness; and let us present in his temple, when it is finished, a book containing the records of our dead, which is worthy of all acceptation. (D&C 128:24.)

To me this means that when all this genealogical and temple work has been finally accomplished, there will be one central book prepared in which all this work will be recorded. Individuals will be recorded therein in their proper order within the family of God. Remember that God's family is a patriarchal family and that these names of individuals must be arranged into sub-families, into families, and into major families in perfect order leading back to Father Adam. When Father Adam turns his family over to Jesus Christ, the work will be complete and perfect and the family will be sealed in perfect family order so that Jesus Christ can then present it to God the Father as a perfected whole.

Let us not be concerned about the lack of such a record today. We are still in the development and construction stages of this work. New developments, new research techniques, and new tools are continually being developed and discovered. Mechanical and electronic equipment is being continually invented and manufactured that will make possible achievements we of today can hardly imagine. It appears obvious to me that the Church as the overall family of God must construct and maintain this overall record that will be able to handle these hundreds of millions of names in an orderly and efficient manner. Already the Genealogical Department has research projects underway to make use of some of these latest scientific developments. Skilled scientists and university faculties are being used in cooperation with genealogists within the Church to see if we cannot al-

264

ready begin to construct such a universal record. We are already doing work at a volume today that ten years ago would have been impossible. Ten years from today the volume of work handled efficiently and accurately will be beyond our present capacity to comprehend, and in the course of time we will develop means of handling this information even more quickly and accurately than is possible today.

The Church is already organizing names for temple ordinance work under a names submission program, and this program is being extended and made more applicable to temple ordinance work as we gain further experience in its use. This work of furnishing additional names to the temples has been done to aid the Saints. However, the latter have not understood this program and have felt it was an invasion of their lineage rights. Not so. Remember that individual Saints are members of this greater family and the greater family is only trying to help them in getting the necessary work done. Our individual Saints working alone or in their immediate families have not made full use of their own abilities to do genealogical research work. They have not submitted sufficient names to keep the temples operating, nor have they organized their families into lineage or patriarchal lines as they should have done. As of this writing the Saints are furnishing only about one-fourth of the names being officiated for in the temples. The other 76 percent of the names are being furnished by the Church or the family of God as a whole. These latter names are handled as individual persons, for it has not yet been possible for the Church to arrange them into family or patriarchal order. It is, however, possible for families to use these carefully indexed names that have been completed by the Church as a whole, to check them for individuals belonging to their lineage lines. Where these are discovered to be part of their heritage, the names can then be put into proper family order. This can be done because Church members have access to additional records that the Church cannot at present use in this name tabulation project. By making use of such records as wills, probates, land records, etc., these individuals can be assembled into family groups and pedigree lineage lines for assembling into the patriarchal family of Adam.

As additional experience in knowing how to organize this information is obtained, it will become possible to arrange the central file of completed ordinance work into patriarchal order also. First things, however, must come first. Anything we know how to do manually by establishing proper rules and principles can be done much faster and more accurately by mechanical and electronic devices. First, however, we need to gain experience by organizing names and other lineage information we now have into proper family order. We need to follow the directions of the Lord and pursue these matters individually and as families as far as it is possible to do so. When that is done, sufficient data and knowledge will have been accumulated to enable us to organize the central family file for the kingdom of God as a whole.

In the construction of a central pedigree file to be developed and maintained by the Church, errors will undoubtedly be found. These come as a result of conflicting pedigree research done by various family organizations. Some is done in an excellent manner, but other work is done in a rather slipshod manner, and errors and conflicts are bound to occur. Some type of pedigree research department will thus have to be organized within the Genealogical Department to coordinate this research and to resolve such problems. As methods and procedures are developed and improved for controlling pedigree research, and as more information is obtained and additional data are gathered, it will become easier to detect these conflicts and make suggestions to the family genealogists as to how these conflicts can be resolved through further genealogical research.

It is doubtful from the revelations already given that the responsibility for resolving such research problems

266

will ever be taken from the individual and from the family. It is our responsibility to see that the temple ordinance work is done for *our own* kindred dead. Although a central file will eventually be prepared and maintained by the Church, it will be an individual and family responsibility to see that such a file contains the names and ordinance data that will release *our* progenitors and their immediate families from their spirit prison. By that time, of course, we will have more intimate and close association with messengers from the other side of the veil who can assist us in resolving such conflicts. We can well understand the necessity of having a thousand years of peace to bring a finishing touch to this work. In the meantime, we have been warned that we must put forth all our efforts now to do all we can with the information already available to us. We have been warned that we will scarcely have time to complete the work, even by putting forth all our efforts during the Millennium, before there is an end to time and the final judgment comes.

267

What will always be needed will be an individual and family effort to do sufficient genealogical and temple work to tie ourselves and our kindred dead into that central file. This suggests that the individual member and the family organization will be responsible at least for a limited number of generations, making sure that each member has been carefully identified and properly sealed in correct family patriarchal order. When we reach a point of entry where those lineage lines fuse into the central file, from that point on the responsibility of maintaining the proper record could fall on the family of God, or the Church, as a whole. Now, if this is to be done, it will have to be done in an orderly and precise fashion. The leadership will have to remain with the priesthood, and the work of the Church will have to be carefully organized.

Temple work beyond that of baptism for the dead is a Melchizedek Priesthood responsibility. It will have to be priesthood directed and led. Responsibilities will have to come through priesthood leadership. At the present time high priests have been given the responsibility to direct and supervise this genealogical and temple work for a very definite and important reason. Directions for such work come through the presidency of the high priests. This assignment of responsibility is very logical as one examines the scriptures. "Wherefore, it must needs be that one be appointed of the High Priesthood to preside over the priesthood, and he shall be called the President of the High Priesthood of the Church: Or, in other words, the Presiding High Priest over the High Priesthood of the Church." (D&C 107:65-66.) He it is who holds all the keys of temple ordinance work and directs the sealing of families in proper patriarchal order. Revelations and directions will come through and from him as the Lord has revealed. (D&C 132:7.) There is never but one on the earth at any one time on whom all this power and all the keys of this priesthood are conferred.

In order to accomplish this work, the Church has been divided into stakes of Zion, each presided over by a high priest who is appointed and set apart as the president of the stake. He is also called and set apart and given keys as the president of the high priests quorum of that stake. He thus holds the keys of high priests presidency in that stake, and, as the president of the high priests quorum, he gives direction for the implementation of genealogical and temple work within that stake. This does not mean that the high priests alone are responsible for all the genealogical and temple work to be done. It only means that they have the responsibility at the present time for directing and supervising this work. The stake president presides over the work of the seventies presidency and over the presidents of the various elders quorums within the stake. He has full authority to direct these presidents to get genealogical and temple work done. They in turn, holding the keys of presidency over their quorums, have the responsibility to

268

teach and train and motivate the members of their quorums to become active in this major priesthood responsibility. Under inspiration from the Lord; the First Presidency and the Council of the Twelve could assign the responsibility for direction of genealogical and temple work to *any* order within the Melchizedek Priesthood. At the present time the high priests have been given this supervisory responsibility.

To motivate members of their quorums and their families to be sealed in proper family order is one of the major responsibilities of these Melchizedek Priesthood quorum presidents. If they do not teach this work to the understanding and comprehension of their quorum members, the garments of these presidents will be stained with the blood of this generation. It is a sobering responsibility and should be impressed upon the home teachers, who are the official agents of the quorum presidency in carrying this program into the home and teaching the father and members of his family their individual responsibilities to get the work done.

269

As the Church grows and temples dot the face of the earth, it is obvious that the overall Church responsibility of keeping the temples supplied with names cannot continue to be handled from Church headquarters alone as at present. The following words are a sobering warning of what we can expect in the future:

The day is coming, not too far ahead of us when all the temples on this earth will be going day and night. There will be shifts and people will be coming in the morning hours and in the night hours and in the day hours, and we may reach the time when we will have no (temple) vacations. . . . There will be a corps of workers night and day almost to exhaustion, because of the importance of the work and the great number of people who lie asleep in the eternity and who are craving and needing the blessings we can bring them. (Spencer W. Kimball, Address at the Dedication of the Washington [D.C.] Temple, November 1974.)

When that day comes we can well expect that the names

for such a great amount of temple work will have to be generated within the stakes comprising that temple district.

Where will the names come from for use in the Sao Paulo Temple in South America? Where will the names come from for the temple in Tokyo, Japan? Where will the names come from in sufficient volume to keep the temple in Seattle, Washington, or in Mexico City, Mexico, busy? Other temples may even be announced before this book is published. How can we continue to furnish such names from Church headquarters in Salt Lake City, Utah, where the people are limited in number and lack the ability to read or even understand the records in which those names are recorded in the various languages of the peoples of those lands? Such a volume of names can never be maintained by paid workers. They will have to be produced on a Church service basis in the stakes through the sacrifice of Church members as they devote time and energy and means to this work.

The times will have to come when records gathered from various archives will be sent to the several stakes of Zion where people live who can read and understand those languages and scripts. As part of their priesthood responsibility, the local stake presidents will correlate this activity. They will assign these tasks to the various quorums of the Melchizedek Priesthood. Presidents of the quorums in turn will have to organize the work of preparing the names for temple ordinance work. This will involve the services not only of the brethren in those areas, but also of their wives and their children.

One other thing we must remember in connection with this work is the principle of revelation. In many cases there will be circumstances in which no records of the deceased are to be found. We are discovering new records daily that we did not know even existed. In areas where we formerly supposed the records had been completely destroyed by war, fire, or flood, we have found copies miraculously preserved. We are now gathering oral genealogies on tape where we formerly supposed no record had ever been made even in the minds of people. Revelation can guide us to these sources. Yet there are millions of people who presently live in areas where no records of births, marriages, and deaths are being recorded. There are hundreds of millions of people who have lived in times past under similar conditions. Yet those people lived. Their spirits are being taught in the spirit world. Many of them will accept the gospel. How will we obtain sufficient information to take care of them?

Those spirits know who they are. They know the names of their fathers and mothers, their spouses and their children. The day will come when they will be permitted to give that information to recorders in the spirit world who will prepare their records for our use in temple ordinance work so they also may be redeemed and exalted. There will be order, however, in this work. Such lists will be brought to the Church authorities charged with the responsibility to see that temple work is done. Such records will not be given to individuals haphazardly, nor revealed in any other than an orderly manner. When such information is given to the proper authority, the work will be assigned and delegated to the various temples in an orderly manner so that the temple work can be done and acceptable records can be prepared on earth that will be "worthy of all acceptation."

We cannot yet comprehend the magnitude of the service that will be required of us when those days come. That they are approaching we can already observe. The problem is to prepare ourselves for that day as it approaches. For this reason, there must not be further delays. We must learn the doctrines and principles that are the basis of this work. We must also become familiar with their operation and actively participate in this work now in order to obtain the necessary expertise to know what to do in the future. God cannot reveal more to us than that which we are now willing to accept and do. When we have made full use of our present knowledge, then God will reveal to us further light and knowledge.

26

The Greatest Gift

Throughout this book reference has been made to those great treasures in heaven which await the faithful. There are many such treasures and blessings, but we might well ask: Which of all the gifts of God is the greatest? No man can answer that question, for no man can comprehend all the gifts, blessings, and treasures that God has prepared for those who love him. God, however, knows and comprehends all things and has revealed the answer as follows: "If thou wilt do good, yea, and hold out faithful to the end, thou shalt be saved in the kingdom of God, which is the greatest of all the gifts of God; for there is *no gift greater than the gift of salvation.*" (D&C 6:13. Italics added.) Applying the principle that if a statement is important it will be repeated frequently, we read: "Seek not for riches but for wisdom; and, behold, the mysteries of God shall be unfolded unto you, and then shall you be made rich. Behold, he that *hath eternal life is rich.*" (D&C 11:7. Italics added.) Again the specific statement of the greatest of all riches is given as follows: "And, if you keep my commandments and endure to the end you shall have eternal life, *which gift is the greatest of all the gifts of God.*" (D&C 14:7. Italics added.) As these scriptures inform us, eternal life in the presence of God the Eternal Father is the greatest gift that God can bestow upon any one of his children.

As I read these statements, the thought comes to me

that it is not the *promise* of eternal life that constitutes that greatest of all gifts. It is the actual *state of being* that constitutes the greatest of all the gifts of God. The promise is given to all the children of God who are willing to pay the price to achieve eternal life. Only those who do pay that price, however, will ever achieve it. Nephi, whose soul delighted in plainness, summarized the difference between following Satan and following God in these words:

> And there is a place prepared, yea, even that awful hell of which I have spoken, and the devil is the foundation of it; wherefore the final state of the souls of men is to dwell in the kingdom of God, or to be cast out because of that justice of which I have spoken.
>
> Wherefore, the wicked are rejected from the righteous, and also from the tree of life, whose fruit is most precious and most desirable above all other fruits; yea, and *it is the greatest of all the gifts of God.* And thus I spake unto my brethren. Amen. (1 Nephi 15:35-36. Italics added.)

The fruit is the end result, or the achievement of the final goal. This is the greatest of all the gifts of God and this is what Paul referred to as he wrote: "For the wages of sin is death; but the gift of God is eternal life through Jesus Christ our Lord." (Romans 6:23.) The wage or end-result comes not only from the choices we make, but also from the things we do.

I realize there are some people in this world who remain terribly discouraged regardless of all the promises I have cited in this book. They feel they are not personally important. They feel rejected and unwanted. Perhaps illness or some other physical, mental, or moral handicap has kept them from doing this work of salvation. They say in their hearts, "This work is all right for others, but not for me. I am not important. God does not love me or I would not have to suffer as I do or be so handicapped. What has family to do with *me?*" Let me assure you that you are important. You are a child of God. He loves every single one of us. You are important and you are loved. This work and these promises are given to you and to every one of God's children. There are no exceptions.

In any educational program where an attempt is made to change people's lives, certain principles must be followed. Principles must be taught or, in other words, information must be given. In this book emphasis has been given to stress the concept that we must not only save ourselves, the living, but we must also make it possible for our kindred dead to be saved. We have been told that our salvation rests on their salvation and that if we exert all our efforts in this direction, we will hardly have time to complete this work before the end of the world, which will come at the end of the Millennium. We have pointed out the magnitude of the task that lies before us. The closer the second coming of Jesus Christ approaches, the more urgent the matter of salvation of both the living and the dead becomes. We must strain ourselves to the utmost to do all we can as saviors on Mount Zion before that time comes, in order to attain our own exaltation. Thus, information has been given in this book in an attempt to enlighten our minds as to the importance of this work.

274

The second principle in the educational process is to repeat that instruction again and again to drill it into the mind of the student. It takes time and it takes practice to learn. Lessons must be taught again and again, because we learn by going over an idea repeatedly until it becomes part of our personal treasure of knowledge. The plea of Jesus Christ is to believe. How often that counsel has been repeated. If we believe and continue to believe, hearing a thing over and over, that belief ripens into knowledge. When we have grasped a concept thoroughly, we say we "know." Knowing is testimony and develops out of belief.

In our church we have done a good job of education up to this point. There are few members of the Church who have not heard about genealogy and about the need to save our kindred dead. Our people have been told over and over again that they will be damned unless they do this work. The statement has been repeated so many times that finally they become resentful. They rebel and say, "I'll be damned if I'll do it!" We have thus lost the value of repetition, which is the second step in the learning process. We have lost that value because we haven't continued the educational process by going on to the third step.

What has been forgotten in our teaching is that with our repetition, we must teach people to their understanding or comprehension and not to their annoyance. They must not only know—they must *understand*. They must comprehend the value of the principle in their own lives. It must mean something to *them*. It must answer the question: "What value does all this have for *me?*" They must have that same need filled which Peter requested of Jesus:

275

Then answered Peter and said unto him, Behold, we have forsaken all, and followed thee; what shall we have therefore? [In other words, what good is all this to us personally? What do we get out of it?]

And Jesus said unto them, Verily I say unto you, That ye which have followed me, in the regeneration [who have been faithful until that time comes when all things are fully completed] when the Son of Man shall sit in the throne of his glory, ye also shall sit upon twelve thrones, judging the twelve tribes of Israel.

And every one that hath forsaken houses, or brethren, or sisters, or father, or mother, or wife, or children, or lands, for my name's sake [in other words, you who have made personal sacrifices to do this work], shall receive an hundredfold, and shall inherit everlasting life. (Matthew 19:27-29.)

Jesus was thus attempting to teach to Peter's understanding. He was answering the question: "What is there in this for me?" He was showing the apostles what great treasures awaited them personally if they would only remain faithful and diligent in the performance of their duties until the final day of judgment comes.

It is only when a person realizes that some idea, concept, or action will be in his own best interest that he will be willing to commit himself fully to that cause. By concentrating on the promises made, of great treasures in heaven that await those who take the time and make the effort to identify them and have their family progenitors sealed together, we can comprehend that priesthood genealogical work is of personal value to us. The values received and the treasures to be gained are more than sufficient to pay for all the time, money, and effort involved in this activity. When one has that inner conviction, he will make his commitment and say, "I'll do it!" It is that commitment which leads to action. Action is the final step in the learning process. This is what we are striving to achieve. We want the lives of people to change. We want them to *do* something! We want *results!*

It has been the purpose of this book to teach understanding. One way to teach understanding is to let the reader know and feel that this work is important and, above all else, is a true principle. I know it is true, for I personally know that God lives. I have a testimony and a witness that Jesus is the Risen Christ. I have heard his voice speak into my mind that these principles of salvation and exaltation for the living and for the dead are true principles and a worthwhile work. As I sit in the temple with the General Authorities and hear the Brethren speak to one another from their hearts in the privacy of that gathering, I know with a surety that prophets and apostles now walk this earth. I know from my heart as well as from my mind that they hold divine power as they speak and teach the words of the Lord. The explanations of the scriptures I have given in this book are my own attempt to follow their example in teaching the truth as I understand it. My desire has been to motivate you to action. I don't want you just to agree with the principle. I desire that you understand the advantages to you personally in doing this work, so you will commit yourself to greater effort and action in the future.

It is this inner conviction, then, that is important. This is what is meant by conversion to a principle. Once we are truly converted to a course of action, nothing can keep us from accomplishing that work. Satan would hinder us from putting God's plan into action if he could, just as Jesus explained to Peter: "And the Lord said, Simon, Simon, behold, Satan hath desired to have you that he may sift you as wheat: But I have prayed for thee, that thy faith fail not: and *when thou art converted, strengthen thy brethren."* (Luke 22:31-32. Italics added.) At that time Peter was not fully converted, but afterwards, strengthened by the Holy Ghost, he became fully, wholly, completely converted. Then nothing could stop him from following the Lord, even if it meant giving up his life. He was thoroughly converted. When he and John were summoned before the Sanhedrin and commanded to cease their teachings, though their very lives were threatened, Peter answered for them both: "Whether it be right in the sight of God to hearken unto you more than unto God, judge ye. For we cannot but speak the things which we have seen and heard." (Acts 4:19-20.) They were converted. They had committed themselves. Not even the threat of punishment or death could stop them once they knew in their hearts that their work was important and true. That is the thought I have tried to put over about this genealogical and temple work for both the living and the dead.

Genealogical work is important in the pattern of priesthood activity. As a person studies the scriptures and learns how important the family is, he obtains knowledge of the gifts and blessings that one can obtain as a heritage right, provided that family is knit together into the family of God in a divinely organized and authorized manner. If I prepare the way and then live for that blessing, I will have the privilege of personal association with the greatest souls who ever lived on this earth. I will have as my teachers, companions, and associates the wisest,

277

most able, the kindest, most gentle people who ever lived. As additional teachers, I will have the Holy Ghost, who bears witness of all truths; Jesus Christ, or Jehovah, the Creator of all things; and Elohim, our Father, the greatest of all. To think of living in their presence with constant communion with them is rapture indeed. What gift could ever surpass that gift? That gift includes not only the privilege of living with them, but also in sharing their power, their knowledge, their work, and their joy.

It is small wonder, then, that the scriptures state of those who achieve this gift: "These are they whose bodies are celestial, whose glory is that of the sun, even the glory of God, the highest of all, whose glory the sun of the firmament is written of as being typical." (D&C 76:70.) It is worth striving for. No matter what the price may be, the promise of eternal life—to live the kind of life that our father and mother in heaven live—is well worth any sacrifice we may have to pay here on earth. That is a goal that every one of us should keep continually in mind. This understanding leads to commitment, and commitment leads to action, and that is the final step in the education process.

Remember, however, that reason alone is not enough. What one can be reasoned into, one can be reasoned out of. We not only need our minds to be illuminated, but our hearts need to be touched also. There is something so personally intimate when our hearts are touched that it is like being on fire. That inner conviction is like a torch burning within us. It is hard to describe but easy to feel. We can also feel that inner fire when it likewise burns in others whose hearts are touched. Soul communes with soul. Faith communes with faith. Conviction within us is strengthened by the conviction we sense in others. We can simply say: "It is true!" If so, what can we do about it? We can now go and do the work that lies before us. We can begin without further delay that work of salvation for ourselves and for others which has been the topic and the burden of this book.

Now one final word of explanation. I have emphasized the concept of an eternal treasure or reward awaiting us in the resurrection. We can all understand the concept of treasures and rewards. These are goals we as people living on the earth can comprehend and work for. If we actively seek for the treasure of eternal life, we shall believe in God and we will do the works of God. Such faith and conduct will then lead us to become like God. We will try to perfect our lives on earth to live as close as we can to the celestial law. That this is required of us can be seen from the following scripture, where the Lord chastizes the members of the Church because they "are not united according to the union required by he law of the celestial kingdom; And Zion cannot be built up unless it is by the principles of the law of the celestial kingdom; otherwise I cannot receive her unto myself." (D&C 105:4-5.) It is this striving to live the celestial law that will bring us closer to the celestial kingdom and to become like God himself.

Now comes the great secret of true godliness. When we become perfected and become like God, we will do all these works of righteousness—not because of any rewards or even hopes of such rewards. We will serve others not because of blessings expected, not because of rewards, duty, or obligation, not because we are forced to do so, or are even required to do so, but simply because it is the best, the right thing to do. God is God and chooses goodness and virtue and service not because of law, not because he has to do so, or is expected to do so, but because he wants to do so. The reason for doing so is because it is right—the best thing to do. It is that action which results in the greatest personal joy and happiness that any individual can ever have.

Until we reach *that* state of godliness and understanding, let us have as our goal the striving for that treasure, the hope for that reward, to attain that gift which is the greatest of all the gifts of God—eternal lives!

Index

Hamor, 112-13
Hazael, 133
Heaven, marriage not
performed in, 2-3; explanation
of kingdom of, 215-18
Heavenly mother, 16
Heavenly parents, we lived
with, 5; existence of, 16-17;
man separated from, 138
Heavenly treasures, should
concentrate on, 9-14
Hebrews, told they are children
of God, 40
History, personal, 253-54;
family, 259-60
Hittite wives, Esau had, 109
Holy Ghost, instructions come
through, 12; testifies to
teachings of Christ, 61-62
Home, emphasis on
strengthening, 202
Husband, Elder Burton talks
with woman concerning death
of her, 1-3; responsibility of, in
marriage, 22-24; importance of
wisdom in choosing a, 123

I

"Illegitimate" children, 74-75
Immortality, accomplished
through the atonement, 34;
often confused with eternal
life, 37; through the atonement,
139-40
Instructions through Holy
Ghost, we should follow, 12
Interview of man by Elder
Burton for priesthood offices,
23-24
Isaac, son of Abraham and
Sarah, 96; Abraham told to
sacrifice, 100-1; faith of, 101;
received promise of great
posterity, 102; wed Rebekah,

103; had twin sons, 103;
marriage of, sealed for eternity,
108; instructed Jacob not to
marry a daughter of Canaan,
111; sacrifice of, preview of
atonement, 145
Isaiah, spoke concerning
treasures to be had, 12; on
Savior's mission to the dead, 78,
173-74
Ishmael, son of Abraham and
Hagar, 96
Israel, family of, moved into
Egypt, 116; gathering of, 118-
19. *See also* Jacob
Israelites, Egyptians made
slaves of, 127

J

Jacob, son of Isaac and
Rebekah, 103; served Laban for
Rachel, 103; tricked into
marrying Leah, 103-4; name
changed to Israel, 104; children
of, 104; obtained birthright
from Esau, 109; received
birthright blessing from father,
110; instructed not to marry a
daughter of Canaan, 111; falls
in love with Rachel, 111;
explains atonement, 142-43
James, received keys of sealing
power, 176-77
Jehovah, was firstborn, 28, 40-
42; explains ranking of
intelligent children to
Abraham, 28; offers to be the
Savior, 32; warns Cain, 64-65;
to bring about atonement, 139;
as God of Old Testament, 139
Jehu, 133
Jeremiah, foreordained, 42-43;
on importance of blood
lineage, 232

285

Nauvoo, Illinois, purpose of
temple at, 205-6
Nephi, born of goodly parents,
72; acquainted with patriarchal
father, 87; given sealing power,
134
Nibley, Hugh W., 7, 152
Nicodemus, talks with Christ
about baptism, 165-67
Noah, also known as Gabriel,
28, 177

O

"O My Father," 16
Obedience, sacrifice a
demonstration of, 99-100;
exaltation depends on, 110
Offering, to the Lord a
commandment, 52-53; of Cain
and Abel, 63-64
Ordinances, must be done in
the flesh, 237

P

Parents, responsibility of, to
teach children, 72-76, 223-24;
must bear blame for failure to
teach children righteousness,
74; of last days are special, 228-
29. *See also* Heavenly parents
Patriarchal blessing, Israel
gives his sons, 117-18; clarifies
lineage, 120-21; highly
personal, 121-22; are individual
revelations, 122
Patriarchal chain, will be
complete from us to God, 122-23
Patriarchal lineage, how passed
on, 84-85
Patriarchal order of the
priesthood, handed down
through descendants of Seth,
82; rights of, limited by lineage,
239

Patriarchs, many, 95; divinely
chosen, 120; seek guidance
from Holy Ghost, 122
Paul, spoke concerning
treasures to be had, 12-13;
explains doctrine of baptism,
157-59; describes resurrected
bodies, 215-16
Pedigree chart, 250-51
Personal history, 253-54
Peter, received keys of sealing
power, 176-77; before
Sanhedrin, 277
Petersen, Mark E., on doing
genealogy for our own dead,
244-45
Pharisees, question Jesus on
marriage, 179-80
Plan of salvation, explains
scripture of Sadducees
questioning Jesus, 3; prepared
by God, 28-36; explained to
Abraham, 29; offers treasures of
eternal life, 37; agreed to in
premortality, 58; sacrifice a
principle of, 99-100
Posterity, need to save own,
202
Potiphar, Joseph sold to, 113;
wife of, attempts to seduce
Joseph, 114
Prayer, importance of, to
Heavenly Father, 17-18
Predestination, 170
Preexistence. *See* Premortality
Premortality, beauty of, 6-7;
possible carryovers of, 27;
promises made in, 38;
scriptures concerning, 39-45; of
blind man, 44
Priesthood, withdrawn from
Cain, 59; withheld from
descendants of Cain, 80-81;
power of, 93-94; passed on to

attempts to deceive us, 60-62;
desired to win Cain over, 65-
66; tempted Cain with greed
and power, 67-68; has no
power to tempt children until
they are eight, 73-74; cast
down to earth, 144; works
harder in last days, 228
Savior, to be provided for us,
32; promised to Adam and Eve,
54; mission of, to dead, 78
Saviors, we are to be, for our
dead, 232; we are to be, for our
own ancestors, 238-39, 241-46,
267
Sealing, power of, restored to
earth today, 3; question of, to
whom, 124-26; Elijah given
keys of power of, 130; keys of
power of, given to Peter,
James, John, 176-77; twelve
apostles given power of, 178;
keys of, restored to Joseph
Smith and Oliver Cowdery,
200-2; Wilford Woodruff on,
within families, 242-44
Second estate, 9
Seth, patriarchal lineage
through, 81-82; ordained by
Adam, 82
Seventy, man interviewed by
Elder Burton to be, 23-24
Shechem, 112
Shem, may be Melchizedek, 90
Simeon, son of Jacob, 113
Sin, Adam brought, 138
Sisters, we are brothers and,
162
Smith, Joseph, knowledge of
heavenly treasures revealed to,
13; speaks of Elohim, 17;
receives revelation concerning
marriage, 21; Lord speaks to, in
Liberty Jail, 52; receives

revelation concerning all
people to hear gospel, 78;
explains story of Melchizedek
and Abraham, 88-89; explains
mission of Elijah, 135; explains
doctrine of translation, 136-37;
translated name of Jesus Christ,
153; restoration of gospel
through, 193; visited by Moses,
Elias, and Elijah, 200-2; on
keeping records, 207;
concerning spirit of Elijah, 208-
9; receives revelation
concerning degrees of glory,
216-18; receives revelation
concerning missionary service
to living and dead, 225-26;
explains how total sealing of
family of God will be done,
234, 241-42
Smith, Joseph F., receives
revelation concerning Christ's
ministry in spirit world, 187
Snow, Eliza R., 16
Sodom and Gomorrah, 96-98
Sons of Levi, function of, 209-
12
Sons of perdition, to be
resurrected, 141
Spirit, gives light to every man,
8
Spirit children, we all lived as,
5; in premortal life, 27-28; plan
of salvation defined for, 29-36
Spirit world, Christ visited,
185-88; all who died without
hearing gospel must go to, 236;
missionary work in, 236-37
Spiritual death, 138
Surname organization, 258-60

T

Teach, we are to, by the power
of the Holy Ghost, 12; people